A BR[...]
A PRO[...]

Enter Sydney On[...]
day-by-day predictions for every aspect of your life. With
expert readings and forecasts, you can chart a course to
romance, adventure, good health, or career opportunities
while gaining valuable insight into yourself and others.
Offering a daily outlook for 18 full months, this fascinating guide shows you:

- The important dates in your life
- What to expect from an astrological reading
- How the stars can help you stay healthy and fit
- Your lucky lottery numbers
  And more!

Let this expert's sound advice guide you through a year
of heavenly possibilities—for today and for every day of
2001!

SYDNEY OMARR'S DAY-BY-DAY
ASTROLOGICAL GUIDE FOR

ARIES—March 21–April 19
TAURUS—April 20–May 20
GEMINI—May 21–June 20
CANCER—June 21–July 22
LEO—July 23–August 22
VIRGO—August 23–September 22
LIBRA—September 23–October 22
SCORPIO—October 23–November 21
SAGITTARIUS—November 22–December 21
CAPRICORN—December 22–January 19
AQUARIUS—January 20–February 18
PISCES—February 19–March 20

IN 2001

WIN A PERSONALIZED HOROSCOPE FOR A FULL YEAR!

Enter the Sydney Omarr Horoscope Sweepstakes!

No purchase necessary. Details below.

Name _____

Address _____

City_____ State_____ Zip_____

Mail to:

Sydney Omarr Horoscope Sweepstakes
c/o Penguin Putnam Inc.
375 Hudson St., 5th floor
New York, NY 10014

All entries must be postmarked by August 31, 2000 and received by September 8, 2000.

1. NO PURCHASE NECESSARY TO ENTER OR WIN A PRIZE. To enter the Sydney Omarr Horoscope Sweepstakes, complete this official entry form or, on 3" x 5" piece of paper, write your name and complete address. Mail your entry to: Sydney Omarr Horoscope Sweepstakes; c/o Penguin Putnam Inc.; 375 Hudson St., 5th floor; New York, NY 10014. Enter as often as you wish, but mail each entry in a separate envelope. No mechanically reproduced or computer generated entries allowed. All entries must be postmarked by 8/31/2000 and received by 9/8/2000 to be eligible. Not responsible for late, lost, damaged, incomplete, illegible, postage due or misdirected mail entries.

2. Winners will be selected from all eligible entries in a random drawing on or about 9/14/00, by Penguin Putnam Inc., whose decisions are final and binding. Odds of winning are dependent upon the number of entries received. Winners will be notified by mail and may be required to execute an affidavit of eligibility and release which must be returned within 14 days of notification or an alternate winner will be selected.

3. One (1) Grand Prize winner will receive a personalized one-year horoscope from an astrologer chosen by Sydney Omarr. One (1) Second Prize winner will receive a personalized one-month horoscope from an astrologer chosen by Sydney Omarr.. Estimated value of all prizes: $250.

4. Sweepstakes open to residents of the U.S. and Canada 18 years of age or older, except employees and the immediate families of Penguin Putnam Inc., its affiliated companies, advertising and promotion agencies. Void in Puerto Rico, the province of Quebec and wherever else prohibited by law. All Federal, State, Local, and Provincial laws apply. Taxes, if any, are the sole responsibility of the prize winners. Canadian winners will be required to answer an arithmetical skill testing question administered by mail. Winners consent to the use of their name and/or photos or likenesses for advertising purposes without additional compensation (except where prohibited).

5. For the names of the prize winners, send a self-addressed, stamped envelope after 9/28/00 to : SYDNEY OMARR HOROSCOPE SWEEPSTAKES WINNERS, Penguin Putnam Inc., 375 Hudson St., 5th floor, New York, NY 10014.

SYDNEY OMARR'S

DAY-BY-DAY ASTROLOGICAL GUIDE FOR

SCORPIO

October 23–November 21

2001

A SIGNET BOOK

SIGNET
Published by New American Library, a division of
Penguin Putnam Inc., 375 Hudson Street,
New York, New York 10014, U.S.A.
Penguin Books Ltd, 27 Wrights Lane,
London W8 5TZ, England
Penguin Books Australia Ltd, Ringwood,
Victoria, Australia
Penguin Books Canada Ltd, 10 Alcorn Avenue,
Toronto, Ontario, Canada M4V 3B2
Penguin Books (N.Z.) Ltd, 182–190 Wairau Road,
Auckland 10, New Zealand

Penguin Books Ltd, Registered Offices:
Harmondsworth, Middlesex, England

First published by Signet, an imprint of New American Library,
a division of Penguin Putnam Inc.

First Printing, June 2000
10 9 8 7 6 5 4 3 2 1

CONTENTS

INTRODUCTION

Changing Times—
Going Global After Y2K

The year 2001 will find more and more of us going global via home computers. And as we travel the expanding cyberworld, we find astrology very much a part of the on-line scenery. Astrology areas are among the most visited on big commercial Web sites. With a more serious educational purpose, there are interactive sites that present new techniques and rediscovered ancient ones as well as offer courses to students of all levels. For the astrologer, computer technology has been a godsend, eliminating long hours of calculation and research, and enabling them to exchange ideas across the planet and access knowledge that is difficult to obtain in many third world cultures.

On the other hand, the year 2001 conjures up vivid memories of the star of Stanley Kubrick's classic sci-fi film, *2001: A Space Odyssey,* an almost-human computer called "Hal," which caused the downfall of the film's space voyage. The film was an eerie premonition of the Y2K alarm that many of the systems we rely on might shut down suddenly at the change of a date. While there's no doubt that the ubiquitous computer will be an important signature of the twenty-first century, we are reminded that, as the original "Hal" forewarned, the computer has a potential fallible dark side manifested in malfunctions and high-tech crimes. Though it has caused our personal universe to expand with unimagined possibilities of global communication, the computer also has presented us with many personal challenges, such as acquiring new skills, protecting our privacy, filtering

1

content from impressionable children, and communicating with cyberfriends from other cultures.

But what of the astrology fan without a computer? There are many valid ways to put astrology into your life that are as relevant now as they have been for millennia past. The basic information hasn't changed, nor have the easy techniques in this book that have been tested over decades.

In addition to daily forecasts that help you make the most of each day, this book tells you what you need to know about your sun sign, your potential for success, your family life, how to create the perfect environment, and how to get along with everyone else under the sun. A chapter on the unique visual language of astrology will help you read the symbols on your horoscope chart. Easy basic information gives you an inside look at how astrology works. Then you can look up the other planets in your horoscope to find out how each contributes to your unique personality.

If you're intrigued by the variety of personal readings advertised, there is guidance on finding a qualified astrologer.

Many readers are fascinated by astrology's insights into the upsides and downsides of relationships. This year, you'll find out who you're likely to click with most and what sun sign combos are more challenging. There's a quiz to rate your relationships that will give you clues about the important people in your life.

For surfers on the Internet, there's our pick of the best of thousands of sites, where you can download a copy of your chart, network with other astrology fans, order books and programs, or enjoy some interactive fun and games. Plus Sydney Omarr's updated "Yellow Pages" of the best astrology resources for books, tapes, and further astrological studies.

As we go on our personal odysseys through cyberspace or relax in our cozy armchair with a good book, we are still searching for the same things that always have made life worth living: love, meaningful work, fulfilling relationships. With Sydney Omarr's astonishingly accurate day-by-day forecasts, you can chart your way to a starlit future and reap happiness, success, and good fortune the whole year through.

CHAPTER 1

What's Hot for 2001!

This year's picks and predictions . . .
worldwide trends that can change your life.

We're entering a decisive decade, when many problems
are coming to the forefront simultaneously: global expansion, territorial disputes, overpopulation, dangers of nuclear warfare, environmental crises. After last year, a time
when one of the most powerful lineups of planets in history
occurred in the sign of Taurus, this year will be a time of
processing the changes that have happened. It looks like a
slower, more thoughtful year, when we'll be formulating
our strategies and philosophies for the future. Here are
key planets calling the shots and the trends to watch.

Masters of the Universe Recognize
a Higher Power

The slow-moving planet Pluto is our guide to the hottest
trends. With this planet, there is no going back. Pluto
brings about a heightened consciousness and transformation of matters related to the sign it is traveling through.
Now in Sagittarius, Pluto's task is to eliminate outworn belief systems to prepare us philosophically and spiritually
for the future.

All that is associated with Sagittarius is sure to be emphasized—religion, advertising, banking, higher education, the travel industry, the legal professions, publishing,
gambling, outdoor sports, pets.

At this writing, churches are filling up again and spiritual advisers are making office calls in New York's canyons of power. Pluto in Sagittarius brings a new emphasis on spirituality, which began in 1995 and will continue in a crescendo until 2008, when it finally moves on to Capricorn. Expect the emphasis to shift from the materialistic and power-hungry nineties to a quest for the meaning of it all, as upward strivers discover that money and power are not enough.

Global environmental crisis and charismatic spiritual leaders are likely to prompt more serious thought and spiritual quests. Extreme forms of religion, a new emphasis on saints, such as Joan of Arc, and other metaphysical beings are other manifestations. Home altars and private sanctuaries are becoming a part of our personal environment. The oriental art of *feng shui* is moving westward, helping to create a more harmonious, spiritual atmosphere in offices and homes, which also promotes luck and prosperity.

In this pet-happy nation, look for extremes related to animal welfare, the life and death of animals. Vegetarianism becomes a more popular alternative lifestyle. The care, feeding, and control of animals becomes an even larger issue as their habitats are destroyed.

The Sagittarian love of the outdoors has already become manifest in the popularity of the extreme sports, especially those that require strong legs like rock climbing or snowboarding. Rugged sporty all-terrain vehicles continue to be popular. Expect the trend toward more adventurous travel and fitness or sports-oriented vacations to continue to be popular: exotic trips to unexplored territories, difficult hikes and mountain-climbing expeditions, spa vacations, sports-associated resorts.

Publishing has been transformed by the new electronic media, with an enormous variety of books available in print. The on-line bookstore will continue to prosper under Pluto in Sagittarius. It is fascinating that the phenomenally popular Amazon.com, the on-line bookstore, took the Sagittarius-influenced name of the fierce female archer-warriors who went to the extreme of removing their right breast to better shoot their arrows.

Mars, the planet of action, triggers things off this year. After racing through all the signs at a breakneck pace last year, it grinds to a slow halt spending almost seven months in Sagittarius, from mid-February to early September. There, it will join Pluto in mid-March, igniting powerful Sagittarius-oriented events. This long stay gives us plenty of time to think about the consequences of our actions, where we're going, and the meaning of it all. We may see a recurrence of events from September 1999, the last meeting of these two power planets.

We can't leave out globalization in all its forms, which has become a main theme of the past few years. We are reforming boundaries, creating new forms of travel that will definitely include space travel. We'll be thinking about more energy efficient ways to get around, especially in the area of mass transit.

Who's Lucky? Make Hay, Gemini and Cancer!

Good fortune, expansion, and big money opportunities are associated with the movement of Jupiter, the planet that embodies the principle of expansion. Jupiter has a twelve-year cycle, staying in each sign for approximately one year.

When Jupiter enters a sign, the fields associated with that sign usually provide excellent opportunities. Areas of speculation associated with the sign Jupiter is passing through will have the hottest market potential—the ones that currently arouse excitement and enthusiasm.

The flip side of Jupiter is that there are no limits . . . you can expand off the planet under a Jupiter transit, which is why the planet is often called the "Gateway to Heaven." If something is going to burst—such as an artery—or overextend or go over the top in some way, it could happen under a supposedly "lucky" Jupiter transit . . . so be aware.

This year, Jupiter won't finish its journey through Gemini until mid-July, when it moves into Cancer. So sun sign Geminis and Cancers or those with strong Gemini or Cancer influence in their horoscopes should have abundant growth opportunities. On the other hand, those born under Sagittarius and Capricorn will need to make adjustments, because this particular expansive tendency is opposed to their natural tendencies. With Saturn coming up more slowly, right behind Jupiter, this is a year to guard against overexpansion, overoptimism, and overextending yourself, without the appropriate organization and structure to back up your ventures. In other words, cover your bases!

Jupiter in Gemini should bring opportunities in all forms of communications, sales, cell phones, E-commerce, talk shows, voice mail, etc. In mid-July, opportunities open up in Cancer-related areas, which include home-related industries, child care, shelter industries, cruises, maternal issues, shipping and boating, water sports.

Saturn Puts on the Brakes in Taurus and Gemini

Saturn key words are focus, time, commitment, accomplishment, discipline, restriction. If Jupiter gives you a handout, then Saturn hands you the bill. With Saturn, nothing's free; you work for what you get, so it's always a good idea to find the areas (or houses) of your horoscope where Saturn is passing, to show where you must focus your energy on what is of lasting value. With Saturn, you must be sure to finish what you start, be responsible, put in the hard work and stick with it.

This year, Saturn finishes up making many demands on Taureans, as well as the other fixed signs (Leo, Scorpio, Aquarius). Saturn is quite powerful in the fixed signs, which are more focused and methodical by nature. In these signs, however, it facilitates more stubborn, tyrannical forces, demanding much wisdom and maturity to handle. Since Taurus is associated with financial matters, the earning and spending of money, possessions of all kinds, and our attitude toward them, expect the forces of limitation to operate here. It will be imperative to curb spending, operate on a budget. When it moves into Gemini on April 21, Taureans should be able to feel the weight lifting.

On the other hand, the normally light-spirited Geminis, who also have Jupiter bringing them many new opportunities until the summer, will have to deal with a serious, sobering influence of Saturn, just when they were enjoying an expansive period. There will be a price to pay, so the Jupiter transit will not be all fun and games. Geminis will have to back up the risks they take and be sure they can deliver on promises. However, learning to balance these two forces can bring lasting rewards. It'll be a powerful challenge for changeable Geminis who will be the ones to pay the piper for the next two years.

Uranus and Neptune in Aquarius— The High-Tech Signs

Uranus and Neptune are pushing us in the future as they continue their long stays in Aquarius. Where there is Neptune, look for imagination and creativity, and since this is the planet of deception and illusion, here comes criminal activity, such as cyber-crime. Uranus overthrows the worn-out status quo and points us toward the future.

Since these planets influence fashion trends, look for clothes of techno-fibers that won't wear out! Fashion will be futuristic, yet also have an elusive, dreamy quality, thanks to Neptune. The hands and breast area are the focus of special attention this year. Perhaps there will be pockets for mini-computers and telephones, since high-tech gadgets are meant to travel with us, creating our own portable command control centers. The inspiration of the futuristic designs of the 1950s and 1970s and of sci-fi films should continue as we redesign our lives.

Our lust for techno-toys should make this a gadget-crazed time. Interactive forms of amusement and communication will rival television for our leisure. In fact, television may be on its way out as we opt for more exciting forms of entertainment.

As these two planets blend with the others, unique trends are formed, such as the high-tech auctions and E-commerce that marked Jupiter/Saturn in Taurus. As they favorably influence Saturn/Jupiter in Gemini, expect an explosion of innovative forms of communication to happen this year. We'll be talking a blue streak across the planet, perhaps by individual satellite lines. Wires disappear as products work by "waves." As Jupiter moves into Cancer, look for news in high-tech home products, innovative ways to become a mother, futuristic cruise ships, new concepts in living quarters, and superfoods that optimize our health.

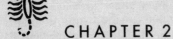

CHAPTER 2

Easy Astrology

You don't have to be an expert in astrology to understand how it works. This chapter is designed to walk you through the basic concepts, to pique your interest and satisfy your curiosity, so you'll know a sign from a house and what the planets mean. But don't expect to stop at this chapter! What makes astrology great is that, like your new PC, you can start using it right away. However, the more you use it, the more you'll crave the extra bells and whistles. Perhaps from here, you'll upgrade your knowledge with a computer program that calculates charts for everyone you know in a nanosecond, or you'll join an astrology class in your city, or you'll want to explore different techniques of astrology, go on to the asteroids and the fixed stars. The sky's the limit, literally. So let's take off!

The Basics—Signs, Houses, Constellations, and the Zodiac

Everyone knows what a sign is . . . or do they? A *sign* is literally a piece of territory marked off on a circle in the sky called the zodiac. Things happen within a sign, but a sign does not DO anything—that's the job of the planets. Signs have certain characteristics that are unique to them and are described by their element (earth, air, fire, water), by their quality or mode (cardinal [active], fixed, mutable), by their polarity (masculine/feminine, yin/yang), and finally by their position in the zodiac.

Now back to celestial real estate. *Signs* are equal 30-

degree portions of the *zodiac,* an imaginary 360-degree belt circling Earth. They're named after *constellations,* patterns of stars that originally marked the twelve divisions, like billboards. However, over the centuries, the constellations have shifted from our point of view here on Earth. So the constellation that once marked a particular sign may now be in the place "owned" by another sign. (Most Western astrologers use the twelve-equal-part division of the zodiac, however there are some methods of astrology that still do use the constellations instead of the signs.) However, the names of the signs remain the same as their original place-markers.

Most people think of themselves in terms of their *sun sign,* which refers to the sign the sun seems to be passing through at a given moment, from our point of view here on Earth. (In reality, we are the ones that are traveling around the sun.) For instance, "I'm an Aries" means that the sun was passing through Aries at my birth. However, there are nine other planets (plus asteroids, fixed stars, and sensitive points) that also form our total astrological personality, and some or many of these will be located in other signs. No one is completely "Aries," with all their astrological components in one sign! (Please note that in astrology the sun and moon are usually referred to as "planets," though of course they're not.)

How to Define a Sign

What makes Aries the sign of go-getters and Taureans savvy with money? And Geminis talk a blue streak and Sagittarians are footloose. Descriptions of the signs are not accidental; they are characterized by different combinations of four concepts: a sign's element, quality, polarity, and place on the zodiac.

Take the element of fire: it's associated with passion, heat. Then have it work in an active energetic way. Give it a jolt of positive energy and place it first in line. And doesn't that sound like the active, me-first, driving, hotheaded, energetic Aries?

Then take the element of earth: it's practical, sensual, where things grow. Add the fixed, stable mode. Give it energy that reacts to its surroundings, that settles in. Make it the consolidating force after the passion of Aries. Now you've got a good idea of how sensual, earthy Taurus operates.

Another way to grasp the idea is to pretend you're doing a magical puzzle based on the numbers that can divide into 12 (the number of signs): 4, 3, and 2. There are four "building blocks" or elements, three ways a sign operates (qualities or modes), and two polarities. These alternate in turn around the zodiac, with a different combination coming up for each sign.

THE FOUR ELEMENTS

Here's how they add up. The *four elements* describe the physical concept of the sign. Is it fiery (dynamic), earthy (practical), airy (mental), watery (emotional)? Divide the twelve signs by the four elements and you get three zodiac signs of each element: fire (Aries, Leo, Sagittarius), earth (Taurus, Virgo, Capricorn), air (Gemini, Libra, Aquarius), water (Cancer, Scorpio, Pisces). These are the same elements that make up our planet: earth, air, fire, and water. But astrology uses the elements as *symbols* that link our body and psyche to the rhythms of the cosmos. If major planets in a horoscope are passing through fire signs, the person will likely have a warm, enthusiastic personality, able to fire up or motivate others. These are people who make ideas catch fire, spring into existence, but they also have hot tempers. Those with major planets in earth signs are the builders of the zodiac who follow through after the initiative of fire signs to make things happen. These people are solid, practical realists who enjoy material things and sensual pleasures. They are interested in ideas that can be used to achieve concrete results. With major planets in air signs, a person will be more mental, a good communicator. Following the consolidating earth signs, air sign people reach out to inspire others through the use of words, social contacts, discussion, and debate. Water sign people complete each

11

four-element series, adding the ingredients of emotion, compassion, and imagination. These people are nonverbal communicators who attune themselves to their surroundings and react through the medium of feelings.

THE THREE QUALITIES

The second consideration when defining a sign is how it will operate. Will it take the initiative, or move slowly and deliberately, or adapt easily? It's *quality* (or modality) will tell. There are three qualities and four signs of each quality: cardinal, fixed, and mutable.

Cardinal signs begin each session (Aries, Cancer, Libra, Capricorn). People with major planets in cardinal signs tend to be active, involved in projects. They are usually on the fast track to success, impatient to get things under way. Those with major planets in *fixed signs* (Taurus, Leo, Scorpio, Aquarius) move steadily, always in control. Since these signs happen in the middle of a season, after the initial character of the season is established, it follows that people with major planets in fixed signs would tend to be more centered; they move more deliberately, do things more slowly, but thoroughly. The fixed signs fall in parts of your horoscope when you take root and integrate your experiences. *Mutable signs* (Gemini, Virgo, Sagittarius, Pisces) embody the principle of distribution. Planets in these signs will break up the cycle, prepare the way for a change by distributing the energy to the next group. People with predominantly mutable planets are likely to be flexible, adaptable, communicative. They can move in many directions easily, darting around obstacles.

THE TWO POLARITIES

In addition to an element and a quality, each sign has a *polarity,* either a positive or negative electrical charge that generates energy around the zodiac, like a giant battery. Polarity refers to opposites, which you could also define as masculine/feminine, yin/yang, active/reactive. Alternating around the zodiac, the six fire and air signs are positive, active, masculine, and yang in polarity. Therefore, planets in these signs are open, expanding outward. The six earth and water signs are negative, reactive, feminine, and yin— in other words, nurturing and receptive in polarity, which allows the energy to develop and take shape.

All positive energy would be like a car without brakes. All negative energy would be like a stalled vehicle, going nowhere. Both polarities are needed in balanced proportion.

THE ORDER OF THE SIGNS
The specific order of the signs is vital to the balance of the zodiac and the transmission of energy around the cycle. Though each sign is quite different from its neighbors on either side, each seems to grow out of its predecessor like links in a chain, transmitting a synthesis of energy accumulated along the chain to the following sign, beginning with the fire-powered, active, positive, cardinal sign of Aries and ending with watery, mutable, reactive Pisces.

Houses of the Horoscope— Where the Action Is

We come to the concept of *houses* once we set up a horoscope, which is a map of the heavens at a given moment in time. The horoscope chart looks somewhat like a wheel divided with twelve spokes. In between each of the "spokes" is a section called a "house." Each house covers a different area of life and is influenced by a particular sign and a planet. In addition, the house is colored by the sign that is passing over the spoke (or cusp) at the moment when the horoscope chart is cast.

Numerically, the house order begins at the left center spoke (or the 9 position if you were reading a clock) and is read counter-clockwise around the chart.

The First House—Home of Aries and Mars

This is the house of "firsts"—the first impression you make, how you initiate matters, the image you choose to project. This is where you advertise yourself, where you project your personality. Planets that fall here will intensify the way you come across to others. Often the first house will project an entirely different type of energy than the sun sign. For instance, a Capricorn with Leo in the first house will come across as much more flamboyant than the average Capricorn. The sign on the cusp of this house is known as your ascendant or rising sign.

The Second House—Home of Taurus and Venus

Here is your contact with the material world. In this house are your attitudes about money, possessions, finances, whatever belongs to you, and what you own, as well as your earning and spending capacity. On a deeper level, this house reveals your sense of self-worth, the inner values that draw wealth in various forms.

The Third House—Home of Gemini and Mercury

This house describes how you communicate with others— are you understood? Here you reach out to others nearby and interact with the immediate environment. This is how your thinking process works, the way you express your thoughts. In relationships, here are your first experiences with brothers and sisters, how you handle people close to you, such as your neighbors or pals. It's also where you take short trips, write letters, or use the telephone. It shows how your mind works in terms of left-brain logical and analytical functions.

The Fourth House—Home of Cancer and the Moon

This shows how you are nurtured and made to feel secure—your roots! Located at the bottom of the chart, the fourth house, like the home, shows the foundation of life, your deepest psychological underpinnings. Here is where you have the deepest confrontation with who you are, and how you make yourself feel secure. It shows your early home environment and the circumstances at the end of your life—your final "home"—as well as the place you call home now. Astrologers look here for information about the primary nurturers in your life.

The Fifth House—Home of Leo and the Sun

This is how you express yourself creatively—your idea of play. The Leo house is where the creative potential develops. Here you show off your talents and also where you procreate, in the sense that children are outgrowths of your creative ability. It most represents your inner childlike self, the part of you that finds joy in play. If inner security has been established by the time you reach this house, you are now free to have fun, romance, love affairs—to give of yourself. This is also the place astrologers look for the playful kind of love affairs, flirtations, and brief romantic encounters (rather than long-term commitments).

The Sixth House—Home of Virgo and Mercury

Here is your "repair and maintenance" department. It shows how you function in daily life, where you get things done, and where you determine how you look after others and fulfill service duties, such as taking care of pets. Here is your daily survival, your "job" (as opposed to your career, which is the domain of the tenth house), your diet, and your health and fitness regimens. Here is where you take care of your body and organize yourself so you can perform efficiently in the world.

The Seventh House—Home of Libra and Venus

This house shows your attitude toward partners and those with whom you enter commitments, contracts, or agree-

ments. This house has to do with your relationships, your close, intimate, one-on-one relationships (even your open enemies—those you "face off" with). Open hostilities, lawsuits, divorces, and marriages happen here. If the first house is the "I," the seventh or opposite house is the "not-I"—the complementary partner you attract by the way you come across. If you are having trouble with partnerships, consider what you are attracting by the interaction of your first and seventh houses.

The Eighth House—Home of Scorpio and Pluto (also Mars)

This refers to how you merge with something or someone, and how you handle power and control. This is one of the most mysterious and powerful houses, where your energy transforms itself from "I" to "we." As you give up your personal power and control by uniting with something or someone, two kinds of energies merge and become something greater, leading to a regeneration of the self on a higher level. Here are your attitudes toward sex, shared resources, taxes (what you share with the government). Because this house involves what belongs to others, you face issues of control and power struggles, or undergo a deep psychological transformation as you bond with another. Here you transcend yourself with the occult, dreams, drugs, or psychic experiences that reflect the collective unconscious.

The Ninth House—Home of Sagittarius and Jupiter

Where you search for wisdom and higher knowledge—your belief system. While the third house represents the "lower mind," its opposite on the wheel, the ninth house, is the "higher mind"—the abstract, intuitive, spiritual mind that asks "big" questions such as "Why are we here?" The ninth house shows what you believe in. After the third house explored what was close at hand, the ninth stretches out to explore more exotic territory, either by traveling, broadening yourself mentally with higher education, or stretching spiritually with religious activity. You take risks in your ninth house, you break rules and boundaries, since you are concerned with how everything is related. Here is where you write a book or extensive thesis, where you pontificate, philosophize, or preach.

The Tenth House—Home of Capricorn and Saturn

Here is your public image and how you handle authority. Located directly overhead at the "high noon" position on the horoscope wheel, this house is associated with high-profile activities, where the world sees you. It deals with your career (but not your routine "job"), and your reputation. Here is where you go public, take on responsibilities (as opposed to the fourth house, where you stay home). This will affect the career you choose and your "public relations." This house is also associated with your father or the main authority figure in your life.

The Eleventh House—Home of Aquarius and Uranus

Here is your support system, how you relate to society and your goals. In this house, you extend your identity to belong to a group, a team, a club, a goal, or a belief system. You worry about being popular, winning the election, or making the team; you define what you really want, the kinds of friends you have, your political affiliations, and the kind of groups you'll belong to. Here is "what other people think." Here is where you could become a socially conscious humanitarian—or a party-going social butterfly. It's where you look to others to stimulate you and discover your kinship to the rest of humanity. The sign on the cusp of this house can help you understand what you gain and lose from friendships.

The Twelfth House—Home of Pisces and Neptune

Here is where the boundaries between yourself and others become blurred, where you become selfless. In your trip around the zodiac, you've gone from the "I" of self-assertion in the first house to the final house symbolizing the dissolution that happens before rebirth. It's where accumulated experiences are processed in the unconscious. Spiritually oriented astrologers look to this house for evidence of past lives and karma. Places where we go for solitude or to do spiritual or reparative work belong here, such as retreats, religious institutions, hospitals. Here are also institutions such as prisons where we withdraw from society or are forced to withdraw because of antisocial behavior. Selfless giving through charitable acts is part of this house as is helpless dependence on charity. In your daily life, the twelfth house reveals your deepest intimacies, your best-kept secrets, especially those you hide from yourself, repressed deep in the unconscious. It is where we surrender a sense of a separate self to a deep feeling of wholeness, such as selfless service in religion or any activity that involves merging with the greater whole. Many sports stars have important planets in the twelfth house that enable them to play in the "zone," find an inner, almost mystical strength that transcends their limits.

The Planets Power Up Your Houses

Houses are stronger or weaker depending on how many planets are inhabiting them. If there are many planets occupying a given house, it follows that the activities of that house will be emphasized in your life. If the planet that rules the house naturally is also located there, this too adds power to the house.

CHAPTER 3

Look Up Your Planets

The Doers in Your Chart— the Planets

The ten planets in your chart will play starring or supporting roles, depending on their position in your horoscope. A planet in the first house, particularly one that's close to your rising sign, is sure to be a featured player. Planets that are grouped together usually operate together like a team, playing off each other, rather than expressing their energy singularly. A planet that stands alone, away from the others, is usually outstanding and sometimes calls the shots.

Each planet has two signs where it is especially at home. These are called its *dignities*. The most favorable place for a planet is in the sign or signs it rules; the next best place is in a sign where it is *exalted*, or especially harmonious. On the other hand, there are places in the horoscope where a planet has to work harder to play its role. These places are called the planets *detriment* and *fall*. The sign opposite a planet's rulership, which embodies the opposite area of life, is its *detriment*. The sign opposite its exaltation is its *fall*. Though these terms may suggest unfortunate circumstances for the planet, that is not always true. In fact, a planet that is debilitated can actually be more complete, because it must stretch itself to meet the challenges of living in a more difficult sign. Like world leaders who've had to struggle for greatness, this planet may actually develop great strength and character.

Here's a list of the best places for each planet to be. Note that as new planets were discovered in this century, they replaced the traditional rulers of signs that best complemented their energies.

ARIES—Mars
TAURUS—Venus, in its most sensual form
GEMINI—Mercury, in its communicative role
CANCER—the moon
LEO—the sun
VIRGO—Mercury, this time in its more critical capacity
LIBRA—Venus, in its more aesthetic, judgmental form
SCORPIO—Pluto, replacing the sign's original ruler, Mars
SAGITTARIUS—Jupiter
CAPRICORN—Saturn
AQUARIUS—Uranus, replacing Saturn, its original ruler
PISCES—Neptune, replacing Jupiter, its original ruler

A person who has many planets in exalted signs is lucky indeed, for here is where the planet can accomplish the most, be its most influential and creative.

The SUN—exalted in Aries, where its energy creates action
The MOON—exalted in Taurus, where instincts and reactions operate on a highly creative level
MERCURY—exalted in Aquarius, where it can reach analytical heights
VENUS—exalted in Pisces, a sign whose sensitivity encourages love and creativity
MARS—exalted in Capricorn, a sign that puts energy to work productively
JUPITER—exalted in Cancer, where it encourages nurturing and growth
SATURN—at home in Libra, where it steadies the scales of justice and promotes balanced, responsible judgment
URANUS—powerful in Scorpio, where it promotes transformation

NEPTUNE—especially favored in Cancer, where it gains the security to transcend to a higher state

PLUTO—exalted in Pisces, where it dissolves the old cycle, to make way for transition to the new

The Sun Is Always Top of the List

Your sun sign is the part of you that shines brightest. Then other planets add special coloration that sets you apart from other members of your sign. If you know a person's sun sign, you will already know some useful generic qualities, but when you know all the planets, you have a much more accurate profile and can predict more accurately how that individual will act. The sun's just one card in your hand—when you know the other planets, you can really play to win!

Since the sun is always the first consideration, it is important to treat it as the star of the show. It is your conscious ego and it is always center stage, even when sharing a house or a sign with several other planets. This is why sun sign astrology works for so many people. In chart interpretations, the sun can also play the parental role.

The sun rules the sign of Leo, gaining strength through the pride, dignity, and confidence of the fixed-fire personality. It is exalted in the "me-first" Aries. In its detriment, Aquarius, the sun-ego is strengthened through group participation and social consciousness, rather than through self-centeredness (note how many Aquarius people are involved in politics, social work, public life . . . follow the demands of their sun sign to be spokesperson for a group). In its fall, Libra, the sun needs the strength of a partner—an "other"—to enhance balance and self-expression.

Like your sun sign, each of the other nine planet personalities is colored by the sign it is passing through at the time. For example, Mercury, the planet that rules the way you communicate, will express itself in a dynamic, headstrong Aries way if it is passing through the sign of

Aries when you were born. You will communicate in a much different way if it is passing through the slower, more patient sign of Taurus. And so on through the list. Here's a rundown of the planets and how they behave in every sign.

The Moon Expresses
Your Inner Feelings

The moon can teach you about the inner side of yourself, your needs and secrets, as well as those of others. It is your most personal planet, the receptive, reflective, female, nurturing side of you. And it reflects who you were nurtured by—the "Mother" or mother figure in your chart. In a man's chart, the moon position also describes his female, receptive, emotional side, and the woman in his life who will have the deepest effect. (Venus reveals the kind of woman who attracts him physically).

The sign the moon was passing through at your birth reflects your instinctive emotional nature, what appeals to you subconsciously. Since accurate moon tables are too extensive for this book, check through these descriptions to find the moon sign that feels most familiar, or better yet, have your chart calculated by a computer service to get your accurate moon placement.

The moon rules maternal Cancer and is exalted in Taurus—both comforting, home-loving signs where the natural emotional energies of the moon are easily and productively expressed. But when the moon is in the opposite signs—in its Capricorn detriment and its Scorpio fall—it leaves the comfortable nest and deals with emotional issues of power and achievement in the outside world. Those of you with the moon in these signs will find your emotional role more challenging in life.

Moon in Aries

You are an idealistic, impetuous person who falls in and out of love easily. This placement makes you both independent and ardent. You love a challenge, but could cool once your quarry is captured. You should cultivate patience and tolerance—or you might tend to gravitate toward those who treat you roughly, just for the sake of challenge and excitement.

Moon in Taurus

You are a sentimental soul who is very fond of the good life and gravitates toward solid, secure relationships. You like displays of affection and creature comforts—all the tangible trappings of a cozy, safe, calm atmosphere. You are sensual and steady emotionally, but very stubborn and determined. You can't be pushed and tend to dislike changes. You should make an effort to broaden your horizons and to take a risk sometimes.

Moon in Gemini

You crave mental stimulation and variety in life, which you usually get through either an ever-varied social life, the excitement of flirtation, and/or multiple professional involvements. You may marry more than once and have a rather chaotic emotional life due to your difficulty with commitment and settling down. Be sure to find a partner who is as outgoing as you are. You will have to learn at some point to focus your energies because you tend to be somewhat fragmented—to do two things at once, to have two homes or even two lovers. If you can find a creative way to express your many-faceted nature, you'll be ahead of the game.

Moon in Cancer

This is the most powerful lunar position, which is sure to make a deep imprint on your character. Your needs are very much associated with your reaction to the needs of others. You are very sensitive and self-protective, though some of you may mask this with a hard shell. This placement also gives you an excellent memory, keen intuition,

23

and an uncanny ability to perceive the needs of others. All of the lunar phases will affect you, especially full moons and eclipses, so you would do well to mark them on your calendar. Because you're happiest at home, you may work at home or turn your office into a second home, where you can nurture and comfort people. (You may tend to "mother the world.") With natural psychic, intuitive ability, you might be drawn to occult work in some way. Or you may get professionally involved with providing food and shelter to others.

Moon in Leo

This warm, passionate moon takes everything to heart. You are attracted to all that is noble, generous, and aristocratic in life (and may be a bit of a snob). You have an innate ability to take command emotionally, but you do need strong support, loyalty, and loud applause from those you love. You are possessive of your loved ones and your turf and will roar if anyone threatens to take over your territory.

Moon in Virgo

You are rather cool until you decide if others measure up. But once someone or something meets your ideal standards, you hold up your end of the arrangement perfectly. You may, in fact, drive yourself too hard to attain some notion of perfection. Try to be a bit easier on yourself and others. Don't always act the censor! You love to be the teacher and are drawn to situations where you can change others for the better, but sometimes you must learn to accept others for what they are—enjoy what you have!

Moon in Libra

A partnership-oriented moon—you may find it difficult to be alone or to do things alone. After you have learned emotional balance by leaning on yourself first, you can have excellent relationships. It is best for you to avoid extremes, however, which set your scales swinging and can make your love life precarious. You thrive in a rather conservative, traditional, romantic relationship, where you receive attention and flattery—but not possessiveness—from your partner. You'll be your most charming in an elegant, harmonious atmosphere.

Moon in Scorpio

This is a moon that enjoys and responds to intense, passionate feelings. You may go to extremes and have a very dramatic emotional life, full of ardor, suspicion, jealousy, and obsession. It would be much healthier to channel your need for power and control into meaningful work. This is a good position for anyone in the fields of medicine, police work, research, the occult, psychoanalysis, or intuitive work, because life-and-death situations don't faze you. However, you do take personal disappointments very hard.

Moon in Sagittarius

You take life's ups and downs with good humor and the proverbial grain of salt. You'll love 'em and leave 'em, take off on a great adventure at a moment's notice. "Born free" could be your slogan. Attracted by the exotic, you have wanderlust mentally and physically. You may be too much in search of new mental and spiritual stimulation to ever settle down.

Moon in Capricorn

Are you ever accused of being too cool and calculating? You have an earthy side, but you take prestige and position very seriously. Your strong drive to succeed extends to your romantic life, where you will be devoted to improving your lifestyle, rising to the top. A structured situation where you can advance methodically makes you feel wonderfully secure. You may be attracted to someone older or very much younger or from a different social world. It may be difficult to look at the lighter side of emotional relationships; however, the "up" side of this moon in the sign of its detriment is that you tend to be very dutiful and responsible to those you care for.

Moon in Aquarius

You are a people collector with many friends of all backgrounds. You are happiest surrounded by people and may feel uneasy when left alone. Though you usually stay friends with lovers, intense emotions and demanding one-on-one relationships turn you off. You don't like anything to be too rigid or scheduled. Though tolerant and understanding, you can be emotionally unpredictable and may opt for an unconventional love life. With plenty of space, you will be able to sustain relationships with liberal, freedom-loving types.

Moon in Pisces

You are very responsive and empathetic to others, especially if they have problems or are the underdog. (Be on guard against attracting too many people with sob stories.) You'll be happiest if you can express your creative imagination in the arts or in the spiritual or healing professions. Because you may tend to escape in fantasies or overreact to the moods of others, you need an emotional anchor to help you keep a firm foothold in reality. Steer clear of too much escapism (especially in alcohol) or reclusiveness. Places near water soothe your moods. Working in a field that gives you emotional variety will also help you be productive.

Close Neighbors—Mercury, Venus, and Mars

These planets work in your immediate personal life.
    Mercury affects how you communicate and how your

mental processes work. Are you a quick study who grasps information rapidly, or do you learn more slowly and thoroughly? How is your concentration? Can you express yourself easily? Are you a good writer? All these questions can be answered by your Mercury placement.

Venus shows what you react to. What turns you on? What appeals to you aesthetically? Are you charming to others? Are you attractive to look at? Your taste, your refinement, and your sense of balance and proportion are all Venus-ruled.

Mars is your outgoing energy, your drive and ambition. Do you reach out for new adventures? Are you assertive? Are you motivated? Self-confident? Hot-tempered? How you channel your energy and drive is revealed by your Mars placement.

Mercury Says It All

Since Mercury never travels far from the sun, read Mercury in your sun sign, then the sign preceding and following it. Then decide which reflects the way your mind works.

Mercury in Aries

Your mind is very active and assertive. You never hesitate to say what you think or shy away from a battle. In fact, you may relish a verbal confrontation. Tact is not your strong point, so you may have to learn not to trip over your tongue.

Mercury in Taurus

Though you may be a slow learner, you have good concentration and mental stamina. You want to make your ideas really happen. You'll attack a problem methodically and consider every angle thoroughly, never jumping to conclusions. You'll stick with a subject until you master it.

Mercury in Gemini

You are a wonderful communicator with great facility for expressing yourself both verbally and in writing. You talk and talk, love gathering all kinds of information. You probably finish other people's sentences, talk with hand gestures. You can talk to anybody anytime . . . and probably have phone bills to prove it. You read anything from sci fi to Shakespeare and might need an extra room just for your book collection. Though you learn fast, you may lack focus and discipline. Watch a tendency to jump from subject to subject.

Mercury in Cancer

You rely on intuition more than logic. Your mental processes are usually colored by your emotions, so you may seem shy or hesitant to voice your opinions. However, this placement gives you the advantage of great imagination and empathy in the way you communicate with others.

Mercury in Leo

You are enthusiastic and very dramatic in the way you express yourself. You like to hold the attention of groups and could be a great public speaker. Your mind thinks big, so you'd prefer to deal with the overall picture rather than with the details.

Mercury in Virgo

This is one of the best places for Mercury. It should give you critical ability, attention to details, and thorough analysis. Your mind focuses on the practical side of things. This type of thinking is very well suited to being a teacher or editor.

Mercury in Libra

You're either a born diplomat who smoothes over ruffled feathers or a talented debater. However, since you're forever weighing the pros and cons of a situation, you may vacillate when making decisions.

Mercury in Scorpio

This is an investigative mind that stops at nothing to get the answers. You may have a sarcastic, stinging wit, a gift for the cutting remark. There's always a grain of truth to your verbal sallies, thanks to your penetrating insight.

Mercury in Sagittarius

You are a super-salesman with a tendency to expound. Though you are very broad-minded, you can be dogmatic when it comes to telling others what's good for them. You won't hesitate to tell the truth as you see it, so watch a tendency toward tactlessness. On the plus side, you have a great sense of humor. This position of Mercury is often considered by astrologers to be at a disadvantage because Sagittarius opposes Gemini, the sign Mercury rules, and squares off with Virgo, another Mercury-ruled sign. What often happens is that Mercury in Sagittarius oversteps its bounds and loses sight of the facts in a situation. Do a reality check before making promises that you may not be able to deliver.

Mercury in Capricorn

This placement endows good mental discipline. You have a love of learning and a very orderly approach to your subjects. You will patiently plod through the facts and figures until you have mastered the tasks. You grasp structured situations easily, but may be short on creativity.

Mercury in Aquarius

With Uranus and Neptune in Aquarius now energizing your Mercury, you're sure to be on the cutting edge of new ideas. An independent, original thinker, you'll have more far-out ideas than the average person and be quick to check out any unusual opportunities. Your opinions are so well researched and grounded in fact that once your mind is made up, it is difficult to change.

Mercury in Pisces

You have the psychic intuitive mind of a natural poet. Learn to make use of your creative imagination. You may think in terms of helping others, but check a tendency to be vague and forgetful of details.

Venus Relates

Venus tells how you relate to others and to your environment. It shows where you receive pleasure, what you love to do. Find your Venus placement on the chart in this book by looking for the year of your birth in the left-hand column. Then follow the line of that year across the page until you reach the time period of your birthday. The sign heading that column will be your Venus. If you were born on a day when Venus was changing signs, check the signs preceding or following that day to determine if that feels more like your Venus nature.

Venus in Aries

You can't stand to be bored, confined, or ordered around. But a good challenge, maybe even a rousing row, turns you on. Confess—don't you pick a fight now and then just to get someone stirred up? You're attracted by the chase, not the catch, which could cause some problems in your love life, if the object of your affection becomes too attainable. You like to wear red and be first with the latest fashion. You'll spot a trend before anyone else.

Venus in Taurus

All your senses work in high gear. You love to be surrounded by glorious tastes, smells, textures, sounds, and visuals—austerity is not for you. Neither is being rushed. You like time to enjoy your pleasures. Soothing surroundings with plenty of creature comforts are your cup of tea. You like to feel secure in your nest, with no sudden jolts or surprises. You like familiar objects—in fact, you may hate to let anything or anyone go.

Venus in Gemini

You are a lively, sparkling personality who thrives in a situation that affords a constant variety and a frequent change of scenery. A varied social life is important to you, with plenty of stimulation and a chance to engage in some light flirtation. Commitment may be difficult, because playing the field is so much fun.

Venus in Cancer

An atmosphere where you feel protected, coddled, and mothered is best for you. You love to be surrounded by children in a cozy, homelike situation. You are attracted to those who are tender and nurturing, who make you feel secure and well provided for. You may be quite secretive about your emotional life or attracted to clandestine relationships.

Venus in Leo

First-class attention in large doses turns you on, and so does the glitter of real gold and the flash of mirrors. You like to feel like a star at all times, surrounded by your admiring audience. The side effect is that you may be attracted to flatterers and tinsel, while the real gold requires some digging.

Venus in Virgo

Everything neatly in its place? On the surface, you are attracted to an atmosphere where everything is in perfect order, but underneath are some basic, earthy urges. You are attracted to those who appeal to your need to teach, be of service, or play out a *Pygmalion* fantasy. You are at your best when you are busy doing something useful.

Venus in Libra

Elegance and harmony are your key words. You can't abide an atmosphere of contention. Your taste tends toward the classic, with light harmonies of color—nothing clashing, trendy, or outrageous. You love doing things with a partner and should be careful to pick one who is decisive, but patient enough to let you weigh the pros and cons. And steer clear of argumentative types.

Venus in Scorpio

Hidden mysteries intrigue you—in fact, anything that is too open and aboveboard is a bit of a bore. You surely have a stack of whodunits by the bed, along with an erotic magazine or two. You like to solve puzzles, may also be fascinated with the occult, crime, or scientific research. Intense, all-or-nothing situations add spice to your life, and you love to ferret out the secrets of others. But you could get burned by your flair for living dangerously. The color black, spicy food, dark wood furniture, and heady perfume all get you in the right mood.

Venus in Sagittarius

If you are not actually a world traveler, your surroundings are sure to reflect your love of faraway places. You like a casual outdoor atmosphere and a dog or two to pet. There should be plenty of room for athletic equipment and suitcases. You're attracted to kindred souls who love to travel and who share your freedom-loving philosophy of life. Athletics and spiritual or New Age pursuits could be other interests.

Venus in Capricorn

No fly-by-night relationships for you! You want substance in life and you are attracted to whatever will help you get where you are going. Status objects turn you on. And so do those who have a serious responsible, businesslike approach, or who remind you of a beloved parent. It is characteristic of this placement to be attracted to someone of a different generation. Antiques, traditional clothing, and dignified behavior favor you.

Venus in Aquarius

This Venus wants to make friends more than to make love. You like to be in a group, particularly one pushing a worthy cause. You feel quite at home surrounded by people, remaining detached from any intense commitment. Original ideas and unpredictable people fascinate you. You don't like everything to be planned out in advance, preferring spontaneity and delightful surprises.

Venus in Pisces

This Venus loves to give of yourself, and you find plenty of takers. Stray animals and people appeal to your heart and your pocketbook, but be careful to look at their motives realistically once in a while. You are extremely vulnerable to sob stories of all kinds. Fantasy, theater, and psychic or spiritual activities also speak to you.

Mars Moves and Shakes

Mars is the mover and shaker in your life. It shows how you pursue your goals and whether you have energy to burn or proceed at a slow, steady pace. Or are you nervous, restless, and unable to sit still? It will also show how you get angry: Do you explode, or do a slow burn, or hold everything inside, then get revenge later?

To find your Mars, turn to the chart on page 68. There you will find an abbreviation of your Mars sign. If the description of your Mars sign doesn't ring true, read the description of the sign preceding and following it. You may have been born on a day when Mars was changing signs, and your Mars would then be in the adjacent sign.

Mars in Aries

In the sign it rules, Mars shows its brilliant fiery nature. You have an explosive temper and can be quite impatient, but on the other hand, you have tremendous courage, energy, and drive. You'll let nothing stand in your way as you race to be first! Obstacles are met head-on and broken through by force. However, those that require patience and persistence can have you exploding in rage. You're a great starter, but not necessarily around for the finish.

Mars in Taurus

Slow, steady, concentrated energy gives you the power. You've great stamina and you never give up. Your tactic is to wear away obstacles with your persistence. Often you come out a winner because you've had the patience to hang in there. When angered, you do a slow burn.

Mars in Gemini

You can't sit still for long. This Mars craves variety. You often have two or more things going on at once—it's all an amusing game to you. Your life can get very complicated, but that only adds spice and stimulation. What drives you into a nervous, hyper state? Boredom, sameness, routine, and confinement. You can do wonderful things with your hands and you have a way with words.

Mars in Cancer

You rarely attack head-on—instead, you'll keep things to yourself, make plans in secret, and always cover your actions. This might be interpreted by some as manipulative, but you are only being self-protective. You get furious when anyone knows too much about you. But you do like to know all about others. Your mothering and feeding instincts can be put to good use, if you work in the food, hotel, or child-care business. You may have to overcome your fragile sense of security, which prompts you not to take risks and get physically upset when criticized. Don't take things so personally!

Mars in Leo

You have a very dominant personality that takes center stage—modesty is not one of your traits, nor is taking a backseat. You prefer giving the orders and have been known to make a dramatic scene if they are not obeyed. Properly used, this Mars confers leadership ability, endurance, and courage.

Mars in Virgo

You are the fault-finder of the zodiac, who notices every detail. Mistakes of any kind make you very nervous. You may worry, even if everything is going smoothly. You may not express your anger directly, but you sure can nag. You have definite likes and dislikes, and you are sure you can do the job better than anyone else. You are certainly more industrious and detail-oriented than other signs. Your Mars energy is often most positively expressed in some kind of teaching role.

Mars in Libra

This Mars will have a passion for beauty, justice, and art. Generally, you will avoid confrontations at all costs. You prefer to spend your energy finding diplomatic solutions or weighing pros and cons. Your other techniques are passive aggression or exercising your well-known charm to get people to do what you want.

Mars in Scorpio

This is a powerful placement, so intense that it demands careful channeling into worthwhile activities. Otherwise, you could become obsessed with your sexuality or might use your need for power and control to manipulate others. You are strong-willed, shrewd, and very private about your affairs, and you'll usually have a secret agenda behind your actions. Your great stamina, focus, and discipline would be excellent assets for careers in the military or medical fields, especially research or surgery. When angry, you don't get mad—you get even!

Mars in Sagittarius

This expansive Mars often propels people into sales, travel, athletics, or philosophy. Your energies function well when you are on the move. You have a hot temper and are inclined to say what you think before you consider the consequences. You shoot for high goals—and talk endlessly about them—but you may be weak on groundwork. This Mars needs a solid foundation. Watch a tendency to take unnecessary risks.

Mars in Capricorn

This is an ambitious Mars with an excellent sense of timing. You have an eye for those who can be of use to you, and you may dismiss people ruthlessly when you're angry. But you drive yourself hard and deliver full value. This is a good placement for an executive. You'll aim for status and a high material position in life, and keep climbing despite the odds. A great Mars to have!

Mars in Aquarius

This is the most rebellious Mars. You seem to have a drive to assert yourself against the status quo. You may enjoy provoking people, shocking them out of traditional views. Or this placement could express itself in an offbeat sex life. Somehow you often find yourself in unconventional situations. You enjoy being a leader of an active group, which pursues forward-looking studies, politics, or goals.

Mars in Pisces

This Mars is a good actor who knows just how to appeal to the sympathies of others. You create and project wonderful fantasies or use your sensitive antennae to crusade for those less fortunate. You get what you want through creating a veil of illusion and glamour. This is a good Mars for someone in the creative fields, a dancer, performer, or photographer, or for someone in motion pictures. Many famous film stars have this placement. Watch a tendency to manipulate by making others feel sorry for you.

Jupiter Gives You the Breaks

Jupiter is the planet in your horoscope that makes you want MORE. This big, bright, swirling mass of gases is associated with abundance, prosperity, and the kind of windfall you get without too much hard work. You're optimistic under Jupiter's influence, when anything seems possible. You'll travel, expand your mind with higher education, and publish to share your knowledge widely. But a strong Jupiter has its downside, too, because Jupiter's influence is neither discriminating nor disciplined. It represents the principle of growth without judgment, and could result in extravagance, weight gain, laziness, and carelessness, if not kept in check.

Be sure to look up your Jupiter in the tables in this book. When the current position of Jupiter is favorable, you may get that lucky break. This is a great time to try new things, take risks, travel, or get more education. Opportunities seem to open up easily, so take advantage of them.

Once a year, Jupiter changes signs. That means you are due for an expansive time every twelve years, when Jupiter travels through your sun sign. You'll also have "up" periods every four years, when Jupiter is in the same element as your sun sign.

Jupiter in Aries

You are the soul of enthusiasm and optimism. Your luckiest times are when you are getting started on an exciting project or selling an idea that you really believe in. You may have to watch a tendency to be arrogant with those who do not share your enthusiasm. You follow your impulses, often ignoring budget or other commonsense limitations. To produce real, solid benefits, you'll need patience and follow-through wherever this Jupiter falls in your horoscope.

Jupiter in Taurus

You'll spend on beautiful material things, especially those that come from nature—items made of rare woods, natural fabrics, or precious gems, for instance. You can't have too much comfort or too many sensual pleasures. Watch a tendency to overindulge in good food, or to overpamper yourself with nothing but the best. Spartan living is not for you! You may be especially lucky in matters of real estate.

Jupiter in Gemini

You are the great talker of the zodiac, and you may be a great writer, too. But restlessness could be your weak point. You jump around, talk too much, and could be a jack of all trades. Keeping a secret is especially difficult, so you'll also have to watch a tendency to spill the beans. Since you love to be at the center of a beehive of activity, you'll have a vibrant social life. Your best opportunities will come through your talent for language—speaking, writing, communicating, and selling.

Jupiter in Cancer

You are luckiest in situations where you can find emotional closeness or deal with basic security needs, such as food, nurturing, or shelter. You may be a great collector and you may simply love to accumulate things—you are the one who stashes things away for a rainy day. You probably have a very good memory and love children—in fact, you may have many children to care for. The food, hotel, child-care, or shipping business holds good opportunities for you.

Jupiter in Leo

You are a natural showman who loves to live in a larger-than-life way. Yours is a personality full of color that always finds its way into the limelight. You can't have too much attention or applause. Showbiz is a natural place for you, and so is any area where you can play to a crowd. Exercising your flair for drama, your natural playfulness, and your romantic nature brings you good fortune. But watch a tendency to be overly extravagant or to monopolize center stage.

Jupiter in Virgo

You actually love those minute details others find boring. To you, they make all the difference between the perfect and the ordinary. You are the fine craftsman who spots every flaw. You expand your awareness by finding the most efficient methods and by being of service to others. Many will be drawn to medical or teaching fields. You'll also have luck in publishing, crafts, nutrition, and service professions. Watch out for a tendency to overwork.

Jupiter in Libra

This is an other-directed Jupiter that develops best with a partner, for the stimulation of others helps you grow. You are also most comfortable in harmonious, beautiful situations, and you work well with artistic people. You have a great sense of fair play and an ability to evaluate the pros and cons of a situation. You usually prefer to play the role of diplomat rather than adversary.

Jupiter in Scorpio

You love the feeling of power and control, of taking things to their limit. You can't resist a mystery, and your shrewd, penetrating mind sees right through to the heart of most situations and people. You have luck in work that provides for solutions to matters of life and death. You may be drawn to undercover work, behind-the-scenes intrigue, psychotherapy, the occult, and sex-related ventures. Your challenge will be to develop a sense of moderation and tolerance for other beliefs. This Jupiter can be fanatical. You may have luck in handling other people's money—insurance, taxes, and inheritance can bring you a windfall.

Jupiter in Sagittarius

Independent, outgoing, and idealistic, you'll shoot for the stars. This Jupiter compels you to travel far and wide, both physically and mentally, via higher education. You may have luck while traveling in an exotic place. You also have luck with outdoor ventures, exercise, and animals, particularly horses. Since you tend to be very open about your opinions, watch a tendency to be tactless and to exaggerate. Instead, use your wonderful sense of humor to make your point.

Jupiter in Capricorn

Jupiter is much more restrained in Capricorn, the sign of rules and authority. Here, Jupiter can make you overwork and heighten any ambition or sense of duty you may have. You'll expand in areas that advance your position, putting you farther up the social or corporate ladder. You are lucky working within the establishment in a very structured situation, where you can show off your ability to organize and reap rewards for your hard work.

Jupiter in Aquarius

This is another freedom-loving Jupiter, with great tolerance and originality. You are at your best when you are working for a humanitarian cause and in the company of many supporters. This is a good Jupiter for a political career. You'll relate to all kinds of people on all social levels. You have an abundance of original ideas, but you are best off away from routine and any situation that imposes rigid rules. You need mental stimulation!

Jupiter in Pisces

You are a giver whose feelings and pocketbook are easily touched by others, so choose your companions with care. You could be the original sucker for a hard-luck story. Better find a worthy hospital or charity to appreciate your selfless support. You have a great creative imagination and may attract good fortune in fields related to oil, perfume, pharmaceuticals, petroleum, dance, footwear,

and alcohol. But beware of overindulgence in alcohol—
focus on a creative outlet instead.

Saturn Puts on the Brakes

Jupiter speeds you up with *lucky breaks,* then along
comes Saturn to slow you down with the *disciplinary
brakes.* Saturn has unfairly been called a malefic planet,
one of the bad guys of the zodiac. On the contrary, Saturn is one of our best friends, the kind who tells you
what you need to hear, even if it's not good news. Under
a Saturn transit, we grow up, take responsibility for our
lives, and emerge from whatever test this planet has in
store, far wiser, more capable, and mature.

When Saturn hits a critical point in your horoscope,
you can count on an experience that will make you slow
up, pull back, and reexamine your life. It is a call to
eliminate what is not working and to shape up. By the
end of its twenty-eight-year trip around the zodiac, Saturn will have tested you in all areas of your life. The
major tests happen in seven-year cycles, when Saturn
passes over the *angles* of your chart—your rising sign,
midheaven, descendant, and nadir. This is when the real
life-changing experiences happen. But you are also in for
a testing period whenever Saturn passes a *planet* in your
chart or stresses that planet from a distance. Therefore,
it is useful to check your planetary positions with the
timetable of Saturn to prepare in advance, or at least to
brace yourself.

When Saturn returns to its location at the time of your
birth, at approximately age twenty-eight, you'll have your
first Saturn return. At this time, a person usually takes
stock or settles down to find his mission in life and as-
sumes full adult duties and responsibilities.

Another way Saturn helps us is to reveal the karmic
lessons from previous lives and gives us the chance to
overcome them. So look at Saturn's challenges as much-
needed opportunities for self-improvement. Under a Jupi-

ter influence, you'll have more fun, but Saturn gives you solid, long-lasting results.

Look up your natal Saturn in the tables in this book for clues on where you need work.

Saturn in Aries

Saturn here puts the brakes on Aries' natural drive and enthusiasm. You don't let anyone push you around and you know what's best for yourself. Following orders is not your strong point, and neither is diplomacy. You tend to be quick to go on the offensive in relationships, attacking first, before anyone attacks you. Because no one quite lives up to your standards, you often wind up doing everything yourself. You'll have to learn to cooperate, tone down self-centeredness.

Saturn in Taurus

A big issue is getting control of the cash flow. There will be lean periods that can be frightening, but you have the patience and endurance to stick them out and the methodical drive to prosper in the end. Learn to take a philosophical attitude like Ben Franklin, who also had this placement and who said, "A penny saved is a penny earned."

Saturn in Gemini

You are a serious student of life who may have difficulty communicating or sharing your knowledge. You may be shy, speak slowly, or have fears about communicating, like Eleanor Roosevelt. You dwell in the realms of science, theory, or abstract analysis, even when you are dealing with the emotions, like Sigmund Freud, who also had this placement.

Saturn in Cancer

Your tests come with establishing a secure emotional base. In doing so, you may have to deal with some very basic fears centering on your early home environment. Most of your Saturn tests will have emotional roots in those early childhood experiences. You may have difficulty remaining objective in terms of what you try to achieve, so it will be especially important for you to deal with negative feelings such as guilt, paranoia, jealousy, resentment, and suspicion. Galileo and Michelangelo also navigated these murky waters.

Saturn in Leo

This is an authoritarian Saturn, a strict, demanding parent who may deny the pleasure principle in your zeal to see that rules are followed. Though you may feel guilty about taking the spotlight, you are very ambitious and loyal. You have to watch a tendency toward rigidity, also toward overwork and holding back affection. Joseph Kennedy and Billy Graham share this placement.

Saturn in Virgo

This is a cautious, exacting Saturn, intensely hard on yourself. Most of all, you give yourself the roughest time with your constant worries about every little detail, often making yourself sick. You may have difficulties setting priorities and getting the job done. Your tests will come in learning tolerance and understanding of others. Charles de Gaulle, Mae West, and Nathaniel Hawthorne had this meticulous Saturn.

Saturn in Libra

Saturn is exalted here, which makes this planet an ally. You may choose very serious, older partners in life, perhaps stemming from a fear of dependency. You need to learn to stand solidly on your own before you commit to another. You are extremely cautious as you deliberate every involvement—with good reason. It is best that you find an occupation that makes good use of your sense of duty and honor. Steer clear of fly-by-night situations.

Both Khrushchev and Mao Tse-tung had this placement, too.

Saturn in Scorpio

You have great staying power. This Saturn tests you in situations involving the control of others. You may feel drawn to some kind of intrigue or undercover work, like J. Edgar Hoover. Or there may be an air of mystery surrounding your life and death, like Marilyn Monroe and Robert Kennedy, who had this placement. There are lessons to be learned from your sexual involvements—often sex is used for manipulation or is somehow out of the ordinary. The Roman emperor Caligula and the transvestite Christine Jorgensen are extreme cases.

Saturn in Sagittarius

Your challenges and lessons will come from tests of your spiritual and philosophical values, as happened to Martin Luther King and Gandhi. You are high-minded and sincere with this reflective, moral placement. Uncompromising in your ethical standards, you could become a benevolent despot.

Saturn in Capricorn

With the help of Saturn at maximum strength, your judgment will improve with age. And, like Spencer Tracy's screen image, you'll be the gray-haired hero with a strong sense of responsibility. You advance in life slowly but steadily, always with a strong hand at the helm and an eye for the advantageous situation. Like Pat Robertson, you're likely to stand for conservative values. Negatively, you may be a loner, prone to periods of melancholy.

Saturn in Aquarius

Your tests come from relationships with groups. Do you care too much about what others think? Do you feel like an outsider, like Greta Garbo? You may fear being different from others and therefore slight your own unique, forward-looking gifts, or, like Lord Byron and Howard Hughes, take the opposite tack and rebel in the extreme. You can apply discipline to accomplish great humanitarian goals, as Albert Schweitzer did.

Saturn in Pisces

Your fear of the unknown and the irrational may lead you to the safety and protection of an institution. You may go on the run like Jesse James, who had this placement, to avoid looking too deeply inside. Or you might go in the opposite, more positive direction and develop a disciplined psychoanalytic approach, which puts you more in control of your feelings. Some of you will take refuge in work with hospitals, charities, or religious institutions. Queen Victoria, who had this placement, symbolized an era when institutions of all kinds were sustained. Discipline applied to artistic work, especially poetry and dance, or spiritual work, such as yoga or meditation, might be helpful.

Uranus, Neptune, and Pluto Affect Your Whole Generation

These three planets remain in signs such a long time that a whole generation bears the imprint of the sign. Mass movements, great sweeping changes, fads that characterize a generation, and even the issues of the conflicts and wars of the time are influenced by the "outer three." When one of these distant planets changes signs, there is a definite shift in the atmosphere, the feeling of the end of an era.

Since these planets are so far away from the sun—too distant to be seen by the naked eye—they pick up signals from the universe at large. These planetary receivers literally link the sun with distant energies, and then perform a similar function in your horoscope by linking your central character with intuitive, spiritual, transformative forces from the cosmos. Each planet has a special domain and will reflect this in the area of your chart where it falls.

Uranus Wakes You Up

There is nothing ordinary about this quirky green planet that seems to be traveling on its side, surrounded by a swarm of moons. Is it any wonder that astrologers assigned it to Aquarius, the most eccentric and gregarious sign? Uranus seems to wend its way around the sun, marching to its own tune.

Uranus energy is electrical, happening in sudden flashes. It is not influenced by karma or past events, nor does it regard tradition, sex, or sentiment. The Uranian key words are surprise and awakening. Uranus wakes you up, jolts you out of your comfortable rut. Suddenly, there's that flash of inspiration, that bright idea, that totally new approach to revolutionize whatever scheme you were undertaking. A Uranus event takes you by surprise, happens from out of the blue, for better or for worse. The Uranus place in your life is where you awaken and become your own person, leaving the structures of Saturn behind. And it is probably the most unconventional place in your chart.

Look up the sign of Uranus at the time of your birth and see where you follow your own tune. If Uranus changed signs on your day of birth, this means you were born on the cusp—a very powerful placement.

Uranus in Aries

BIRTH DATES:
March 31, 1927–November 4, 1927
January 13, 1928–June 6, 1934
October 10, 1934–March 28, 1935
Your generation is original, creative, pioneering. It developed the computer, the airplane, and the cyclotron. You

let nothing hold you back from exploring the unknown and have a powerful mixture of fire and electricity behind you. Women of your generation were among the first to be liberated. You were the unforgettable style setters. You have a surprise in store for everyone. Like Yoko Ono, Grace Kelly, and Jacqueline Onassis, your life may be jolted by sudden and violent changes.

Uranus in Taurus

BIRTH DATES:
June 6, 1934–October 10, 1934
March 28, 1935–August 7, 1941
October 5, 1941–May 15, 1942

World War II began during your generation. You are probably self-employed or would like to be. You have original ideas about making money, and you brace yourself for sudden changes of fortune. This Uranus can cause shake-ups, particularly in finances, but it can also make you a born entrepreneur.

Uranus in Gemini

BIRTH DATES:
August 7, 1941–October 5, 1941
May 15, 1942–August 30, 1948
November 12, 1948–June 10, 1949

You were the first children to be influenced by television, and now in your adult years, your generation stocks up on answering machines, cordless phones, car phones, computers, and fax machines—any new way you can communicate. You have an inquiring mind, but your interests may be rather short-lived. This Uranus can be easily fragmented if there is no structure and focus.

Uranus in Cancer

BIRTH DATES:
August 30, 1948–November 12, 1948
June 10, 1949–August 24, 1955

January 28–June 10, 1956

This generation came at a time when divorce was becoming commonplace, so your home image is unconventional. You may have an unusual relationship with your parents; you may have come from a broken home or an unconventional one. You'll have unorthodox ideas about parenting, intimacy, food, and shelter. You may also be interested in dreams, psychic phenomena, and memory work.

Uranus in Leo

BIRTH DATES:
August 24, 1955–January 28, 1956
June 10, 1956–November 1, 1961
January 10, 1962–August 10, 1962

This generation understood how to use electronic media. Many of your group are now leaders in the high-tech industries, and you also understand how to use the new media to promote yourself. Like Isadora Duncan, you may have a very eccentric kind of charisma and a life that is sparked by unusual love affairs. Your children, too, may have traits that are out of the ordinary. Where this planet falls in your chart, you'll have a love of freedom, be a bit of an egomaniac, and show the full force of your personality in a unique way, like tennis great Martina Navratilova.

Uranus in Virgo

BIRTH DATES:
November 1, 1961–January 10, 1962
August 10, 1962–September 28, 1968
May 20, 1969–June 24, 1969

You'll have highly individual work methods, and many will be finding newer, more practical ways to use computers. Like Einstein, who had this placement, you'll break the rules brilliantly. Your generation came at a time of student rebellions, the civil rights movement, and the general acceptance of health foods. Chances are, you're concerned about pollution and cleaning up the environment. You may also be involved with nontraditional healing methods. Heavyweight champ Mike Tyson has this placement.

Uranus in Libra

BIRTH DATES:
September 28, 1968–May 20, 1969
June 24, 1969–November 21, 1974
May 1, 1975–September 8, 1975

Your generation will always be changing partners. Born during the era of women's liberation, you may have come from a broken home and have no clear image of what a marriage entails. There will be many sudden splits and experiments before you settle down. Your generation will be much involved in legal and political reforms and in changing artistic and fashion looks.

Uranus in Scorpio

BIRTH DATES:
November 21, 1974–May 1, 1975
September 8, 1975–February 17, 1981
March 20, 1981–November 16, 1981

Interest in transformation, meditation, and life after death signaled the beginning of New Age consciousness. Your generation recognizes no boundaries, no limits, and no external controls. You'll have new attitudes toward death and dying, psychic phenomena and the occult. Like Mae West and Casanova, you'll shock 'em sexually, too.

Uranus in Sagittarius

BIRTH DATES:
February 17, 1981–March 20, 1981
November 16, 1981–February 15, 1988
May 27, 1988–December 2, 1988

Could this generation be the first to travel in outer space? The last generation with this placement included Charles Lindbergh—at that time, the first zeppelins and the Wright Brothers were conquering the skies. Uranus here forecasts great discoveries, mind expansion, and long-distance travel. Like Galileo and Martin Luther, those born in these years will generate new theories about the cosmos and man's relation to it.

Uranus in Capricorn

BIRTH DATES:
December 20, 1904–January 30, 1912
September 4, 1912–November 12, 1912
February 15, 1988–May 27, 1988
December 2, 1988–April 1, 1995
June 9, 1995–January 12, 1996

This generation will challenge traditions with the help of electronic gadgets. In these years, we got organized with the help of technology put to practical use. Great leaders, who were movers and shakers of history, like Julius Caesar and Henry VIII, were born under this placement.

Uranus in Aquarius

BIRTH DATES:
January 30, 1912–September 4, 1912
November 12, 1912–April 1, 1919
August 16, 1919–January 22, 1920
April 1, 1995–June 9, 1995
January 12, 1996–March 11, 2003

The last generation with this placement produced great innovative minds such as Leonard Bernstein and Orson Welles. The next will become another radical breakthrough generation, much concerned with global issues that involve all humanity. Intuition, innovation, and sudden changes will surprise everyone when Uranus is in its home sign. This will be a time of experimentation on every level.

Uranus in Pisces

BIRTH DATES:
April 1, 1919–August 16, 1919

January 22, 1920–March 31, 1927
November 4, 1927–January 12, 1928
March 11, 2003–May 28, 2010

In this century, Uranus in Pisces focused attention on the rise of electronic entertainment—radio and the cinema—and the secretiveness of Prohibition. This produced a generation of idealists exemplified by Judy Garland's theme, "Somewhere Over the Rainbow."

Neptune Takes You Out of This World

Under Neptune's influence, you see what you want to see. But Neptune also encourages you to create, lets your fantasies and daydreams run free. Neptune is often maligned as the planet of illusions, drugs and alcohol, where you can't bear to face reality. But it also embodies the energy of glamour, subtlety, mystery, and mysticism, and governs anything that takes you beyond the mundane world, including out-of-body experiences.

Neptune acts to break through your ordinary perceptions and take you to another level of reality, where you experience either confusion or ecstasy. Neptune's force can pull you off course, just as this planet affects it neighbor, Uranus, but only if you allow this to happen. Those who use Neptune wisely can translate their daydreams into poetry, theater, design, or inspired moves in the business world, avoiding the tricky "con artist" side of this planet.

Find your Neptune listed here:

Neptune in Cancer

BIRTH DATES:
July 19, 1901–December 25, 1901
May 21, 1902–September 23, 1914
December 14, 1914–July 19, 1915
March 19, 1916–May 2, 1916

Dreams of the homeland, idealistic patriotism, and glamorization of the nurturing assets of women characterized this time. You who were born here have unusual psychic ability and deep insights into the basic needs of others.

Neptune in Leo

BIRTH DATES:
September 23, 1914–December 14, 1914
July 19, 1915–March 19, 1916
May 2, 1916–September 21, 1928
February 19, 1929–July 24, 1929

Neptune here brought us the glamour and high living of the 1920s and the big spenders of that time. Neptunian temptations of gambling, seduction, theater, and lavish entertaining distracted from the realities of the age. Those born in that generation also made great advances in the arts.

Neptune in Virgo

BIRTH DATES:
September 21, 1928–February 19, 1929
July 24, 1929–October 3, 1942
April 17, 1943–August 2, 1943

Neptune in Virgo encompassed the Great Depression and World War II, while those born at this time later spread the gospel of health and fitness. This generation's devotion to spending hours at the office inspired the term "workaholic."

Neptune in Libra

BIRTH DATES:
October 3, 1942–April 17, 1943
August 2, 1943–December 24, 1955
March 12, 1956–October 19, 1956
June 15, 1957–August 6, 1957

Neptune in Libra was the romantic generation who would later be concerned with relating. As this generation matured, there was a new trend toward marriage and commitment. Racial and sexual equality became important issues, as they redesigned traditional roles to suit modern times.

Neptune in Scorpio

BIRTH DATES:
December 24, 1955–March 12, 1956
October 19, 1956–June 15, 1957
August 6, 1957–January 4, 1970
May 3, 1970–November 6, 1970

Neptune in Scorpio brought in a generation that would become interested in transformative power. Born in an era that glamorized sex, drugs, rock and roll, and Eastern religion, they matured in a more sobering time of AIDS, cocaine abuse, and New Age spirituality. As they evolve, they will become active in healing the planet from the results of the abuse of power.

Neptune in Sagittarius

BIRTH DATES:
January 4, 1970–May 3, 1970
November 6, 1970–January 19, 1984
June 23, 1984–November 21, 1984

Neptune in Sagittarius was the time when space and astronaut travel became a reality. The Neptune influence glamorized new approaches to mysticism, religion, and mind expansion. This generation will take a new approach to spiritual life, with emphasis on visions, mysticism, and clairvoyance.

Neptune in Capricorn

BIRTH DATES:
January 19, 1984–June 23, 1984
November 21, 1984–January 29, 1998

Neptune in Capricorn brought a time when delusions about material power were first glamorized, then dashed on the rocks of reality. It was also a time when the psychic and occult worlds spawned a new category of business enterprise, and sold services on television.

Neptune in Aquarius

BIRTH DATES:
January 29, 1998–April 4, 2111

This should continue to be a time of breakthroughs, when the creative influence of Neptune reaches a universal audience. This is a time of dissolving barriers, of globalization, when we truly become one world.

Pluto Transforms You

Pluto is a mysterious little planet with a strange elliptical orbit that occasionally runs inside the orbit of its neighbor Neptune. Because of its eccentric path, the length of time Pluto stays in any given sign can vary from thirteen to thirty-two years. It has covered only seven signs in the last century. Though it is a tiny planet, its influence is great. When Pluto zaps a strategic point in your horoscope, your life changes dramatically.

This little planet is the power behind the scenes; it affects you at deep levels of consciousness, causing events to come to the surface that will transform you and your generation. Nothing escapes, or is sacred, with this probing planet. The Pluto place in your horoscope is where you have invisible power (Mars governs the visible power), where you can transform, heal, and affect the unconscious needs of the masses. Pluto tells lots about how your generation projects power, what makes it seem "cool" to others. And when Pluto changes signs, there's a whole new concept of what's cool.

Pluto in Gemini

BIRTH DATES:
Late 1800s–May 26, 1914

This was a time of mass suggestion and breakthroughs

in communications, when many brilliant writers, such as Ernest Hemingway and F. Scott Fitzgerald, were born. Henry Miller, D. H. Lawrence, and James Joyce scandalized society by using explicit sexual images and language in their literature. "Muckraking" journalists exposed corruption. Pluto-ruled Scorpio President Theodore Roosevelt said, "Speak softly, but carry a big stick." This generation had an intense need to communicate and made major breakthroughs in knowledge. A compulsive restlessness and a thirst for a variety of experiences characterizes many of this generation.

Pluto in Cancer

BIRTH DATES:
May 26, 1914–June 14, 1939
Dictators and mass media arose to wield emotional power over the masses. Women's rights was a popular issue. Deep sentimental feelings, acquisitiveness, and possessiveness characterized these times and people. Most of the great stars of the Hollywood era that embodied the American image were born during this period: Grace Kelly, Esther Williams, Frank Sinatra, Lana Turner, etc.

Pluto in Leo

BIRTH DATES:
June 14, 1939–August 19, 1957
The performing arts, under Leo's rule, never wielded more power over the masses than during this era. Pluto in Leo transforms via creative self-expression, exemplified by the almost shamanistic rock and roll stars such as Mick Jagger and John Lennon, who were born at this time. (So were Bill and Hillary Clinton.) People born with Pluto in Leo often tend to be self-centered and love to "do their own thing"—for better or for worse.

Pluto in Virgo

BIRTH DATES:
August 19, 1957–October 5, 1971
April 17, 1972–July 30, 1972

This became the "yuppie" generation that sparked a mass clean-up shape-up movement toward fitness, health, and obsessive careerism. It's a much more sober, serious, driven generation than the fun-loving Pluto in Leo. During this time, inventions took on a practical turn, as answering machines, fax machines, car phones, and home office equipment have all transformed the workplace.

Pluto in Libra

BIRTH DATES:
October 5, 1971–April 17, 1972
July 30, 1972–August 28, 1984

A mellower generation, people born at this time are concerned with partnerships, working together, and finding diplomatic solutions to problems. Marriage is important to this generation, who redefine it along more traditional, but equal-partnership lines. This was a time of women's liberation, gay rights, ERA, and legal battles over abortion, all of which transformed our ideas about relationships.

Pluto in Scorpio

BIRTH DATES:
August 28, 1984–January 17, 1995

Pluto was in its ruling sign for a comparatively short period of time. In 1989, it was at its perihelion, or the closest point to the sun and Earth. We have all felt this transforming power somewhere in our lives. This was a time of record achievements, destructive sexually transmitted diseases, nuclear power controversies, and explosive political issues. Pluto destroys in order to create new understanding—think of it as a phoenix rising from the ashes, which should be some consolation for those of you who have felt Pluto's force before 1995. Sexual shockers were par for the course during these intense years, when black clothing, transvestites, body piercing, tattoos, and sexually explicit advertising pushed the boundaries of good taste.

Pluto in Sagittarius

BIRTH DATES:
January 17, 1995–January 27, 2008

During our current Pluto transit through Sagittarius, we are being pushed to expand our horizons and find deeper meaning in life. For many of us, this will mean traveling the globe via our modems as we explore the vastness of the Internet. It signals a time of spiritual transformation and religion will exert much power in politics as well. Since Sagittarius is the sign that rules travel, there's a good possibility that Pluto, the planet of extremes, will make space travel a reality for some of us. Discovery of life on Mars, traveling here as minute life forms on meteors, could transform our ideas about where we came from. At this writing, a giant telescope in Puerto Rico has been reactivated to search the faraway galaxies for pulsing hints of life.

New dimensions in electronic publishing, concern with animal rights and the environment, and an increasing emphasis on extreme forms of religion are signs of Pluto in Sagittarius. Look for charismatic religious leaders to arise now. We'll also be developing far-reaching philosophies designed to elevate our lives with a new sense of purpose.

Look Up Your Planets

The following tables are provided so that you can look up the signs of the other major planets—Venus, Mars,

Saturn, and Jupiter. We do not have room for tables for the moon and Mercury, which change signs often.

How to Use the Venus Table

Find the year of your birth in the vertical column on the left, then follow across the page until you find the correct date. Your Venus sign is at the top of that column.

VENUS SIGNS 1901–2001

	Aries	Taurus	Gemini	Cancer	Leo	Virgo
1901	3/29–4/22	4/22–5/17	5/17–6/10	6/10–7/5	7/5–7/29	7/29–8/23
1902	5/7–6/3	6/3–6/30	6/30–7/25	7/25–8/19	8/19–9/13	9/13–10/7
1903	2/28–3/24	3/24–4/18	4/18–5/13	5/13–6/9	6/9–7/7	7/7–8/17
						9/6–11/8
1904	3/13–5/7	5/7–6/1	6/1–6/25	6/25–7/19	7/19–8/13	8/13–9/6
1905	2/3–3/6	3/6–4/9	7/8–8/6	8/6–9/1	9/1–9/27	9/27–10/21
	4/9–5/28	5/28–7/8				
1906	3/1–4/7	4/7–5/2	5/2–5/26	5/26–6/20	6/20–7/16	7/16–8/11
1907	4/27–5/22	5/22–6/16	6/16–7/11	7/11–8/4	8/4–8/29	8/29–9/22
1908	2/14–3/10	3/10–4/5	4/5–5/5	5/5–9/8	9/8–10/8	10/8–11/3
1909	3/29–4/22	4/22–5/16	5/16–6/10	6/10–7/4	7/4–7/29	7/29–8/23
1910	5/7–6/3	6/4–6/29	6/30–7/24	7/25–8/18	8/19–9/12	9/13–10/6
1911	2/28–3/23	3/24–4/17	4/18–5/12	5/13–6/8	6/9–7/7	7/8–11/8
1912	4/13–5/6	5/7–5/31	6/1–6/24	6/24–7/18	7/19–8/12	8/13–9/5
1913	2/3–3/6	3/7–5/1	7/8–8/5	8/6–8/31	9/1–9/26	9/27–10/20
	5/2–5/30	5/31–7/7				
1914	3/14–4/6	4/7–5/1	5/2–5/25	5/26–6/19	6/20–7/15	7/16–8/10
1915	4/27–5/21	5/22–6/15	6/16–7/10	7/11–8/3	8/4–8/28	8/29–9/21
1916	2/14–3/9	3/10–4/5	4/6–5/5	5/6–9/8	9/9–10/7	10/8–11/2
1917	3/29–4/21	4/22–5/15	5/16–6/9	6/10–7/3	7/4–7/28	7/29–8/21
1918	5/7–6/2	6/3–6/28	6/29–7/24	7/25–8/18	8/19–9/11	9/12–10/5
1919	2/27–3/22	3/23–4/16	4/17–5/12	5/13–6/7	6/8–7/7	7/8–11/8
1920	4/12–5/6	5/7–5/30	5/31–6/23	6/24–7/18	7/19–8/11	8/12–9/4
1921	2/3–3/6	3/7–4/25	7/8–8/5	8/6–8/31	9/1–9/25	9/26–10/20
	4/26–6/1	6/2–7/7				
1922	3/13–4/6	4/7–4/30	5/1–5/25	5/26–6/19	6/20–7/14	7/15–8/9
1923	4/27–5/21	5/22–6/14	6/15–7/9	7/10–8/3	8/4–8/27	8/28–9/20
1924	2/13–3/8	3/9–4/4	4/5–5/5	5/6–9/8	9/9–10/7	10/8–11/12
1925	3/28–4/20	4/21–5/15	5/16–6/8	6/9–7/3	7/4–7/27	7/28–8/21

Libra	Scorpio	Sagittarius	Capricorn	Aquarius	Pisces
8/23–9/17	9/17–10/12	10/12–1/16	1/16–2/9	2/9–3/5	3/5–3/29
			11/7–12/5	12/5–1/11	
10/7–10/31	10/31–11/24	11/24–12/18	12/18–1/11	2/6–4/4	1/11–2/6
					4/4–5/7
8/17–9/6	12/9–1/5			1/11–2/4	2/4–2/28
11/8–12/9					
9/6–9/30	9/30–10/25	1/5–1/30	1/30–2/24	2/24–3/19	3/19–4/13
		10/25–11/18	11/18–12/13	12/13–1/7	
10/21–11/14	11/14–12/8	12/8–1/1/06			1/7–2/3
8/11–9/7	9/7–10/9	10/9–12/15	1/1–1/25	1/25–2/18	2/18–3/14
	12/15–12/25	12/25–2/6			
9/22–10/16	10/16–11/9	11/9–12/3	2/6–3/6	3/6–4/2	4/2–4/27
			12/3–12/27	12/27–1/20	
11/3–11/28	11/28–12/22	12/22–1/15			1/20–2/4
8/23–9/17	9/17–10/12	10/12–11/17	1/15–2/9	2/9–3/5	3/5–3/29
			11/17–12/5	12/5–1/15	
10/7–10/30	10/31–11/23	11/24–12/17	12/18–12/31	1/1–1/15	1/16–1/28
				1/29–4/4	4/5–5/6
11/19–12/8	12/9–12/31		1/1–1/10	1/11–2/2	2/3–2/27
9/6–9/30	1/1–1/4	1/5–1/29	1/30–2/23	2/24–3/18	3/19–4/12
	10/1–10/24	10/25–11/17	11/18–12/12	12/13–12/31	
10/21–11/13	11/14–12/7	12/8–12/31		1/1–1/6	1/7–2/2
8/11–9/6	9/7–10/9	10/10–12/5	1/1–1/24	1/25–2/17	2/18–3/13
	12/6–12/30	12/31			
9/22–10/15	10/16–11/8	1/1–2/6	2/7–3/6	3/7–4/1	4/2–4/26
		11/9–12/2	12/3–12/26	12/27–12/31	
11/3–11/27	11/28–12/21	12/22–12/31		1/1–1/19	1/20–2/13
8/22–9/16	9/17–10/11	1/1–1/14	1/15–2/7	2/8–3/4	3/5–3/28
		10/12–11/6	11/7–12/5	12/6–12/31	
10/6–10/29	10/30–11/22	11/23–12/16	12/17–12/31	1/1–4/5	4/6–5/6
11/9–12/8	12/9–12/31		1/1–1/9	1/10–2/2	2/3–2/26
9/5–9/30	1/1–1/3	1/4–1/28	1/29–2/22	2/23–3/18	3/19–4/11
	9/31–10/23	10/24–11/17	11/18–12/11	12/12–12/31	
10/21–11/13	11/14–12/7	12/8–12/31		1/1–1/6	1/7–2/2
8/10–9/6	9/7–10/10	10/11–11/28	1/1–1/24	1/25–2/16	2/17–3/12
	11/29–12/31				
9/21–10/14	1/1	1/2–2/6	2/7–3/5	3/6–3/31	4/1–4/26
	10/15–11/7	11/8–12/1	12/2–12/25	12/26–12/31	
11/13–11/26	11/27–12/21	12/22–12/31		1/1–1/19	1/20–2/12
8/22–9/15	9/16–10/11	1/1–1/14	1/15–2/7	2/8–3/3	3/4–3/27
		10/12–11/6	11/7–12/5	12/6–12/31	

VENUS SIGNS 1901–2001

	Aries	Taurus	Gemini	Cancer	Leo	Virgo
1926	5/7–6/2	6/3–6/28	6/29–7/23	7/24–8/17	8/18–9/11	9/12–10/5
1927	2/27–3/22	3/23–4/16	4/17–5/11	5/12–6/7	6/8–7/7	7/8–11/9
1928	4/12–5/5	5/6–5/29	5/30–6/23	6/24–7/17	7/18–8/11	8/12–9/4
1929	2/3–3/7	3/8–4/19	7/8–8/4	8/5–8/30	8/31–9/25	9/26–10/19
	4/20–6/2	6/3–7/7				
1930	3/13–4/5	4/6–4/30	5/1–5/24	5/25–6/18	6/19–7/14	7/15–8/9
1931	4/26–5/20	5/21–6/13	6/14–7/8	7/9–8/2	8/3–8/26	8/27–9/19
1932	2/12–3/8	3/9–4/3	4/4–5/5	5/6–7/12	9/9–10/6	10/7–11/1
			7/13–7/27	7/28–9/8		
1933	3/27–4/19	4/20–5/28	5/29–6/8	6/9–7/2	7/3–7/26	7/27–8/20
1934	5/6–6/1	6/2–6/27	6/28–7/22	7/23–8/16	8/17–9/10	9/11–10/4
1935	2/26–3/21	3/22–4/15	4/16–5/10	5/11–6/6	6/7–7/6	7/7–11/8
1936	4/11–5/4	5/5–5/28	5/29–6/22	6/23–7/16	7/17–8/10	8/11–9/4
1937	2/2–3/8	3/9–4/13	7/7–8/3	8/4–8/29	8/30–9/24	9/25–10/18
	4/14–6/3	6/4–7/6				
1938	3/12–4/4	4/5–4/28	4/29–5/23	5/24–6/18	6/19–7/13	7/14–8/8
1939	4/25–5/19	5/20–6/13	6/14–7/8	7/9–8/1	8/2–8/25	8/26–9/19
1940	2/12–3/7	3/8–4/3	4/4–5/5	5/6–7/4	9/9–10/5	10/6–10/31
			7/5–7/31	8/1–9/8		
1941	3/27–4/19	4/20–5/13	5/14–6/6	6/7–7/1	7/2–7/26	7/27–8/20
1942	5/6–6/1	6/2–6/26	6/27–7/22	7/23–8/16	8/17–9/9	9/10–10/3
1943	2/25–3/20	3/21–4/14	4/15–5/10	5/11–6/6	6/7–7/6	7/7–11/8
1944	4/10–5/3	5/4–5/28	5/29–6/21	6/22–7/16	7/17–8/9	8/10–9/2
1945	2/2–3/10	3/11–4/6	7/7–8/3	8/4–8/29	8/30–9/23	9/24–10/18
	4/7–6/3	6/4–7/6				
1946	3/11–4/4	4/5–4/28	4/29–5/23	5/24–6/17	6/18–7/12	7/13–8/8
1947	4/25–5/19	5/20–6/12	6/13–7/7	7/8–8/1	8/2–8/25	8/26–9/18
1948	2/11–3/7	3/8–4/3	4/4–5/6	5/7–6/28	9/8–10/5	10/6–10/31
			6/29–8/2	8/3–9/7		
1949	3/26–4/19	4/20–5/13	5/14–6/6	6/7–6/30	7/1–7/25	7/26–8/19
1950	5/5–5/31	6/1–6/26	6/27–7/21	7/22–8/15	8/16–9/9	9/10–10/3
1951	2/25–3/21	3/22–4/15	4/16–5/10	5/11–6/6	6/7–7/7	7/8–11/9

Libra	Scorpio	Sagittarius	Capricorn	Aquarius	Pisces
10/6–10/29	10/30–11/22	11/23–12/16	12/17–12/31	1/1–4/5	4/6–5/6
11/10–12/8	12/9–12/31	1/1–1/7	1/8	1/9–2/1	2/2–2/26
9/5–9/28	1/1–1/3	1/4–1/28	1/29–2/22	2/23–3/17	3/18–4/11
	9/29–10/23	10/24–11/16	11/17–12/11	12/12–12/31	
10/20–11/12	11/13–12/6	12/7–12/30	12/31	1/1–1/5	1/6–2/2
8/10–9/6	9/7–10/11	10/12–11/21	1/1–1/23	1/24–2/16	2/17–3/12
	11/22–12/31				
9/20–10/13	1/1–1/3	1/4–2/6	2/7–3/4	3/5–3/31	4/1–4/25
	10/14–11/6	11/7–11/30	12/1–12/24	12/25–12/31	
11/2–11/25	11/26–12/20	12/21–12/31		1/1–1/18	1/19–2/11
8/21–9/14	9/15–10/10	1/1–1/13	1/14–2/6	2/7–3/2	3/3–3/26
		10/11–11/5	11/6–12/4	12/5–12/31	
10/5–10/28	10/29–11/21	11/22–12/15	12/16–12/31	1/1–4/5	4/6–5/5
11/9–12/7	12/8–12/31		1/1–1/7	1/8–1/31	2/1–2/25
9/5–9/27	1/1–1/2	1/3–1/27	1/28–2/21	2/22–3/16	3/17–4/10
	9/28–10/22	10/23–11/15	11/16–12/10	12/11–12/31	
10/19–11/11	11/12–12/5	12/6–12/29	12/30–12/31	1/1–1/5	1/6–2/1
8/9–9/6	9/7–10/13	10/14–11/14	1/1–1/22	1/23–2/15	2/16–3/11
	11/15–12/31				
9/20–10/13	1/1–1/3	1/4–2/5	2/6–3/4	3/5–3/30	3/31–4/24
	10/14–11/6	11/7–11/30	12/1–12/24	12/25–12/31	
11/1–11/25	11/26–12/19	12/20–12/31		1/1–1/18	1/19–2/11
8/21–9/14	9/15–10/9	1/1–1/12	1/13–2/5	2/6–3/1	3/2–3/26
		10/10–11/5	11/6–12/4	12/5–12/31	
10/4–10/27	10/28–11/20	11/21–12/14	12/15–12/31	1/1–4/4	4/6–5/5
11/9–12/7	12/8–12/31		1/1–1/7	1/8–1/31	2/1–2/24
9/3–9/27	1/1–1/2	1/3–1/27	1/28–2/20	2/21–3/16	3/17–4/9
	9/28–10/21	10/22–11/15	11/16–12/10	12/11–12/31	
10/19–11/11	11/12–12/5	12/6–12/29	12/30–12/31	1/1–1/4	1/5–2/1
8/9–9/6	9/7–10/15	10/16–11/7	1/1–1/21	1/22–2/14	2/15–3/10
	11/8–12/31				
9/19–10/12	1/1–1/4	1/5–2/5	2/6–3/4	3/5–3/29	3/30–4/24
	10/13–11/5	11/6–11/29	11/30–12/23	12/24–12/31	
11/1–11/25	11/26–12/19	12/20–12/31		1/1–1/17	1/18–2/10
8/20–9/14	9/15–10/9	1/1–1/12	1/13–2/5	2/6–3/1	3/2–3/25
		10/10–11/5	11/6–12/5	12/6–12/31	
10/4–10/27	10/28–11/20	11/21–12/13	12/14–12/31	1/1–4/5	4/6–5/4
11/10–12/7	12/8–12/31		1/1–1/7	1/8–1/31	2/1–2/24

VENUS SIGNS 1901–2001

	Aries	Taurus	Gemini	Cancer	Leo	Virgo
1952	4/10–5/4	5/5–5/28	5/29–6/21	6/22–7/16	7/17–8/9	8/10–9/3
1953	2/2–3/3 4/1–6/5	3/4–3/31 6/6–7/7	7/8–8/3	8/4–8/29	8/30–9/24	9/25–10/18
1954	3/12–4/4	4/5–4/28	4/29–5/23	5/24–6/17	6/18–7/13	7/14–8/8
1955	4/25–5/19	5/20–6/13	6/14–7/7	7/8–8/1	8/2–8/25	8/26–9/18
1956	2/12–3/7	3/8–4/4	4/5–5/7 6/24–8/4	5/8–6/23 8/5–9/8	9/9–10/5	10/6–10/31
1957	3/26–4/19	4/20–5/13	5/14–6/6	6/7–7/1	7/2–7/26	7/27–8/19
1958	5/6–5/31	6/1–6/26	6/27–7/22	7/23–8/15	8/16–9/9	9/10–10/3
1959	2/25–3/20	3/21–4/14	4/15–5/10	5/11–6/6	6/7–7/8 9/21–9/24	7/9–9/20 9/25–11/9
1960	4/10–5/3	5/4–5/28	5/29–6/21	6/22–7/15	7/16–8/9	8/10–9/2
1961	2/3–6/5	6/6–7/7	7/8–8/3	8/4–8/29	8/30–9/23	9/24–10/17
1962	3/11–4/3	4/4–4/28	4/29–5/22	5/23–6/17	6/18–7/12	7/13–8/8
1963	4/24–5/18	5/19–6/12	6/13–7/7	7/8–7/31	8/1–8/25	8/26–9/18
1964	2/11–3/7	3/8–4/4	4/5–5/9 6/18–8/5	5/10–6/17 8/6–9/8	9/9–10/5	10/6–10/31
1965	3/26–4/18	4/19–5/12	5/13–6/6	6/7–6/30	7/1–7/25	7/26–8/19
1966	5/6–6/31	6/1–6/26	6/27–7/21	7/22–8/15	8/16–9/8	9/9–10/2
1967	2/24–3/20	3/21–4/14	4/15–5/10	5/11–6/6	6/7–7/8 9/10–10/1	7/9–9/9 10/2–11/9
1968	4/9–5/3	5/4–5/27	5/28–6/20	6/21–7/15	7/16–8/8	8/9–9/2
1969	2/3–6/6	6/7–7/6	7/7–8/3	8/4–8/28	8/29–9/22	9/23–10/17
1970	3/11–4/3	4/4–4/27	4/28–5/22	5/23–6/16	6/17–7/12	7/13–8/8
1971	4/24–5/18	5/19–6/12	6/13–7/6	7/7–7/31	8/1–8/24	8/25–9/17
1972	2/11–3/7	3/8–4/3	4/4–5/10 6/12–8/6	5/11–6/11 8/7–9/8	9/9–10/5	10/6–10/30
1973	3/25–4/18	4/18–5/12	5/13–6/5	6/6–6/29	7/1–7/25	7/26–8/19
1974	5/5–5/31	6/1–6/25	6/26–7/21	7/22–8/14	8/15–9/8	9/9–10/2
1975	2/24–3/20	3/21–4/13	4/14–5/9	5/10–6/6	6/7–7/9 9/3–10/4	7/10–9/2 10/5–11/9

Libra	Scorpio	Sagittarius	Capricorn	Aquarius	Pisces
9/4–9/27	1/1–1/2	1/3–1/27	1/28–2/20	2/21–3/16	3/17–4/9
	9/28–10/21	10/22–11/15	11/16–12/10	12/11–12/31	
10/19–11/11	11/12–12/5	12/6–12/29	12/30–12/31	1/1–1/5	1/6–2/1
8/9–9/6	9/7–10/22	10/23–10/27	1/1–1/22	1/23–2/15	2/16–3/11
	10/28–12/31				
9/19–10/13	1/1–1/6	1/7–2/5	2/6–3/4	3/5–3/30	3/31–4/24
	10/14–11/5	11/6–11/30	12/1–12/24	12/25–12/31	
11/1–11/25	11/26–12/19	12/20–12/31		1/1–1/17	1/18–2/11
8/20–9/14	9/15–10/9	1/1–1/12	1/13–2/5	2/6–3/1	3/2–3/25
		10/10–11/5	11/6–12/6	12/7–12/31	
10/4–10/27	10/28–11/20	11/21–12/14	12/15–12/31	1/1–4/6	4/7–5/5
11/10–12/7	12/8–12/31		1/1–1/7	1/8–1/31	2/1–2/24
9/3–9/26	1/1–1/2	1/3–1/27	1/28–2/20	2/21–3/15	3/16–4/9
	9/27–10/21	10/22–11/15	11/16–12/10	12/11–12/31	
10/18–11/11	11/12–12/4	12/5–12/28	12/29–12/31	1/1–1/5	1/6–2/2
8/9–9/6	9/7–12/31		1/1–1/21	1/22–2/14	2/15–3/10
9/19–10/12	1/1–1/6	1/7–2/5	2/6–3/4	3/5–3/29	3/30–4/23
	10/13–11/5	11/6–11/29	11/30–12/23	12/24–12/31	
11/1–11/24	11/25–12/19	12/20–12/31		1/1–1/16	1/17–2/10
8/20–9/13	9/14–10/9	1/1–1/12	1/13–2/5	2/6–3/1	3/2–3/25
		10/10–11/5	11/6–12/7	12/8–12/31	
10/3–10/26	10/27–11/19	11/20–12/13	2/7–2/25	1/1–2/6	4/7–5/5
			12/14–12/31	2/26–4/6	
11/10–12/7	12/8–12/31		1/1–1/6	1/7–1/30	1/31–2/23
9/3–9/26	1/1	1/2–1/26	1/27–2/20	2/21–3/15	3/16–4/8
	9/27–10/21	10/22–11/14	11/15–12/9	12/10–12/31	
10/18–11/10	11/11–12/4	12/5–12/28	12/29–12/31	1/1–1/4	1/5–2/2
8/9–9/7	9/8–12/31		1/1–1/21	1/22–2/14	2/15–3/10
9/18–10/11	1/1–1/6	1/8–2/5	2/6–3/4	3/5–3/29	3/30–4/23
	10/12–11/5	11/6–11/29	11/30–12/23	12/24–12/31	
	11/25–12/18	12/19–12/31		1/1–1/16	1/17–2/10
10/31–11/24					
8/20–9/13	9/14–10/8	1/1–1/12	1/13–2/4	2/5–2/28	3/1–3/24
		10/9–11/5	11/6–12/7	12/8–12/31	
			1/30–2/28	1/1–1/29	
10/3–10/26	10/27–11/19	11/20–12/13	12/14–12/31	3/1–4/6	4/7–5/4
			1/1–1/6	1/7–1/30	1/31–2/23
11/10–12/7	12/8–12/31				

VENUS SIGNS 1901–2001

	Aries	Taurus	Gemini	Cancer	Leo	Virgo
1976	4/8–5/2	5/2–5/27	5/27—6/20	6/20–7/14	7/14–8/8	8/8–9/1
1977	2/2–6/6	6/6–7/6	7/6–8/2	8/2–8/28	8/28–9/22	9/22–10/17
1978	3/9–4/2	4/2–4/27	4/27–5/22	5/22–6/16	6/16–7/12	7/12–8/6
1979	4/23–5/18	5/18–6/11	6/11–7/6	7/6–7/30	7/30–8/24	8/24–9/17
1980	2/9–3/6	3/6–4/3	4/3–5/12 6/5–8/6	5/12–6/5 8/6–9/7	9/7–10/4	10/4–10/30
1981	3/24–4/17	4/17–5/11	5/11–6/5	6/5–6/29	6/29–7/24	7/24–8/18
1982	5/4–5/30	5/30–6/25	6/25–7/20	7/20–8/14	8/14–9/7	9/7–10/2
1983	2/22–3/19	3/19–4/13	4/13–5/9	5/9–6/6	6/6–7/10 8/27–10/5	7/10–8/27 10/5–11/9
1984	4/7–5/2	5/2–5/26	5/26–6/20	6/20–7/14	7/14–8/7	8/7–9/1
1985	2/2–6/6	6/7–7/6	7/6–8/2	8/2–8/28	8/28–9/22	9/22–10/16
1986	3/9–4/2	4/2–4/26	4/26–5/21	5/21–6/15	6/15–7/11	7/11–8/7
1987	4/22–5/17	5/17–6/11	6/11–7/5	7/5–7/30	7/30–8/23	8/23–9/16
1988	2/9–3/6	3/6–4/3	4/3–5/17 5/27–8/6	5/17–5/27 8/28–9/22	9/7–10/4 9/22–10/16	10/4–10/29
1989	3/23–4/16	4/16–5/11	5/11–6/4	6/4–6/29	6/29–7/24	7/24–8/18
1990	5/4–5/30	5/30–6/25	6/25–7/20	7/20–8/13	8/13–9/7	9/7–10/1
1991	2/22–3/18	3/18–4/13	4/13–5/9	5/9–6/6	6/6–7/11 8/21–10/6	7/11–8/21 10/6–11/9
1992	4/7–5/1	5/1–5/26	5/26–6/19	6/19–7/13	7/13–8/7	8/7–8/31
1993	2/2–6/6	6/6–7/6	7/6–8/1	8/1–8/27	8/27–9/21	9/21–10/16
1994	3/8–4/1	4/1–4/26	4/26–5/21	5/21–6/15	6/15–7/11	7/11–8/7
1995	4/22–5/16	5/16–6/10	6/10–7/5	7/5–7/29	7/29–8/23	8/23–9/16
1996	2/9–3/6	3/6–4/3	4/3–8/7	8/7–9/7	9/7–10/4	10/4–10/29
1997	3/23–4/16	4/16–5/10	5/10–6/4	6/4–6/28	6/28–7/23	7/23–8/17
1998	5/3–5/29	5/29–6/24	6/24–7/19	7/19–8/13	8/13–9/6	9/6–9/30
1999	2/21–3/18	3/18–4/12	4/12–5/8	5/8–6/5	6/5–7/12 8/15–10/7	7/12–8/15 10/7–11/9
2000	4/6–5/1	5/1–5/25	5/25–6/13	6/13–7/13	7/13–8/6	8/6–8/31
2001	2/2–6/6	6/6–7/5	7/5–8/1	8/1–8/26	8/26–9/20	9/20–10/15

Libra	Scorpio	Sagittarius	Capricorn	Aquarius	Pisces
9/1–9/26	9/26–10/20	1/1–1/26	1/26–2/19	2/19–3/15	3/15–4/8
		10/20–11/14	11/14–12/8	12/9–1/4	
10/17–11/10	11/10–12/4	12/4–12/27	12/27–1/20/78		1/4–2/2
8/6–9/7	9/7–1/7			1/20–2/13	2/13–3/9
9/17–10/11	10/11–11/4	1/7–2/5	2/5–3/3	3/3–3/29	3/29–4/23
		11/4–11/28	11/28–12/22	12/22–1/16/80	
10/30–11/24	11/24–12/18	12/18–1/11/81			1/16–2/9
8/18–9/12	9/12–10/9	10/9–11/5	1/11–2/4	2/4–2/28	2/28–3/24
			11/5–12/8	12/8–1/23/82	
10/2–10/26	10/26–11/18	11/18–12/12	1/23–3/2	3/2–4/6	4/6–5/4
			12/12–1/5/83		
11/9–12/6	12/6–1/1/84			1/5–1/29	1/29–2/22
9/1–9/25	9/25–10/20	1/1–1/25	1/25–2/19	2/19–3/14	3/14–4/7
		10/20–11/13	11/13–12/9	12/10–1/4	
10/16–11/9	11/9–12/3	12/3–12/27	12/28–1/19		1/4–2/2
8/7–9/7	9/7–1/7			1/20–2/13	2/13–3/9
9/16–10/10	10/10–11/3	1/7–2/5	2/5–3/3	3/3–3/28	3/28–4/22
		11/3–11/28	11/28–12/22	12/22–1/15	
10/29–11/23	11/23–12/17	12/17–1/10			1/15–2/9
8/18–9/12	9/12–10/8	10/8–11/5	1/10–2/3	2/3–2/27	2/27–3/23
			11/5–12/10	12/10–1/16/90	
10/1–10/25	10/25–11/18	11/18–12/12	1/16–3/3	3/3–4/6	4/6–5/4
			12/12–1/5		
11/9–12/6	12/6–12/31	12/31–1/25/92		1/5–1/29	1/29–2/22
8/31–9/25	9/25–10/19	10/19–11/13	1/25–2/18	2/18–3/13	3/13–4/7
			11/13–12/8	12/8–1/3/93	
10/16–11/9	11/9–12/2	12/2–12/26	12/26–1/19		1/3–2/2
8/7–9/7	9/7–1/7			1/19–2/12	2/12–3/8
9/16–10/10	10/10–11/13	1/7–2/4	2/4–3/2	3/2–3/28	3/28–4/22
		11/3–11/27	11/27–12/21	12/21–1/15	
10/29–11/23	11/23–12/17	12/17–1/10/97			1/15–2/9
8/17–9/12	9/12–10/8	10/8–11/5	1/10–2/3	2/3–2/27	2/27–3/23
			11/5–12/12	12/12–1/9	
9/30–10/24	10/24–11/17	11/17–12/11	1/9–3/4	3/4–4/6	4/6–5/3
11/9–12/5	12/5–12/31	12/31–1/24		1/4–1/28	1/28–2/21
8/31–9/24	9/24–10/19	10/19–11/13	1/24–2/18	2/18–3/12	3/13–4/6
			11/13–12/8	12/8	
10/15–11/8	11/8–12/2	12/2–12/26	12/26/2001–1/19/2002	12/8/2000–1/3/2001	1/3–2/2

How to Use the Mars, Jupiter, and Saturn Tables

Find the year of your birth on the left side of each column. The dates when the planet entered each sign are listed on the right side of each column. (Signs are abbreviated to the first three letters.) Your birthday should fall on or between each date listed, and your planetary placement should correspond to the earlier sign of that period.

MARS SIGN 1901–2001

Year	Month	Day	Sign		Year	Month	Day	Sign
1901	MAR	1	Leo		1905	JAN	13	Scp
	MAY	11	Vir			AUG	21	Sag
	JUL	13	Lib			OCT	8	Cap
	AUG	31	Scp			NOV	18	Aqu
	OCT	14	Sag			DEC	27	Pic
	NOV	24	Cap		1906	FEB	4	Ari
1902	JAN	1	Aqu			MAR	17	Tau
	FEB	8	Pic			APR	28	Gem
	MAR	19	Ari			JUN	11	Can
	APR	27	Tau			JUL	27	Leo
	JUN	7	Gem			SEP	12	Vir
	JUL	20	Can			OCT	30	Lib
	SEP	4	Leo			DEC	17	Scp
	OCT	23	Vir		1907	FEB	5	Sag
	DEC	20	Lib			APR	1	Cap
1903	APR	19	Vir			OCT	13	Aqu
	MAY	30	Lib			NOV	29	Pic
	AUG	6	Scp		1908	JAN	11	Ari
	SEP	22	Sag			FEB	23	Tau
	NOV	3	Cap			APR	7	Gem
	DEC	12	Aqu			MAY	22	Can
1904	JAN	19	Pic			JUL	8	Leo
	FEB	27	Ari			AUG	24	Vir
	APR	6	Tau			OCT	10	Lib
	MAY	18	Gem			NOV	25	Scp
	JUN	30	Can		1909	JAN	10	Sag
	AUG	15	Leo			FEB	24	Cap
	OCT	1	Vir			APR	9	Aqu
	NOV	20	Lib			MAY	25	Pic

	JUL	21	Ari		AUG	19	Can
	SEP	26	Pic		OCT	7	Leo
	NOV	20	Ari	1916	MAY	28	Vir
1910	JAN	23	Tau		JUL	23	Lib
	MAR	14	Gem		SEP	8	Scp
	MAY	1	Can		OCT	22	Sag
	JUN	19	Leo		DEC	1	Cap
	AUG	6	Vir	1917	JAN	9	Aqu
	SEP	22	Lib		FEB	16	Pic
	NOV	6	Scp		MAR	26	Ari
	DEC	20	Sag		MAY	4	Tau
1911	JAN	31	Cap		JUN	14	Gem
	MAR	14	Aqu		JUL	28	Can
	APR	23	Pic		SEP	12	Leo
	JUN	2	Ari		NOV	2	Vir
	JUL	15	Tau	1918	JAN	11	Lib
	SEP	5	Gem		FEB	25	Vir
	NOV	30	Tau		JUN	23	Lib
1912	JAN	30	Gem		AUG	17	Scp
	APR	5	Can		OCT	1	Sag
	MAY	28	Leo		NOV	11	Cap
	JUL	17	Vir		DEC	20	Aqu
	SEP	2	Lib	1919	JAN	27	Pic
	OCT	18	Scp		MAR	6	Ari
	NOV	30	Sag		APR	15	Tau
1913	JAN	10	Cap		MAY	26	Gem
	FEB	19	Aqu		JUL	8	Can
	MAR	30	Pic		AUG	23	Leo
	MAY	8	Ari		OCT	10	Vir
	JUN	17	Tau		NOV	30	Lib
	JUL	29	Gem	1920	JAN	31	Scp
	SEP	15	Can		APR	23	Lib
1914	MAY	1	Leo		JUL	10	Scp
	JUN	26	Vir		SEP	4	Sag
	AUG	14	Lib		OCT	18	Cap
	SEP	29	Scp		NOV	27	Aqu
	NOV	11	Sag	1921	JAN	5	Pic
	DEC	22	Cap		FEB	13	Ari
1915	JAN	30	Aqu		MAR	25	Tau
	MAR	9	Pic		MAY	6	Gem
	APR	16	Ari		JUN	18	Can
	MAY	26	Tau		AUG	3	Leo
	JUL	6	Gem		SEP	19	Vir

Year	Month	Day	Sign		Year	Month	Day	Sign
	NOV	6	Lib			APR	7	Pic
	DEC	26	Scp			MAY	16	Ari
1922	FEB	18	Sag			JUN	26	Tau
	SEP	13	Cap			AUG	9	Gem
	OCT	30	Aqu			OCT	3	Can
	DEC	11	Pic			DEC	20	Gem
1923	JAN	21	Ari		1929	MAR	10	Can
	MAR	4	Tau			MAY	13	Leo
	APR	16	Gem			JUL	4	Vir
	MAY	30	Can			AUG	21	Lib
	JUL	16	Leo			OCT	6	Scp
	SEP	1	Vir			NOV	18	Sag
	OCT	18	Lib			DEC	29	Cap
	DEC	4	Scp		1930	FEB	6	Aqu
1924	JAN	19	Sag			MAR	17	Pic
	MAR	6	Cap			APR	24	Ari
	APR	24	Aqu			JUN	3	Tau
	JUN	24	Pic			JUL	14	Gem
	AUG	24	Aqu			AUG	28	Can
	OCT	19	Pic			OCT	20	Leo
	DEC	19	Ari		1931	FEB	16	Can
1925	FEB	5	Tau			MAR	30	Leo
	MAR	24	Gem			JUN	10	Vir
	MAY	9	Can			AUG	1	Lib
	JUN	26	Leo			SEP	17	Scp
	AUG	12	Vir			OCT	30	Sag
	SEP	28	Lib			DEC	10	Cap
	NOV	13	Scp		1932	JAN	18	Aqu
	DEC	28	Sag			FEB	25	Pic
1926	FEB	9	Cap			APR	3	Ari
	MAR	23	Aqu			MAY	12	Tau
	MAY	3	Pic			JUN	22	Gem
	JUN	15	Ari			AUG	4	Can
	AUG	1	Tau			SEP	20	Leo
1927	FEB	22	Gem			NOV	13	Vir
	APR	17	Can		1933	JUL	6	Lib
	JUN	6	Leo			AUG	26	Scp
	JUL	25	Vir			OCT	9	Sag
	SEP	10	Lib			NOV	19	Cap
	OCT	26	Scp			DEC	28	Aqu
	DEC	8	Sag		1934	FEB	4	Pic
1928	JAN	19	Cap			MAR	14	Ari
	FEB	28	Aqu			APR	22	Tau

	JUN	2	Gem		AUG	19	Vir
	JUL	15	Can		OCT	5	Lib
	AUG	30	Leo		NOV	20	Scp
	OCT	18	Vir	1941	JAN	4	Sag
	DEC	11	Lib		FEB	17	Cap
1935	JUL	29	Scp		APR	2	Aqu
	SEP	16	Sag		MAY	16	Pic
	OCT	28	Cap		JUL	2	Ari
	DEC	7	Aqu	1942	JAN	11	Tau
1936	JAN	14	Pic		MAR	7	Gem
	FEB	22	Ari		APR	26	Can
	APR	1	Tau		JUN	14	Leo
	MAY	13	Gem		AUG	1	Vir
	JUN	25	Can		SEP	17	Lib
	AUG	10	Leo		NOV	1	Scp
	SEP	26	Vir		DEC	15	Sag
	NOV	14	Lib	1943	JAN	26	Cap
1937	JAN	5	Scp		MAR	8	Aqu
	MAR	13	Sag		APR	17	Pic
	MAY	14	Scp		MAY	27	Ari
	AUG	8	Sag		JUL	7	Tau
	SEP	30	Cap		AUG	23	Gem
	NOV	11	Aqu	1944	MAR	28	Can
	DEC	21	Pic		MAY	22	Leo
1938	JAN	30	Ari		JUL	12	Vir
	MAR	12	Tau		AUG	29	Lib
	APR	23	Gem		OCT	13	Scp
	JUN	7	Can		NOV	25	Sag
	JUL	22	Leo	1945	JAN	5	Cap
	SEP	7	Vir		FEB	14	Aqu
	OCT	25	Lib		MAR	25	Pic
	DEC	11	Scp		MAY	2	Ari
1939	JAN	29	Sag		JUN	11	Tau
	MAR	21	Cap		JUL	23	Gem
	MAY	25	Aqu		SEP	7	Can
	JUL	21	Cap		NOV	11	Leo
	SEP	24	Aqu		DEC	26	Can
	NOV	19	Pic	1946	APR	22	Leo
1940	JAN	4	Ari		JUN	20	Vir
	FEB	17	Tau		AUG	9	Lib
	APR	1	Gem		SEP	24	Scp
	MAY	17	Can		NOV	6	Sag
	JUL	3	Leo		DEC	17	Cap

1947	JAN	25	Aqu		MAR	20	Tau
	MAR	4	Pic		MAY	1	Gem
	APR	11	Ari		JUN	14	Can
	MAY	21	Tau		JUL	29	Leo
	JUL	1	Gem		SEP	14	Vir
	AUG	13	Can		NOV	1	Lib
	OCT	1	Leo		DEC	20	Scp
	DEC	1	Vir	1954	FEB	9	Sag
1948	FEB	12	Leo		APR	12	Cap
	MAY	18	Vir		JUL	3	Sag
	JUL	17	Lib		AUG	24	Cap
	SEP	3	Scp		OCT	21	Aqu
	OCT	17	Sag		DEC	4	Pic
	NOV	26	Cap	1955	JAN	15	Ari
1949	JAN	4	Aqu		FEB	26	Tau
	FEB	11	Pic		APR	10	Gem
	MAR	21	Ari		MAY	26	Can
	APR	30	Tau		JUL	11	Leo
	JUN	10	Gem		AUG	27	Vir
	JUL	23	Can		OCT	13	Lib
	SEP	7	Leo		NOV	29	Scp
	OCT	27	Vir	1956	JAN	14	Sag
	DEC	26	Lib		FEB	28	Cap
1950	MAR	28	Vir		APR	14	Aqu
	JUN	11	Lib		JUN	3	Pic
	AUG	10	Scp		DEC	6	Ari
	SEP	25	Sag	1957	JAN	28	Tau
	NOV	6	Cap		MAR	17	Gem
	DEC	15	Aqu		MAY	4	Can
1951	JAN	22	Pic		JUN	21	Leo
	MAR	1	Ari		AUG	8	Vir
	APR	10	Tau		SEP	24	Lib
	MAY	21	Gem		NOV	8	Scp
	JUL	3	Can		DEC	23	Sag
	AUG	18	Leo	1958	FEB	3	Cap
	OCT	5	Vir		MAR	17	Aqu
	NOV	24	Lib		APR	27	Pic
1952	JAN	20	Scp		JUN	7	Ari
	AUG	27	Sag		JUL	21	Tau
	OCT	12	Cap		SEP	21	Gem
	NOV	21	Aqu		OCT	29	Tau
	DEC	30	Pic	1959	FEB	10	Gem
1953	FEB	8	Ari		APR	10	Can

	JUN	1	Leo		NOV	14	Cap
	JUL	20	Vir		DEC	23	Aqu
	SEP	5	Lib	1966	JAN	30	Pic
	OCT	21	Scp		MAR	9	Ari
	DEC	3	Sag		APR	17	Tau
1960	JAN	14	Cap		MAY	28	Gem
	FEB	23	Aqu		JUL	11	Can
	APR	2	Pic		AUG	25	Leo
	MAY	11	Ari		OCT	12	Vir
	JUN	20	Tau		DEC	4	Lib
	AUG	2	Gem	1967	FEB	12	Scp
	SEP	21	Can		MAR	31	Lib
1961	FEB	5	Gem		JUL	19	Scp
	FEB	7	Can		SEP	10	Sag
	MAY	6	Leo		OCT	23	Cap
	JUN	28	Vir		DEC	1	Aqu
	AUG	17	Lib	1968	JAN	9	Pic
	OCT	1	Scp		FEB	17	Ari
	NOV	13	Sag		MAR	27	Tau
	DEC	24	Cap		MAY	8	Gem
1962	FEB	1	Aqu		JUN	21	Can
	MAR	12	Pic		AUG	5	Leo
	APR	19	Ari		SEP	21	Vir
	MAY	28	Tau		NOV	9	Lib
	JUL	9	Gem		DEC	29	Scp
	AUG	22	Can	1969	FEB	25	Sag
	OCT	11	Leo		SEP	21	Cap
1963	JUN	3	Vir		NOV	4	Aqu
	JUL	27	Lib		DEC	15	Pic
	SEP	12	Scp	1970	JAN	24	Ari
	OCT	25	Sag		MAR	7	Tau
	DEC	5	Cap		APR	18	Gem
1964	JAN	13	Aqu		JUN	2	Can
	FEB	20	Pic		JUL	18	Leo
	MAR	29	Ari		SEP	3	Vir
	MAY	7	Tau		OCT	20	Lib
	JUN	17	Gem		DEC	6	Scp
	JUL	30	Can	1971	JAN	23	Sag
	SEP	15	Leo		MAR	12	Cap
	NOV	6	Vir		MAY	3	Aqu
1965	JUN	29	Lib		NOV	6	Pic
	AUG	20	Scp		DEC	26	Ari
	OCT	4	Sag	1972	FEB	10	Tau

	MAR	27	Gem	1978	JAN	26	Can
	MAY	12	Can		APR	10	Leo
	JUN	28	Leo		JUN	14	Vir
	AUG	15	Vir		AUG	4	Lib
	SEP	30	Lib		SEP	19	Scp
	NOV	15	Scp		NOV	2	Sag
	DEC	30	Sag		DEC	12	Cap
1973	FEB	12	Cap	1979	JAN	20	Aqu
	MAR	26	Aqu		FEB	27	Pic
	MAY	8	Pic		APR	7	Ari
	JUN	20	Ari		MAY	16	Tau
	AUG	12	Tau		JUN	26	Gem
	OCT	29	Ari		AUG	8	Can
	DEC	24	Tau		SEP	24	Leo
1974	FEB	27	Gem		NOV	19	Vir
	APR	20	Can	1980	MAR	11	Leo
	JUN	9	Leo		MAY	4	Vir
	JUL	27	Vir		JUL	10	Lib
	SEP	12	Lib		AUG	29	Scp
	OCT	28	Scp		OCT	12	Sag
	DEC	10	Sag		NOV	22	Cap
1975	JAN	21	Cap		DEC	30	Aqu
	MAR	3	Aqu	1981	FEB	6	Pic
	APR	11	Pic		MAR	17	Ari
	MAY	21	Ari		APR	25	Tau
	JUL	1	Tau		JUN	5	Gem
	AUG	14	Gem		JUL	18	Can
	OCT	17	Can		SEP	2	Leo
	NOV	25	Gem		OCT	21	Vir
1976	MAR	18	Can		DEC	16	Lib
	MAY	16	Leo	1982	AUG	3	Scp
	JUL	6	Vir		SEP	20	Sag
	AUG	24	Lib		OCT	31	Cap
	OCT	8	Scp		DEC	10	Aqu
	NOV	20	Sag	1983	JAN	17	Pic
1977	JAN	1	Cap		FEB	25	Ari
	FEB	9	Aqu		APR	5	Tau
	MAR	20	Pic		MAY	16	Gem
	APR	27	Ari		JUN	29	Can
	JUN	6	Tau		AUG	13	Leo
	JUL	17	Gem		SEP	30	Vir
	SEP	1	Can		NOV	18	Lib
	OCT	26	Leo	1984	JAN	11	Scp

	AUG	17	Sag			JUL	12	Tau
	OCT	5	Cap			AUG	31	Gem
	NOV	15	Aqu			DEC	14	Tau
	DEC	25	Pic		1991	JAN	21	Gem
1985	FEB	2	Ari			APR	3	Can
	MAR	15	Tau			MAY	26	Leo
	APR	26	Gem			JUL	15	Vir
	JUN	9	Can			SEP	1	Lib
	JUL	25	Leo			OCT	16	Scp
	SEP	10	Vir			NOV	29	Sag
	OCT	27	Lib		1992	JAN	9	Cap
	DEC	14	Scp			FEB	18	Aqu
1986	FEB	2	Sag			MAR	28	Pic
	MAR	28	Cap			MAY	5	Ari
	OCT	9	Aqu			JUN	14	Tau
	NOV	26	Pic			JUL	26	Gem
1987	JAN	8	Ari			SEP	12	Can
	FEB	20	Tau		1993	APR	27	Leo
	APR	5	Gem			JUN	23	Vir
	MAY	21	Can			AUG	12	Lib
	JUL	6	Leo			SEP	27	Scp
	AUG	22	Vir			NOV	9	Sag
	OCT	8	Lib			DEC	20	Cap
	NOV	24	Scp		1994	JAN	28	Aqu
1988	JAN	8	Sag			MAR	7	Pic
	FEB	22	Cap			APR	14	Ari
	APR	6	Aqu			MAY	23	Tau
	MAY	22	Pic			JUL	3	Gem
	JUL	13	Ari			AUG	16	Can
	OCT	23	Pic			OCT	4	Leo
	NOV	1	Ari			DEC	12	Vir
1989	JAN	19	Tau		1995	JAN	22	Leo
	MAR	11	Gem			MAY	25	Vir
	APR	29	Can			JUL	21	Lib
	JUN	16	Leo			SEP	7	Scp
	AUG	3	Vir			OCT	20	Sag
	SEP	19	Lib			NOV	30	Cap
	NOV	4	Scp		1996	JAN	8	Aqu
	DEC	18	Sag			FEB	15	Pic
1990	JAN	29	Cap			MAR	24	Ari
	MAR	11	Aqu			MAY	2	Tau
	APR	20	Pic			JUN	12	Gem
	MAY	31	Ari			JUL	25	Can

	SEP	9	Leo		MAY	5	Lib
	OCT	30	Vir		JUL	5	Scp
1997	JAN	3	Lib		SEP	2	Sag
	MAR	8	Vir		OCT	17	Cap
	JUN	19	Lib		NOV	26	Aqu
	AUG	14	Scp	2000	JAN	4	Pic
	SEP	28	Sag		FEB	12	Ari
	NOV	9	Cap		MAR	23	Tau
	DEC	18	Aqu		MAY	3	Gem
1998	JAN	25	Pic		JUN	16	Can
	MAR	4	Ari		AUG	1	Leo
	APR	13	Tau		SEP	17	Vir
	MAY	24	Gem		NOV	4	Lib
	JUL	6	Can		DEC	23	Scp
	AUG	20	Leo	2001	FEB	14	Sag
	OCT	7	Vir		SEP	8	Cap
	NOV	27	Lib		OCT	27	Aqu
1999	JAN	26	Scp		DEC	8	Pic

JUPITER SIGN 1901–2001

1901	JAN	19	Cap	1916	FEB	12	Ari
1902	FEB	6	Aqu		JUN	26	Tau
1903	FEB	20	Pic		OCT	26	Ari
1904	MAR	1	Ari	1917	FEB	12	Tau
	AUG	8	Tau		JUN	29	Gem
	AUG	31	Ari	1918	JUL	13	Can
1905	MAR	7	Tau	1919	AUG	2	Leo
	JUL	21	Gem	1920	AUG	27	Vir
	DEC	4	Tau	1921	SEP	25	Lib
1906	MAR	9	Gem	1922	OCT	26	Scp
	JUL	30	Can	1923	NOV	24	Sag
1907	AUG	18	Leo	1924	DEC	18	Cap
1908	SEP	12	Vir	1926	JAN	6	Aqu
1909	OCT	11	Lib	1927	JAN	18	Pic
1910	NOV	11	Scp		JUN	6	Ari
1911	DEC	10	Sag		SEP	11	Pic
1913	JAN	2	Cap	1928	JAN	23	Ari
1914	JAN	21	Aqu		JUN	4	Tau
1915	FEB	4	Pic	1929	JUN	12	Gem

1930	JUN	26	Can		MAR	20	Lib
1931	JUL	17	Leo		SEP	7	Scp
1932	AUG	11	Vir	1959	FEB	10	Sag
1933	SEP	10	Lib		APR	24	Scp
1934	OCT	11	Scp		OCT	5	Sag
1935	NOV	9	Sag	1960	MAR	1	Cap
1936	DEC	2	Cap		JUN	10	Sag
1937	DEC	20	Aqu		OCT	26	Cap
1938	MAY	14	Pic	1961	MAR	15	Aqu
	JUL	30	Aqu		AUG	12	Cap
	DEC	29	Pic		NOV	4	Aqu
1939	MAY	11	Ari	1962	MAR	25	Pic
	OCT	30	Pic	1963	APR	4	Ari
	DEC	20	Ari	1964	APR	12	Tau
1940	MAY	16	Tau	1965	APR	22	Gem
1941	MAY	26	Gem		SEP	21	Can
1942	JUN	10	Can		NOV	17	Gem
1943	JUN	30	Leo	1966	MAY	5	Can
1944	JUL	26	Vir		SEP	27	Leo
1945	AUG	25	Lib	1967	JAN	16	Can
1946	SEP	25	Scp		MAY	23	Leo
1947	OCT	24	Sag		OCT	19	Vir
1948	NOV	15	Cap	1968	FEB	27	Leo
1949	APR	12	Aqu		JUN	15	Vir
	JUN	27	Cap		NOV	15	Lib
	NOV	30	Aqu	1969	MAR	30	Vir
1950	APR	15	Pic		JUL	15	Lib
	SEP	15	Aqu		DEC	16	Scp
	DEC	1	Pic	1970	APR	30	Lib
1951	APR	21	Ari		AUG	15	Scp
1952	APR	28	Tau	1971	JAN	14	Sag
1953	MAY	9	Gem		JUN	5	Sc
1954	MAY	24	Can		SEP	11	Sag
1955	JUN	13	Leo	1972	FEB	6	Cap
	NOV	17	Vir		JUL	24	Sag
1956	JAN	18	Leo		SEP	25	Cap
	JUL	7	Vir	1973	FEB	23	Aqu
	DEC	13	Lib	1974	MAR	8	Pic
1957	FEB	19	Vir	1975	MAR	18	Ari
	AUG	7	Lib	1976	MAR	26	Tau
1958	JAN	13	Scp		AUG	23	Gem

	OCT	16	Tau		NOV	30	Tau
1977	APR	3	Gem	1989	MAR	11	Gem
	AUG	20	Can		JUL	30	Can
	DEC	30	Gem	1990	AUG	18	Leo
1978	APR	12	Can	1991	SEP	12	Vir
	SEP	5	Leo	1992	OCT	10	Lib
1979	FEB	28	Can	1993	NOV	10	Scp
	APR	20	Leo	1994	DEC	9	Sag
	SEP	29	Vir	1996	JAN	3	Cap
1980	OCT	27	Lib	1997	JAN	21	Aqu
1981	NOV	27	Scp	1998	FEB	4	Pic
1982	DEC	26	Sag	1999	FEB	13	Ari
1984	JAN	19	Cap		JUN	28	Tau
1985	FEB	6	Aqu		OCT	23	Ari
1986	FEB	20	Pic	2000	FEB	14	Tau
1987	MAR	2	Ari		JUN	30	Gem
1988	MAR	8	Tau	2001	JUL	14	Can
	JUL	22	Gem				

SATURN SIGN 1903–2001

1903	JAN	19	Aqu	1924	APR	6	Lib
1905	APR	13	Pic		SEP	13	Scp
	AUG	17	Aqu	1926	DEC	2	Sag
1906	JAN	8	Pic	1929	MAR	15	Cap
1908	MAR	19	Ari		MAY	5	Sag
1910	MAY	17	Tau		NOV	30	Cap
	DEC	14	Ari	1932	FEB	24	Aqu
1911	JAN	20	Tau		AUG	13	Cap
1912	JUL	7	Gem		NOV	20	Aqu
	NOV	30	Tau	1935	FEB	14	Pic
1913	MAR	26	Gem	1937	APR	25	Ari
1914	AUG	24	Can		OCT	18	Pic
	DEC	7	Gem	1938	JAN	14	Ari
1915	MAY	11	Can	1939	JUL	6	Tau
1916	OCT	17	Leo		SEP	22	Ari
	DEC	7	Can	1940	MAR	20	Tau
1917	JUN	24	Leo	1942	MAY	8	Gem
1919	AUG	12	Vir	1944	JUN	20	Can
1921	OCT	7	Lib	1946	AUG	2	Leo
1923	DEC	20	Scp	1948	SEP	19	Vir

1949	APR	3	Leo		JUN	5	Leo
	MAY	29	Vir	1977	NOV	17	Vir
1950	NOV	20	Lib	1978	JAN	5	Leo
1951	MAR	7	Vir		JUL	26	Vir
	AUG	13	Lib	1980	SEP	21	Lib
1953	OCT	22	Scp	1982	NOV	29	Scp
1956	JAN	12	Sag	1983	MAY	6	Lib
	MAY	14	Scp		AUG	24	Scp
	OCT	10	Sag	1985	NOV	17	Sag
1959	JAN	5	Cap	1988	FEB	13	Cap
1962	JAN	3	Aqu		JUN	10	Sag
1964	MAR	24	Pic		NOV	12	Cap
	SEP	16	Aqu	1991	FEB	6	Aqu
	DEC	16	Pic	1993	MAY	21	Pic
1967	MAR	3	Ari		JUN	30	Aqu
1969	APR	29	Tau	1994	JAN	28	Pic
1971	JUN	18	Gem	1996	APR	7	Ari
1972	JAN	10	Tau	1998	JUN	9	Tau
	FEB	21	Gem		OCT	25	Ari
1973	AUG	1	Can	1999	MAR	1	Tau
1974	JAN	7	Gem	2000	AUG	10	Gem
	APR	18	Can		OCT	16	Tau
1975	SEP	17	Leo	2001	APR	21	Gem
1976	JAN	14	Can				

CHAPTER 4

The Astro-Visuals: What Those Mysterious Glyphs on Your Chart Mean

When you first try to decipher your horoscope chart, you may recognize the tiny moon and the symbol for your sign. Perhaps you'll also recognize Mars and Venus, since they are often used as male and female gender symbols outside of astrology. But the other marks could look as strange as Japanese to the uninitiated. Those little characters, called glyphs (or sigils), were created centuries ago so that any astrologer from Russia to Argentina could read your chart and know what it means. Since there are only twenty-two major glyphs, for the twelve signs and ten planets (not counting a few asteroids and other space creatures some astrologers use), it's a lot easier than learning to read Japanese!

There are several good reasons why you should learn the glyphs. First, they're interesting. The glyphs are much more than little drawings. They are magical codes that contain within them keys to the meanings of the planets. Cracking their codes teaches you immediately, in a visual way, much about the deeper meaning of a planet or sign.

Another good reason: if you ever get your horoscope chart done, either by an astrologer or by a computer, the chart will be written in glyphs! Though some charts have a list of the planets in plain English on the main page, others do not, leaving you mystified. You might pick out the symbol for the sun and the trident of Neptune. But then there's Jupiter, which looks something like the number 4, and Mercury, which looks like Venus wearing a hat.

Here's a code-cracker for the glyphs, beginning with the glyphs for the planets. To those who already *know* their glyphs, don't just skim over the chapter! There are hidden meanings to discover, so test your glyph-ese.

Think you know it all? Take the test at the end of the chapter to find out.

The Glyphs for the Planets

Almost all the glyphs of the planets are combinations of the most basic forms: the circle, the half circle or arc, and the cross. Artists and glyph designers have stylized these forms over the years, but the basic concept is always visible. Each component of the glyph has a special meaning in relation to the others, which combines to create the meaning of the completed symbol.

For instance, the circle, which has no beginning or end, is one of the oldest symbols of spirit or spiritual forces. The early diagrams of the heavens are shown in circular form. The semicircle or arc symbolizes the receptive, finite soul, which contains spiritual potential in the curving line. The vertical line symbolizes movement from heaven to Earth. The horizontal line describes temporal movement, here and now, within the confines of time and space. Superimposed together, the vertical and horizontal planes symbolize manifestation in the material world.

The Sun Glyph ⊙

The sun is always shown by this powerful solar symbol, a circle with a point in the center. It is you, your spiritual center, your infinite personality incarnating the point into the finite cycles of birth and death.

This symbol was brought into common use in the sixteenth century, after a German occultist and scholar, Cornelius Agrippa (1486–1535), wrote a book called *Die Occulta Philosophia,* which became accepted as the standard work in its field. Agrippa collected many medieval astrological and magical symbols in this book, which were used by astrologers thereafter, copied from those found in Agrippa's book.

The Moon Glyph ☽

This is surely the easiest symbol to spot on a chart. The moon glyph is a left-facing arc stylized into the crescent moon, which perfectly captures the reactive, receptive, emotional nature of the moon. As part of a circle, the arc symbolizes the potential fulfillment of the entire circle. It is the life force that is still incomplete.

The Mercury Glyph ☿

This is the "Venus with a hat" glyph. With another stretch of the imagination, can't you see the winged cap of Mercury the messenger? The upturned crescent could be antennae that tune in and transmit messages from the sun, signifying that Mercury is the way you communicate, the way your mind works. The upturned arc is receiving energy into the spirit or solar circle, which will later be translated into action on the material plane, symbolized by the cross. All the elements are equally sized because Mercury is neutral . . . it doesn't play favorites! This planet symbolizes objective, detached, unemotional thinking.

The Venus Glyph ♀

Here the relationship is between two elements—the circle or spirit above the cross of matter. Spirit is elevated over matter, pulling it upward. Venus asks, "What is beautiful? What do you like best, what do you love to have done to you?" Venus determines both your ideal of beauty and what feels good sensually. It governs your own allure and power to attract, as well as what attracts and pleases you.

The Mars Glyph ♂

In this glyph, the cross of matter is stylized into an arrow-head pointed up and outward, propelled by the circle of spirit. You can deduce that Mars embodies your spiritual energy projected into the outer world. It's your assert-iveness, your initiative, your aggressive drive, what you like to do to others, your temper. If you know someone's Mars, you know whether they'll blow up when angry or do a slow burn. Your task is to use your outgoing Mars energy wisely and well.

The Jupiter Glyph ♃

Jupiter is the basic cross of matter, with a large stylized crescent perched on the left side of the horizontal, tem-poral plane. You might think of the crescent as an open hand—one meaning of Jupiter is "luck," what's handed to you. You don't work for what you get from Jupiter—it comes to you, if you're open to it.

The Jupiter glyph might also remind you of a jumbo jet plane with a huge tail fin, about to take off. This is the planet of travel, mental and spiritual, of expanding your horizons via new ideas, new spiritual dimensions, and new places. Jupiter embodies the optimism and en-thusiasm of the traveler about to embark on an excit-ing adventure.

The Saturn Glyph ♄

Flip Jupiter over and you've got Saturn. (This might not be immediately apparent, because Saturn is usually styl-ized in an "h" form like the one shown here.) But the principle it expresses is the opposite of Jupiter's expan-sive tendencies. Saturn pulls you back to Earth—the re-ceptive arc is pushed down underneath the cross of matter. Before there are any rewards or expansion, the duties and obligations of the material world must be con-sidered. Saturn says, "Stop, wait, finish your chores be-fore you take off!"

Saturn's glyph also resembles the sickle of old Father Time. Saturn was first known as Chronos, the Greek god of time, for time brings all matter to an end. When it was thought to be the most distant planet (before the discovery of Uranus), Saturn was believed to be the place that time stopped. After the soul, having departed from Earth, journeyed back to the outer reaches of the universe, it finally stopped at Saturn, or at "the end of time."

The Uranus Glyph ♅

The glyph for Uranus is often stylized to form a capital "H" after Sir William Herschel, the name of the planet's discoverer. But the more esoteric version curves the two pillars of the H into crescent antennae, or "ears," or like satellite discs receiving signals from space. These are perched on the horizontal material line of the cross (matter) and pushed from below by the circle of the spirit. To many sci-fi fans, Uranus looks like an orbiting satellite.

Uranus channels the highest energy of all, the white electrical light of the universal spiritual sun, the force that holds the cosmos together. This pure electrical energy is gathered from all over the universe. Because it doesn't follow an ordinary celestial drumbeat, it can't be controlled or predicted, which is also true of those who are strongly influenced by this eccentric planet. In the symbol, this energy is manifested through the balance of polarities (the two opposite arms of the glyph) like the two polarized wires of a lightbulb.

The Neptune Glyph ♆

Neptune's glyph is usually stylized to look like a trident, the weapon of the Roman god Neptune. However, on a more esoteric level, it shows the large upturned crescent of the soul pierced through by the cross of matter. Neptune nails down, or materializes, soul energy, bringing impulses from the soul level into manifestation. That is why Neptune is associated with imagination or "imagining in," making an image of the soul. Neptune works through feeling, sensitivity, and mystical capacity to bring the divine into the earthly realm.

The Pluto Glyph ♀

Pluto is written two ways. One is a composite of the letters PL, the first two letters of the word Pluto and coincidentally the initials of Percival Lowell, one of the planet's discoverers. The other, more esoteric symbol is a small circle, above a large open crescent that surmounts the cross of matter. This depicts Pluto's power to regenerate—you might imagine from this glyph a new little spirit emerging from the sheltering cup of the soul. Pluto rules the forces of life and death—after a Pluto experience, you are transformed, reborn in some way.

Sci-fi fans might visualize this glyph as a small satellite (the circle) being launched. It was shortly after Pluto's discovery that we learned how to harness the nuclear forces that made space exploration possible. Pluto rules the transformative power of atomic energy, which totally changed our lives and from which there was no turning back.

The Glyphs for the Signs

On an astrological chart, the glyph for the sign will appear after that of the planet. When you see the moon glyph followed by a number and the glyph for the sign, this means that the moon was passing over a certain degree of an astrological sign at the time of the chart. On the dividing points between the segments or "houses" on your chart, you'll find the symbol for the sign that rules the house.

Since sun sign symbols do not always bring together the same basic components of the planetary glyphs, where do their meanings come from? Many have been passed down from ancient Egyptian and Chaldean civilizations with few modifications. Others have been adapted over the centuries. In deciphering many of the glyphs, you'll often find that many symbols reveal a dual nature of the sign, which is not always apparent in sun sign descriptions. For instance, the Gemini glyph is similar to the Roman numeral for two, and reveals this sign's longing to discover a twin soul. The Cancer glyph may be interpreted as either resembling nurturing breasts or the self-protective claws of the crab. Libra's glyph embodies the duality of the spirit balanced with material reality. The Sagittarius glyph shows that the aspirant must also carry along the earthly animal nature in his quest. The Capricorn sea goat is another symbol with dual emphasis. The goat climbs high yet is always pulled back by the deep waters of the unconscious. Aquarius embodies the double waves of mental detachment, balanced by the desire for connection with others in a friendly way. And finally, the two fishes of Pisces, which are forever tied together, show the duality of the soul and the spirit that must be reconciled.

The Aries Glyph ♈

Since the symbol for Aries is the ram, this glyph's most obvious association is with a ram's horns, which characterize one aspect of the Aries personality—an aggressive, me-first, leaping-headfirst attitude. But the symbol may have other meanings for you, too. Some astrologers liken it to a fountain of energy, which Aries people also embody. The first sign of the zodiac bursts on the scene eagerly, ready to go. Another analogy is to the eyebrows and nose of the human head, which Aries rules, and the thinking power that is initiated in the brain. Another interesting theory is that the symbol represents spirit descending from a higher realm into the mind of man, which would be the point of the V shape in the Aries glyph, corresponding to the center of the eyebrows, the place of the "third eye," which the Hindus mark with a red bindi dot.

The origin of this symbol links it to the Egyptian god Amun, represented by a ram. As Amon-Ra, this god was believed to embody the creator of the universe, the leader of all the other gods. This relates easily to the zodiac, which begins at the spring equinox, a time of the year when nature is renewed.

The Taurus Glyph ♉

·This is another easy glyph to draw and identify. It takes little imagination to decipher the bull's head with long, curving horns. Like the bull, the archetypal Taurus is slow to anger but ferocious when provoked, as well as stubborn, steady, and sensual. Another association is the larynx (and thyroid) of the throat area (ruled by Taurus) and the Eustachian tubes (the "horns" of the glyph) running up to the ears, which coincides with the relationship of Taurus to the voice, song, and music. Many famous singers, musicians, and composers have prominent Taurus influences.

Many ancient religions involved a bull as the central figure in fertility rites or initiations, usually symbolizing the victory of man over his animal nature. Another possible origin is in the sacred bull of Egypt, who embodied the incarnate form of Osiris, god of death and resurrection. In early Christian imagery, the Taurean bull, representing St. Luke, appears in many art forms along with symbols of the other fixed signs: the lion (Leo and St. Mark), the man (Aquarius and St. Matthew), and the eagle (Scorpio and St. John).

The Gemini Glyph ♊

The standard glyph immediately calls to mind the Roman numeral for two and the symbol for Gemini, the "twins." In almost all images for this sign, the relationship between two persons is emphasized. This is the sign of communication and human contact, and it manifests the desire to share. Many of the figurative images of Gemini show twins with their arms around each other, emphasizing that they are sharing the same ideas and the same ground. In the glyph, the top line indicates mental communication, while the bottom line indicates shared physical space.

The most famous Gemini legend is that of the twin sons, Castor and Pollux, one of whom had a mortal father, while the other was the son of Zeus, king of the gods. When it came time for the mortal twin to die, his grief-stricken brother pleaded with Zeus, who agreed to let them spend half the year on earth, in mortal form, and half in immortal life, with the gods on Mt. Olympus. This reflects a basic concept of humankind, which possesses an immortal soul, yet is also subject to the limits of mortality.

The Cancer Glyph ♋

Two convenient images relate to the Cancer glyph. The easiest to picture is the curving claws of the Cancer symbol, the crab. Like the crab, Cancer's element is water. This sensitive sign also has a hard protective shell to shield its tender interior. It must be wily to escape predators, scampering sideways and hiding shyly under the rocks. The crab also responds to the cycles of the moon, as do all shellfish. The other image is that of two female breasts, which Cancer rules, showing that this is a sign that nurtures and protects others as well as itself. In ancient Egypt, Cancer was also represented by the scarab beetle, a symbol of regeneration and eternal life.

The Leo Glyph ♌

Lions have belonged to the sign of Leo since earliest times and it is not difficult to imagine the king of beasts with his sweeping mane and curling tail from this glyph. The upward sweep of the glyph easily describes the positive energy of Leos—the flourishing tail of the glyph depicts their flamboyant qualities. Another analogy, which is a stretch, is that of a heart leaping up with joy and enthusiasm, also very typical of Leo. Notice that the Leo glyph seems to be an extension of Cancer's glyph, with a significant difference. In the Cancer glyph, the figures are folding inward, protectively, while the Leo glyph expresses energy outwardly, with no duality in the symbol (or in Leo). In early Christian imagery, the Leo lion represented St. Mark.

The Virgo Glyph ♍

You can read much into this mysterious glyph. For instance, it could represent the initials of "Mary Virgin," or a young woman holding a staff of wheat, or stylized female genitalia, all common interpretations. The "M" shape might also remind you that Virgo is ruled by Mercury. The cross beneath the symbol could indicate the grounded, practical nature of this earth sign.

The earliest zodiacs link Virgo with the Egyptian goddess Isis, who gave birth to the god Horus after her husband Osiris had been killed, in the archetype of a miraculous conception. There are many statues of Isis nursing her baby son, which are reminiscent of medieval Virgin and Child motifs. This sign has also been associated with the image of the Holy Grail, when the Virgo symbol was substituted with a chalice.

The Libra Glyph ♎

It is not difficult to read the standard image for Libra, the scales, into this glyph. There is another meaning, however, that is equally relevant: the setting sun as it descends over the horizon. Libra's natural position on the zodiac wheel is the descendant or sunset position (as Aries' natural position is the ascendant, or rising sign). Both images relate to Libra's personality. Libra is always weighing pros and cons for a balanced decision. In the sunset image, the sun (male) hovers over the horizontal Earth (female) before setting. Libra is the space between these lines, harmonizing yin and yang, spiritual and material, ideal and real worlds. The glyph has also been linked to the kidneys, which are ruled by Libra.

The Scorpio Glyph ♏

With its barbed tail, this glyph is easy to identify with the sign of the Scorpion. It also represents the male sexual parts, over which the sign rules. However, some earlier symbols for Scorpio, such as the Egyptian, represent it as an erect serpent. You can also draw the conclusion that Mars is its ruler by the arrowhead.

Another image for Scorpio, which is not identifiable in this glyph, is the eagle. Scorpios can go to extremes, soaring like the eagle or self-destructing like the Scorpion. In early Christian imagery, which often used zodiacal symbols, the Scorpio eagle was chosen to symbolize the intense apostle St. John the Evangelist.

The Sagittarius Glyph ♐

This glyph is one of the easiest to spot and draw—an upward pointing arrow lifting up a cross. The arrow is pointing skyward, while the cross represents the four elements of the material world, which the arrow must convey. Elevating materiality into spirituality is an important Sagittarius quality, which explains why this sign is associated with higher learning, religion, philosophy, travel—the aspiring professions. Sagittarius can also send barbed arrows of frankness in their pursuit of truth. (This is also the sign of the super-salesman.)

Sagittarius is symbolically represented by the centaur, a mythological creature who is half man, half horse, aiming his arrow toward the skies. Though Sagittarius is motivated by spiritual aspiration, it also must balance the powerful appetites of the animal nature. The centaur Chiron, a figure in Greek mythology, became a wise teacher, after many adventures and world travels.

The Capricorn Glyph ♑

One of the most difficult symbols to draw, this glyph may take some practice. It is a representation of the sea goat: a mythical animal that is a goat with a curving fish's tail.

The goat part of Capricorn wants to leave the waters of the emotions and climb to the elevated areas of life. But the fish tail part of the symbol is the unconscious, the deep chaotic psychic level that draws the goat back. Capricorn is often trying to escape the deep, feeling part of life by submerging himself in work, steadily climbing to the top. To some people, the glyph represents a seated figure with a bent knee, a reminder that Capricorn governs the knee area of the body.

An interesting aspect of this figure is how the sharp pointed horns of the symbol, which represent the penetrating, shrewd, conscious side of Capricorn, contrast with the swishing tail, which represents its serpentine, unconscious, emotional force. One Capricorn legend, which dates from Roman times, tells of the earthly fertility god, Pan, who tried to save himself from uncontrollable sexual desires by jumping into the Nile. His upper body then turned into a goat, while the lower part became a fish. Later, Jupiter gave him a safe haven in the skies, as a constellation.

The Aquarius Glyph ≈

This ancient water symbol can be traced back to an Egyptian hieroglyph representing streams of life force. Symbolized by the water bearer, Aquarius is distributor of the waters of life—the magic liquid of regeneration. The two waves can also be linked to the positive and negative charges of the electrical energy that Aquarius rules, a sort of universal wavelength. Aquarius is tuned in intuitively to higher forces via this electrical force. The duality of the glyph could also refer to the dual nature of Aquarius, a sign that runs hot and cold, is friendly but also detached in the mental world of air signs.

In Greek legends, Aquarius is represented by Ganymede, who was carried to heaven by an eagle in order to become the cup bearer of Zeus, and to supervise the annual flooding of the Nile. The sign became associated with aviation and notions of flight.

The Pisces Glyph)(

Here is an abstraction of the familiar image of Pisces, two fishes swimming in opposite directions, bound together by a cord. The fishes represent spirit, which yearns for the freedom of heaven, while the soul remains attached to the desires of the temporal world. During life on earth, the spirit and the soul are bound together and when they complement each other, instead of pulling in opposite directions, this facilitates the creative expression for which Pisceans are known. The ancient version of this glyph, taken from the Egyptians, had no connecting line, which was added in the fourteenth century.

Another interpretation is that the left fish indicates the direction of involution or the beginning of the cycle, the right-hand fish, the direction of evolution, the way to completion of a cycle. It's an appropriate meaning for Pisces, the last sign of the zodiac.

How Well Do You Know the Glyphs?

Take this test after you've practiced drawing the glyphs.

1. Draw the glyphs of Mercury, Venus, and Mars. How do the differences in form help explain the nature of the planets?
2. How do the glyphs for the sign of Pisces and the planet Uranus relate to the balance of opposites?
3. How do the glyphs for Virgo and Scorpio express sexuality? Can you guess from the Scorpio glyph that Mars was once the ruling planet of Scorpio?
4. What do the central spaces in the Libra and Aquarius glyphs convey?
5. Draw the glyph for Capricorn. Is it the most difficult? Can you see horns and tail of the sea goat in this glyph?
6. Draw the glyphs for Saturn and Jupiter. Can you see how they complement each other?

7. Draw the glyphs for the three horned animals in the zodiac: Aries, Taurus, and Capricorn.
8. Compare the glyphs for the dual signs: the Twins, the Fishes, the Scales.
9. Compare the glyphs of Cancer and Leo. Can you see the Leo glyph as an extension of the Cancer one?
10. What does the dot in the center of the sun glyph mean? Which way is the moon glyph facing?

CHAPTER 5

How to Choose the Right Time

To find out if there is truth to the saying "to every thing there is a season and to every time there is a purpose unto heaven," try using some easy astrological principles to coordinate your schedule with the most beneficial times. When that tricky planet Mercury will be creating havoc with communications, be sure to back up the hard drive on your computer, keep duplicates of your correspondence, record those messages, and read between the lines of contracts. When Venus is in your sign, get a new hairstyle, entertain a VIP client, circulate where you'll be seen and admired.

To mark your own calendar for love, career moves, vacations, and important events, use the information in this chapter and the section in the previous one titled "Look Up Your Planets," as well as the moon sign listing under your daily forecast. Here are the happenings to note on your agenda:

- Dates of your sun sign period. This is a high energy time when you are beginning a new solar cycle. You are "reborn" for the year. A time to get a new lease on life. The sign before yours is a time of gestation, when you are winding up the previous cycle, a good time to review what has happened and make plans for your year ahead. It can be an especially loving time, if there is someone in your life who can provide extra attention now.
- Dates of planets in your sign this year. As each planet enters your sign, it will energize your life in a special way. Mercury will improve communications,

Venus will make you more appealing to others, Mars will energize you, Jupiter brings luck and opportunities, Saturn brings tests and discipline, etc.

- Full and new moons. Pay special attention when these fall in your sun sign. This is your axis of beginning and culminating.
- Eclipses. These bring changes in the area of life where they fall.
- When the moon is in your sun sign every month, as well as the moon in the opposite sign. These will be listed in the daily forecasts in the back of the book. Pay special attention to these high and low power times.
- Mercury retrogrades. These happen three times a year.
- Other retrograde periods.

Power Up on Your Birthday!

Every birthday starts a cycle of solar energy for you. You should feel a surge of vitality as the sun enters your sign, the time when predominant energies are most favorable to you. Start new projects, make your big moves. You'll get the recognition you deserve now, because your sun sign is most prominent. The tables in this book will tell you if other planets will also be passing through your sun sign at this time. Venus (love, beauty), Mars (energy, drive), or Mercury (communication, mental sharpness) reinforce the sun, boosting your luck.

Venus will rev up your social and love life, making you attractive to the opposite sex, charming to others. Mars revs up your energy and drive. Mercury fuels your brain power and helps your message reach the right people. Jupiter brings a lucky period of expansion when opportunities could fall into your lap.

There are two "down" times related to the sun. During the month before your birthday period, when you are winding up your annual cycle, you could be feeling especially vulnerable and depleted, so get extra rest, watch your diet, don't overstress yourself. Use this time to gear up for a big "push" when the sun enters your sign. On a positive note, at this time when the creative imagination is strong, your dreams, psychic life, and fantasies can be marvelous. It's a great time to escape the world with someone special on a marvelous vacation.

Another "down" time is when the sun is in the opposite sign (six months from your birthday), when the prevailing energies are very different from yours. You may feel at odds with the world, and things might not come easily. You'll have to work harder for recognition, because the world at large is attuned to the sign opposite yours and might not be receptive to your sun sign personality. However, this could be a good time to work on a team, in cooperation with others or behind the scenes.

Winding Up, Winding Down with the Moon Phases

Working with the moon's phases is as easy as looking up at the night sky. The new moon, when both sun and moon are in the same sign, is the best time to begin new ventures, especially the activities that are favored by the moon's sign. Then you'll naturally be focused outward, toward action. Postpone activities that are associated with the end of a cycle, such as breaking off, terminating, deliberating, reflecting, or activities that require introspection and passive work. Instead, focus on initiating, moving forward.

Get your project under way during the first quarter, then go public at the full moon, a culminating time of high intensity, when feelings come out into the open. This is the time to express yourself. Be aware, however, that because pressures are being released, other people are also letting off steam and confrontations are possible. Things are coming to "light." Traditionally, astrologers often advise against surgery at this time, which could produce heavier bleeding.

From the last quarter to the new moon is a winding-down phase, a time to cut off unproductive relationships, do serious thinking and inward-directed activities.

You'll feel some new and full moons more strongly than others, especially those new moons that fall in your sun sign and full moons in your opposite sign. Because that particular full moon happens at your low-energy time of year, it is likely to be an especially stressful time in a relationship, when hidden problems or unexpressed emotions could surface.

The Year 2001—Full and New Moons

(Note: these are calculated for EST)

JANUARY
Full Moon: January 9—(Lunar Eclipse) Cancer
New Moon: January 24—Aquarius
FEBRUARY
Full Moon: February 8—Leo
New Moon: February 23—Pisces
MARCH
Full Moon: March 9—Virgo
New Moon: March 24—Aries
APRIL
Full Moon: April 7—Libra
New Moon: April 23—Taurus
MAY
Full Moon: May 7—Scorpio
New Moon: May 23—Gemini
JUNE
Full Moon: June 5—Sagittarius
New Moon: June 21—(Solar Eclipse) Cancer
JULY
Full Moon: July 5—(Lunar Eclipse) Capricorn
New Moon: July 20—also in Cancer (as above)
AUGUST
Full Moon: August 4—Aquarius
New Moon: August 18—Leo

SEPTEMBER
Full Moon: September 2—Pisces
New Moon: September 17—Virgo
OCTOBER
Full Moon: October 2—Aries
New Moon: October 16—Libra
NOVEMBER
Full Moon: November 1—Taurus
New Moon: November 15—Scorpio
Full Moon: November 30—Gemini
DECEMBER
New Moon: December 14—(Solar Eclipse) Sagittarius
Full Moon: December 30—(Lunar Eclipse) Cancer

Don't Be Eclipsed!

Both solar and lunar eclipses are times when our natural rhythms are altered, often producing important changes in our lives. There are five eclipses this year, which will affect the houses of your horoscope (areas of life) where the eclipses fall. If the eclipses fall in your sun sign, especially on or close to your birthday, you may experience a turning point in your life. This year's eclipses fall in Cancer, Capricorn, or Sagittarius, and will be felt more strongly in members of those signs.

Lunar eclipses happen when the Earth is on a level plane with the sun and moon and moves exactly between them during the time of the full moon, breaking the powerful monthly cycle of opposition of these two forces. We might say the Earth "short-circuits" the connection between them. The effect can be either confusion or clarity, as our subconscious energies, which normally react to the pull of opposing sun and moon, are turned off. This momentary "turnoff" could help us turn our lives around. When we are temporarily freed from the subconscious attachments, we may have "Aha!" insights that could help us change destructive emotional patterns, such as addictions. On the other hand, this break in the normal cycle could cause a bewildering disorientation that intensifies our insecurities.

The solar eclipse occurs during a new moon, when the moon blocks the sun's energies as it passes exactly between the sun and the Earth. This means the objective, conscious force, represented by the sun, will be temporarily darkened. Subconscious lunar forces, activating our deepest emotions, will now dominate, putting us in a highly subjective state. Emotional truths can be revealed or emotions can run wild, as our objectivity is cut off and hidden patterns surface. If your sign is affected, you may find yourself beginning a period of work on a deep inner level, you may have psychic experiences or a surfacing of deep feelings.

You'll start feeling the energies of an upcoming eclipse a few days after the previous new or full moon. The energy continues to intensify until the actual eclipse, then disperses for three or four days. So plan ahead at least a week or more before an eclipse and allow several days afterward for the natural rhythms to return. Try not to make major moves during this period (it's not a great time to get married, change jobs, or buy a home).

Eclipses in 2001

January 9—Lunar Eclipse in Cancer
June 21—Solar Eclipse in Cancer
July 5—Lunar Eclipse in Capricorn
December 14—Solar Eclipse in Sagittarius
December 30—Lunar Eclipse in Cancer

Moon Sign Timing

You can forecast the daily emotional "weather," to determine your monthly high and low days, or to synchronize your activities with the cycles and the sign of the moon. Take note of the moon's daily sign under your daily forecast at the end of the book. Here are some of the activities favored and moods you are likely to encounter under each sign.

Moon in Aries

Get moving! The new moon in Aries is an ideal time to start new projects. Everyone is pushy, raring to go, rather impatient and short-tempered. Leave details and follow-up for later. Competitive sports or martial arts are great ways to let off steam. Quiet types could use some assertiveness, but it's a great day for dynamos. Be careful not to step on too many toes.

Moon in Taurus

It's time to do solid, methodical tasks. This is the time to tackle follow-through or backup work. Lay the foundations for success. Make investments, buy real estate, do appraisals, do some hard bargaining. Attend to your property—get out in the country. Spend some time in your garden. Enjoy creature comforts, music, a good dinner, sensual lovemaking. Forget starting a diet.

Moon in Gemini

Talk means action today. Telephone, write letter, fax! Make new contacts, stay in touch with steady customers. You can handle lots of tasks at once. A great day for mental activity of any kind. Don't try to pin people down—they too are feeling restless. Keep it light. Flirtations and socializing are good. Watch gossip—and don't give away secrets.

Moon in Cancer

This is a moody, sensitive, emotional time. People respond to personal attention, mothering. Stay at home, have a family dinner, call your mother. Nostalgia, memories, and psychic powers are heightened. You'll want to hang on to people and things (don't clean out your closets now). You could have some shrewd insights into what others really need and want now. Pay attention to dreams, intuition, gut reactions.

Moon in Leo

Everybody is in a much more confident, enthusiastic, generous mood. It's a good day to ask for a raise, show what you can do, dress like a star. People will respond to flattery, enjoy a bit of drama and theater. You may be feeling extravagant, so treat yourself royally and show off a bit (but don't break the bank!). Be careful that you don't promise more than you can deliver!

Moon in Virgo

Do practical down-to-earth chores. Review your budget. Make repairs. Be an efficiency expert. (Not a day to ask for a raise.) Have a health checkup. Revamp your diet. Buy vitamins or health food. Make your home spotless. Take care of details, piled-up chores. Reorganize your work and life so they run more smoothly and efficiently. Save money. Be prepared for others to be in a critical, fault-finding mood.

Moon in Libra

Relationships of all kinds are favored. Attend to legal matters. Negotiate contracts. Arbitrate. Do things with your favorite partner. Socialize. Be romantic. Buy a special gift or a beautiful object. Decorate yourself or your surroundings. Buy new clothes. Throw a party. Have an elegant, romantic evening. Smooth over any ruffled feathers. Avoid confrontations, stick to civilized discussions.

Moon in Scorpio

This is a day to do things with passion. You'll have excellent concentration and focus. Try not to get too intense emotionally, however, and avoid sharp exchanges with loved ones. Others many tend to go to extremes, get jealous, overreact. Great for troubleshooting, problem-solving, research, scientific work—and making love. Pay attention to psychic vibes.

Moon in Sagittarius

A great time for travel. Have philosophical discussions. Set long-range career goals. Work out, do sports, or buy athletic equipment. Others will be feeling upbeat, exuberant, adventurous, risk-taking. You may feel like taking a gamble, betting on the horses, visiting a local casino, buying a lottery ticket. Teaching, writing, and spiritual activities also get the green light. Relax outdoors. Take care of animals.

Moon in Capricorn

You can accomplish a lot today, so get on the ball! Issues concerning your basic responsibilities, duties, family, and parents could crop up. You'll be expected to deliver on promises and stick to your schedule now. Weed out the dead wood from your life and attack chores systematically. Get a dental checkup or attend to aching knees.

Moon in Aquarius

A great day for doing things in groups— clubs, meetings, outings, politics, parties. Campaign for your candidate. Work for a worthy cause. Deal with larger issues that affect the welfare of humanity. Buy a computer or electronic gadget. Watch TV. Wear something outrageous. Try something you've never done before. Present an original idea. Don't stick to a rigid schedule—go with the flow. Take a class in meditation, mind control, yoga.

Moon in Pisces

This can be a very creative day, so let your imagination work overtime. Film, theater, music, and ballet could inspire you. Spend some time alone, resting and reflecting, reading, watching a favorite film, or writing poetry. Daydreams can also be profitable. Help those less fortunate or lend a listening ear to someone who may be feeling blue. Don't overindulge in self-pity or escapism via adult beverages, since people are especially vulnerable to substance abuse now. Turn your thoughts to romance and someone special.

When the Planets Seem to Go Backward

All the planets, except for the sun and moon, have times when they appear to move backward—or retrograde—in the sky, or so it seems from our point of view on earth. Astrologers often compare retrograde motion to the optical illusion that occurs when we ride on a train that passes another train traveling at a different speed—the second train appears to be moving in reverse.

At these times, planets do not work as they usually do, so it's best to "take a break" from that planet's energies in our life and do some work on an inner level.

How to Outwit Mercury Mischief

Mercury goes retrograde three times each year, and its effects can be especially irritating, since the Mercury-ruled areas of your life, such as analytical thought processes, communications, scheduling, are subject to all kinds of confusion.

This year Mercury retrogrades in the air signs (Aquarius, Gemini, and Libra), which are associated with mental processes, so expect people to change their minds, renege on commitments. Communications equipment might break down. Schedules must be changed on short notice. People show up late for appointments or don't show up at all. Traffic jams are par for the course. Major purchases may malfunction, not work out, or get delivered in the wrong color. Letters might not arrive or may be sent to the wrong address. Employees make errors that have to be corrected later. Contracts don't work out or must be renegotiated.

Since most of us can't put our lives on "hold" for nine weeks every year (three Mercury retrograde periods), we should learn to tame the trickster and make it work for us. The key is in the prefix "re." This is the time to go back over things in your life. Reflect on what you've done during the previous months. Look for deeper insights, spot errors you've missed, take time to REview and REevaluate what has happened. This time is very good for inner spiritual work and meditations. Rest and reward yourself—it's a good time to take a vacation, especially if you REvisit a favorite place. REorganize your work and finish up projects that are backed up. Clean out your desk and closets. Throw away what you can't REcycle. If you must sign contracts or agreements, do so with a contingency clause that lets you REnegotiate the terms later.

Postpone major purchases or commitments. Don't get married (unless you're RE-marrying the same person). Try not to rely on other people keeping appointments, contracts, or agreements to the letter—have several alternatives. Double-check and read between the lines. Don't buy anything connected with communications or transportation (if you must, be sure to cover yourself). Mercury retrograding through your sun sign will intensify its effect on your life.

If Mercury was retrograde when you were born, you may be one of the lucky people who won't suffer the frustrations of this period. If so, your mind probably works in a very intuitive, insightful way.

The sign Mercury is retrograding through can give you an idea of what's in store—as well as the sun signs that will be especially challenged.

MERCURY RETROGRADE PERIODS IN 2001
February 3–February 25 in Aquarius

June 4–28 in Gemini
October 1–22 in Libra

Venus Retrograde—Make Peace!

Retrograding Venus can cause relationships to take a backward step or it can make you extravagant and impractical. *Not* a good time to redecorate—you'll hate the color of the walls later. Postpone getting a new hairstyle and try not to fall in love. But, if you wish to make amends in an already troubled relationship, make peaceful overtures then. Aries and Libra (its opposite sign) must take special note this year.

VENUS RETROGRADE IN 2001
   March 8–April 19 in Aries

Mars Tips—When to Push and When to Hold Back!

Mars shows how and when to get where you want to go. Timing your moves with Mars on your side can give you a big push. On the other hand, pushing Mars the wrong way can guarantee that you'll run into frustrations in every corner. Your best times to forge ahead are during the weeks when Mars is traveling through your sun sign or your Mars sign (look these up in the chapter on how to find your planets). Also consider times when Mars is in a compatible sign (fire with air signs, or earth with water signs). You'll be sure to have planetary power on your side.

   Hold your fire when Mars retrogrades, especially if you are Sagittarius or Gemini this year. Now is the time to exercise patience, let someone else run with the ball, especially if it's the opposing team. You may feel that you're not accomplishing much, but that's the right idea. Slow down and work off any frustrations at the gym. It's also best to postpone buying mechanical devices, which are Mars-rules, and take extra care when handling sharp objects. Sports, especially those requiring excellent balance, should be played with care. Be sure to use the appropriate protective gear and don't take unnecessary chances. This is not the time for daredevil moves! Pace yourself and pay extra attention to your health, since you may be especially vulnerable at this time.

MARS RETROGRADES IN 2001
May 11–July 19 in Sagittarius

When Other Planets Retrograde

The slower-moving planets stay retrograde for months at a time (Saturn, Jupiter, Neptune, Uranus, and Pluto). When Saturn is retrograde, you may feel more like hanging out than getting things done. It's an uphill battle with self-discipline at this time. Neptune retrograde promotes a dreamy escapism from reality, whereas Uranus retrograde may mean setbacks in areas where there have been sudden changes. Think of this as an adjustment period, a time to think things over and allow new ideas to develop. Pluto retrograde is a time to work on establishing proportion and balance in areas where there have been recent dramatic transformations.

When the planets start moving forward again, there's a shift in the atmosphere. Activities connected with each planet start moving ahead, plans that were stalled get rolling. Make a special note of those days on your calendar and proceed accordingly.

OTHER RETROGRADES IN 2001

- Pluto retrograde: March 17–August 23 in Sagittarius
- Neptune retrograde: May 10–October 17 in Aquarius
- Uranus retrograde: May 29–October 30 in Aquarius
- Saturn retrograde: September 26, 2001–February 7, 2002 in Gemini
- Jupiter retrograde: November 2, 2001–March 1, 2002 in Cancer

CHAPTER 6

Love Clicks and Crashes

Are you a Leo with a fatal attraction to a sexy Scorpio? Or an Aquarius with an immaculate Virgo who complains that you'll rush off leaving a pile of towels on the bathroom floor. Or you're that Virgo, in love with Aquarius, who hadn't bargained for a lifetime of picking up after your mate. Old-fashioned astrologers would say, "This combination is doomed from the start!" It used to be that some sun sign combinations were treated like champagne and tomato juice—never the twain should meet. Others were blessed by the stars as perfectly compatible.

Today we make allowance for the fact that hearts don't follow horoscopes. Although some combinations will be more challenging, too many long-lasting relationships happen between so-called incompatible sun signs to brand ANY combination as totally unworkable. We've gone far beyond stereotyping to respecting and enjoying the differences between people and using astrology to help us get along with them.

Here is a guide to finding out in advance how well you'll get along. Or, if you've already fallen for someone, checking out the potential for clicking long-term or avoiding a crash in the future. Though the comparisons here apply to sun signs, you can apply other planets that could influence your relationship to these sun sign descriptions. The moon (emotions), Mercury (communication), Mars (sex drive), and Venus (allure, tastes) can make a big difference to the longevity of a relationship.

To understand your astrological connection with another person you need to identify the spatial relationship between signs. The sign "next door" is something like your next-door neighbor who loans you his lawn mower or feeds your cats—or disputes your property boundaries. Signs distant from yours also have attitudes based on their "neighborhoods." Since the zodiac is a circle, the signs also relate to each other according to the angle of the distance between them. Between signs of the *same polarity,* but different elements, such as earth signs with water signs or fire and air combinations, energy flows most easily (with one exception: the sign opposite yours). Between signs of *different polarity,* you'll experience tension or challenge (and possibly a very sexy "charge").

Your Sign Mates—It's a Click or a Ho-Hum

Those of your own sign could be the soul mate you've been looking for—one who understands and sympathizes with you like no other sign can! Your sign mate understands your need for space, yet knows how and when to be "there" for you. There are many examples of long-term partnerships between sun sign twins—Roy Rogers and Dale Evans (both Scorpios), Abigail and John Adams (both Scorpios), George and Barbara Bush (both Geminis), Bob and Delores Hope (both Geminis), Frank and Kathie Lee Gifford (both Leos). Working relationships fare especially well when there are common sun signs, though you may have to delegate unwanted tasks to others. In a public lifestyle or one where there is much separation or stimulation, your similarities can also hold you together—there is the feeling of "you and me against the world." The problem is when there is too much of a good thing with no stimulation or challenge—or when there is no "chemistry," which can often happen between signs that share so much. The solution is to bring plenty of outside excitement into your lives.

The Sign Next Door—
Where's the Chemistry?

These signs are your next-door neighbors on the zodiac wheel. Your relationships is based on evolution—you've evolved out of the previous sign carrying energies that have been accumulating and developing through the zodiac cycle. The sign following yours is where your energy is headed, the next step. In a way, it's like sitting at a dinner table and passing the plate from left to right. You receive certain qualities from the previous sign and pass on those, plus your own, to the next.

This is also a sibling relationship where the sign before yours is like a protective older brother or sister, who's "been there," and the next sign is your eager younger sibling. Every sign also has a compensating factor for its predecessor—this sign embodies lessons you should have learned (and which could trip you up if you've forgotten them).

But although both are in the same "family," sibling signs actually have little in common, because you have different basic values (elements), ways of operating (qualities), and types of energy (polarity). You probably won't feel sparks of chemistry or deep rapport unless other planets in your horoscope provide this bond. Instead, the emphasis is on pals, best friends, working partners, who are enhanced by the sibling sign position.

The sign ahead can inspire you—they're where you are heading, but you may be afraid to take the first brave step. For example, to Pisces, Aries embodies dynamic, forceful, self-oriented will—whereas Pisces is the formless, selfless, imaginative state where Aries originated. So Aries energizes Pisces, gets Pisces moving. This sign behind backs you up, supports you. This relationship often makes one of the most lasting and contented unions—a couple of famous examples are the Duke and Duchess of Windsor (Cancer/Gemini), Paul Newman and Joanne Woodward (Aquarius/Pisces).

Your Squared-Off Relationships—
Three Signs Away

If you recognize that stress in a relationship often stimulates growth and that sexual tension can be heightened by a challenge, you might succeed with signs that are three signs away from yours. Relationships between these signs, which have a similar quality or way of acting, are charged with erotic energy and sparks of passion. Some of these can thrive on difficulty. But, even though you might declare a truce with this sign, the person probably won't be easy to live with. However, these will also be your least boring partners.

Since you will both operate in the same way, you'll understand how the other acts, though you won't necessarily share the same basic values or type of energy. It often happens that you'll continually confront each other—here is a sign that is just as restless, stubborn, or driven as you are! This person isn't one to provide security, settle down, or back you up. So will you choose to compete or to join forces to forge an equal partnership?

Mutable signs (Gemini, Virgo, Sagittarius, Pisces), which are the most changeable, understand each other's restlessness and low tolerance for boredom. This is a couple that can easily fragment, however, going off in different directions. This union often falls apart under stress, but challenges mutables to make order out of chaos. In other words, get your act together.

Cardinal couples (Aries, Cancer, Libra, Capricorn) with equal drive and energy often are characterized by goal-driven intensity—they never sit still. Fixed signs (Taurus, Leo, Scorpio, Aquarius) can be the most stable partners, or negatively, they can wrestle for control, war over territory, or have a stubborn Mexican standoff.

Positively, this is one of the sexiest aspects—these two signs challenge each other, bring about growth. Here are some of the issues likely to arise between signs that square off:

Aries—Cancer

Aries is forced by Cancer to consider the consequences of actions, particularly those that threaten security and hurt feelings. However, introspection cramps Aries' style—this sign wants perfect freedom to act as they please and has no patience for Cancer's self-pity or self-protectiveness. Although Cancer admires Aries' courage, the interaction will have to confront the conflict between the Aries' out-directed desire to have their own way and Cancer's inward-turning drive to create safety and security.

Cancer—Libra

Cancer is most satisfied by symbiotic, intimate, emotionally dependent relationships. So when you meet someone who is very independent, you feel hurt, rejected, and throw up a defensive shell or get moody and depressed. Unfortunately, you risk this happening with Libra, a romantic, but rather emotionally cool sign. Libras want an equal partner, tend to judge their partner on a detached, idealistic level, by their looks, style, ideas, conversation. Libra recognizes that the best partnerships are between equals, but the issue here is what do you have to share? Libra won't be able to escape emotions through social activities or intellectual analysis here.

Libra—Capricorn

Both of you love the good life, but you may have conflicting ideas about how to get it. Capricorn is a very disciplined, goal-directed, ordered worker who requires concrete results. Libra is more about style, abstract principles, and can be quite self-indulgent. Libran indulgence versus Capricorn discipline could be the cruncher here. Another bone to pick would be differing ideas about what's fair and just. Capricorn often believes that the "end justifies the means." Libra upholds fairness over bottom-line concerns.

Capricorn—Aries

Both are survivors who love to win. But Capricorn works for status and material rewards, while Aries works for glory, heroism, challenge, for the joy of being first. Capricorn wants to stay in control. Aries wants freedom. In a positive way, Aries must grow up with Capricorn, but, in return, it can give this tradition-oriented sign a younger lease on life.

Taurus—Leo

Leo has an insatiable appetite for admiration; Taurus for pleasure. Taurus sensuality can make Leo feel like a star. Leo's romantic gestures appeal to Taurus on a grand scale. Taurus will have to learn courtship and flattery to keep Leo happy—bring on the champagne and caviar! Leo will have to learn not to tease the bull, especially by withholding affection—and to enjoy simple meat-and-potatoes kinds of pleasures as well. Money can be so important here. Leo likes to spend royally; Taurus likes to accumulate and hoard.

Leo—Scorpio

Scorpio wants adventure in the psychic underworld. Leo wants to stay in the throne room. Scorpio challenges Leo to experience life intensely, which can bring out the best in Leo. Leo burns away Scorpio negativity—with low tolerance for dark moods. Scorpio is content to work behind the scenes, giving Leo center stage. But Leo must never mistake a quiet Scorpio for a gentle pussycat. There will be plenty of action behind the scenes. Settle issues of control without playing power games.

Scorpio—Aquarius

Aquarius' love of freedom and Scorpio's possessiveness could clash here. Scorpio wants to own you—Aquarius wants to remain friends. This is one unpredictable sign

Scorpio can't figure out, but has fun trying. Aquarius' flair for group dynamics could bring Scorpio out. However, too many outside interests could put a damper on this combination.

Aquarius—Taurus

Taurus lives in the touchable realm of the earth. Aquarius is in the electric, invisible realm of air, which can't be fenced in. It's anyone's guess if Taurus can ground Aquarius or if Aquarius can uplift Taurus. Taurus' talent as a realist could be the anchor this free spirit needs. Aquarian originality opens new territory to Taurus.

Gemini—Virgo

Nerves can be stimulated or frayed when these Mercury-ruled signs sound off. Both have much to say to each other—from different points of view. Gemini deals in abstractions. Virgo in down-to-earth facts. Common interests could keep this pair focused on each other.

Virgo—Sagittarius

Safety versus risk could be the hallmark of this relationship. Virgo plays it safe and cautious. Sagittarius operates on faith and enthusiasm. You're two natural teachers who have different philosophies and have much to learn from each other. When Virgo picks things apart or gets bogged down in details, Sagittarius urges them to look for the *truth*—the big picture. Sagittarius' lack of organization or follow-through will either drive Virgo crazy or provide a job. Virgo puts Sagittarius down with facts, deflating overblown promises and sales pitches.

Sagittarius—Pisces

There should be many philosophical and spiritual discussions and debates here. When Sagittarius says, "I'm right," Pisces says, "Everything's relative. We're all right

and wrong, so what?" Sagittarius is about elevating the
self and Pisces is about merging the self, losing the self.
On a less cosmic level, these two high-flying signs may
never get down to earth. Pisces' supersensitive feelings
are easily wounded by Sagittarius' moments of truth-tell-
ing. But Sagittarius can help sell those creative Piscean
ideas; that is, if you don't wander off in different
direction.

Pisces—Gemini

Gemini is always trying to understand, abstract, rational-
ize. Pisces wants to merge and flow, find a soul mate, go
beyond the mind. Pisces' moods get on Gemini's nerves.
Gemini runs away from emotional mergers, which really
matter to Pisces. Yet Pisces' glamour can intrigue Gemini
and Gemini's lightness and wit help Pisces laugh away
the blues.

Your Easiest Love Clicks—
Too Much of a Good Thing?

Signs of your same element (four signs away from yours)
are considered the easiest relationships possible . . . the
most compatible partners. But sometimes there is too
much of a good thing. These tend to lack dynamism and
sexy sparks. They can be too comfortable as you adjust
very easily to each other. If it's too easy, you might look
for excitement and challenge elsewhere.

Relationships between the three earth signs (Taurus,
Virgo, Capricorn) are mutually profitable, both professionally and personally. You won't find the other sign
tampering with your financial security, frittering away
hard-earned funds, or flirting with danger. You could fulfill your dreams of a comfortable life together. Too much
comfort could leave you yawning, however—you need
someone to shake you up once in a while.

Fire signs (Aries, Leo, Sagittarius) can ignite each

other, but watch out for temper and jealousy. You both demand exclusive attention, are happiest when your ego is stoked and you feel like number one, so you may have to curb any tendency to flirt. Because you tend to be big risk-takers and free spenders, you may have to delegate the financial caretaking carefully or find an expert adviser.

Water signs (Cancer, Scorpio, Pisces) have found partners who aren't afraid of emotional depths or heights. These are the ones who can understand and sympathize with your moods. This could be your solution to who gives you the emotional security you need. When moods collide, however, you could find it difficult to get each other out of deep water.

Air signs (Gemini, Libra, Aquarius) communicate well together. There is no heavy emotionalism or messy ego or possessiveness to deal with. You both respect the need for freedom and personal space and can make your own rules for an open, equal partnership. Staying in touch is the problem here. You could become so involved in your own pursuits that you let romance fly by or are never there for each other. Be sure to cultivate things in common, because unless there are many shared interests, it is easy to float away.

On Different Wavelengths: The Potential Crashes

Here are the relationships that challenge your sign the most, where you have to stretch yourself to make this work. You have different basic values (element), ways of acting (quality), kinds of energy (polarity), and unlike your next-door signs, who also have those differences, you don't have the proximity of being next in line. Instead of being beside you, the other sign is off on the other side of the zodiac. On the other hand, this very separateness can have an exotic quality, the attraction of the unknown (and unattainable). This is someone you'll never quite figure out. And this sign also has many threatening traits—if you get into this relationship, there will be risks, you won't quite know what to expect. The relationship is the proverbial square peg and round hole. Even though the stress of making this relationship work can be great, so can the stimulation and creativity that result from trying to find out what makes each other tick.

When positive and negative signs come together, lights go on, as you discover different ways of viewing the world, which can move you out of the doldrums. Here is how your sign relates to these partners.

Aries: Scorpio/Virgo

Scorpio, who tends to be secretive and manipulative, embodies everything that is foreign to Aries. Aries is clear-cut, openly demanding. If an Aries attacks, it will be swift and open. Scorpio will wait for the time when an opponent is most vulnerable—years, if necessary—to deal the lethal blow. Aries burns out much sooner. Yet your very strong differences only make the conquest more exciting.

Virgo thinks the way to solve problems is to get organized, think things through—steamrolling Aries wants fast action, quick results. Both Scorpio and Virgo will challenge Aries to go against the grain—be careful, organized, persevering, delve deeply, look at the long haul. Aries will have to tone down impulsiveness with these signs.

Taurus: Libra/Sagittarius

Libra, also Venus-ruled, is involved with the abstract, idealistic side of the planet, whereas Taurus is involved with the sensual, materialistic, self-indulgent side. Libra challenges Taurus to abstract, to get into the mind as well as the body. Taurus will bring Libra down to earth and provide stability for this sign.

Sagittarius challenges Taurus to expand its territory. Taurus is the most rooted of signs, and can be immobile.

Sagittarius is the happy wanderer. Taurus moves outside its turf with Sagittarius, who challenges it intellectually, spiritually, and physically.

Gemini: Scorpio/Capricorn

Here, playful, verbal, mental Gemini is confronted by the failure to probe, the failure to deal with passion. Gemini gets into deep real emotional stuff with Scorpio. Contact with Scorpio often precipitates a crisis in Gemini's life, as this sign realizes there is something powerful it's been missing. Scorpio challenges Gemini to delve deeply and make commitments rather than deals.

Capricorn makes Gemini develop discipline, set goals, and do practical bottom-line things the sign is not prepared to do. Capricorn has no tolerance for fragmented efforts and forces Gemini to focus and produce.

Cancer: Sagittarius/Aquarius

Fearful, frugal Cancer must take risks to make a relationship work with Sagittarius, who loves to gamble, has faith in the universe. Everyone's buddy, Aquarius makes Cancer give love with an open hand, placing less emphasis on personal security, property.

Cancer must give up possessiveness with both these signs, who actually enjoy the kind of freedom (insecurity) that Cancer most fears. In these relationships, Cancer's expectations of what a relationship should be have to change. It gets no protection from either sign and its favorite sympathy-winning techniques (playing "poor little me," whining, clinging, or complaining) only alienate these signs further. In the process of coping with these distant signs however, Cancer can eventually become more independent and truly secure within itself.

Leo: Capricorn/Pisces

Capricorn demands that Leo deliver on promises. With this down-to-earth sign, Leo can't coast for long on looks

117

and star power. Capricorn wants results, pushes Leo to produce, casts a cold eye on shows of ego, and sees through bluffs. Conversely, both enjoy many of the same things, such as a high-profile lifestyle, if for different reasons.

Pisces is on another planet from solar Leo—the Neptunian embodies all that is not-self. This is a sign that devalues the ego. Pisces teaches Leo to be unselfish, to exercise compassion and empathy, to walk in others' shoes. Leo has to give up arrogance and false pride for a lasting relationship with Pisces.

Virgo: Aquarius/Aries

Aquarius sheds light on Virgo's problem without getting bogged down in details. Interaction with Aquarius expands Virgo, prepares this sign for the unpredictable, the sudden, the unexpected. Aquarius gets Virgo to broaden scope—to risk experimenting. Aries gives Virgo positive energy and draws Virgo away from self-criticism and out into the world.

Libra: Pisces/Taurus

Looking for a decision-maker—Libra won't find it in Pisces! Pisces and Libra both share an artistic nature, but executed in a different way. Libra can't project its need for direction onto Pisces. Libra says, "What should I do?" Pisces says, "I know how you feel. It's tough not knowing what to do." Pisces challenges Libra to go within, to understand where others are coming from, rather than expecting them to conform to an abstract ideal.

Taurus brings Libra into the practical material world and gives this sign ground, but Taurus will also insist on material value. Taurus will ask, "How much does it cost?" Libra says, "I don't care, it's so pretty." Libra would rather not worry about function and operations, which become Taurus' task. Libra will either desperately need Taurus' practicality or find it a drag.

Scorpio: Aries/Gemini

Listen for the clanking of iron shields on a Mars-ruled Aries and Scorpio get-together. Both of you thrive on challenge and find it in each other. The issue here: who's the conqueror when neither will give in or give up? You'll have to respect each other's courage and bravery, and enjoy the sparks.

Gemini is the sign you can never pin down or possess—and this is super-fascinating for Scorpio. Their quicksilver wit and ability to juggle many people and things are talents not found in the Scorpio repertoire. Scorpios never stop trying to fathom the power of Gemini. Just when they've almost got them pegged, Gemini's onto something or someone else! As long as you don't expect devotion, you won't be disappointed.

Sagittarius: Taurus/Cancer

This is a dialogue between the rooted and the rootless. Both Taurus and Cancer are the most home-loving signs of the zodiac, while Sagittarius is the eternal wanderer—mentally, physically, or both. Will they be content to keep the home fires burning for Sagittarius? Another sticky point: both signs are very careful with money. However, these two financially savvy signs could help Sagittarius achieve miracles instead of talking about them. Sagittarius will have to learn patience with Taurus, who will inevitably try to tie Sagittarius down. Cancer could dampen Sagittarius' spirits with self-pity if they feel neglected in any way. Sagittarius will have to learn sensitivity to feelings. If Sagittarius can give up the position as teacher and become a student, these relationships might last.

Capricorn: Gemini/Leo

Both of these signs are social charmers who need organization, which is Capricorn's forte. They can help Capricorn get a desired position with Gemini's deft charm or

Leo's warmth and poise. The trade-off is that Capricorn will have to learn to take life less seriously, be as devoted to the partnership as to work. Otherwise, these two signs will look for amusement elsewhere. Gemini should inspire Capricorn to diversify, communicate, and spread wings socially. Leo adds confidence, authority, status. They'll appreciate Capricorn's adding structure to their lives.

Aquarius: Cancer/Virgo

Aquarius, the most freedom-loving sign, here encounters two different dimensions, both of which tend to bring this sign back to the realities of operating on a day-to-day level (Virgo) and honoring emotional attachments, the level of feeling (Cancer). Cancer is the home-loving sign who values security, family, emotional connections—an area often dismissed by Aquarius. Virgo is about organization, critical judgment, efficiency—which enhance Aquarius' accomplishments.

Pisces: Leo/Libra

With Leo, Pisces learns to find and project itself. Leo enjoys Pisces' talent and often profits by it. In return, Leo gives this often-insecure sign confidence. With Leo, Pisces can't hide any longer, must come out from the depths—but Leo will not sympathize or indulge Pisces' blue moods or self-pity. Pisces has to give up negativity with Leo.

Libra's instinct is to separate and analyze. Pisces wants an emotional merger with no boundaries. However, the more Pisces gets emotional, the more Libra becomes cool and detached. On a more positive note, Pisces can gain objectivity from this relationship, which insists on seeing both sides of any matter equally. Libra can provide the balance that keeps Pisces from drowning in the emotional depths.

Opposites Click or Freeze Up

This sign opposite yours is your other half, who manifests qualities that you think you don't have. There are many marriages between "opposite numbers," because one sign expresses what the other suppresses.

Because most lasting relationships are between equals, the attraction to your "opposite number" could backfire, if you suddenly develop strength in the opposite sign's own stronghold. What happens if you're an easygoing Aquarius married to a star-quality Leo and you decide it's time to show off your natural charisma on center stage? Or a disorganized Pisces with an efficient Virgo partner who goes on a cleanup, shape-up program and out-organizes the Virgo? No longer does the opposite partner have exclusive rights to certain talents or attitudes. If they can make adjustments to the new you, fine. Otherwise, someone could be out of a job.

It's an excellent idea to ask yourself if you are attracting your opposite sign in relationships, what the signs are acting out for you. It could be a clue to a side of your character you need to develop. Sometimes, after the initial chemistry dies down, and two opposite signs actually begin living together, you'll be irritated by the same qualities that at first attracted you. That's because they reveal the part you are afraid of within yourself—the part you haven't really claimed for yourself, and you resent this other person taking it over. Here's how it works out with opposite numbers: the more you learn to express "both sides of the same coin," the better chance your relationship will have.

Aries—Libra

Aries brings out Libra's placating, accommodating talents. And, at first, Libra is happy to play the charmer, in exchange for Aries' decisiveness. Aries revels in the chance to take charge and to be so openly needed. But in close quarters, Aries seems too pushy, too bossy. And when Libra decided to make its own decisions, Aries had better learn to charm.

Taurus—Scorpio

This is one of the most powerful attractions and is often found in marriages and long-term relationships. Some of these couples manage to balance out their differences nicely; others are just too stubborn to give up or give in. The uncomplicated, earthy, sensual Taurus likes safety, comfort, pleasurable physical things. Scorpio, who enjoys the challenges and dangers of intense feelings (and could live in a monk's cell), is often attracted to danger and risk. Scorpio wants a deep powerful merger. Taurus likes to stay aboveground, enjoying innocent pleasures. Both are possessive and jealous, with a need to control their own territory. Scorpio marvels at the uncomplicated basic drives of Taurus—couldn't they get into trouble together? Taurus enjoys teasing Scorpio with promises of innocent pleasure, but learns that Scorpios will sting when teased. Settle issues of control early on—and never underestimate each other's strength.

Gemini—Sagittarius

Gemini is the eager student of the world. Sagittarius is the perfect guide, only too happy to teach, enlighten, and expound. This is a very stimulating combination. Sagittarius enjoys telling others what to believe, however, and Gemini can't be bossed. Gemini also turns off fiery confrontations and absolute declarations of truth, and may deflate Sagittarius with barbs of wit. On a positive note, this could be a wonderful combination both socially and professionally. Romantically it works best if they can be both student and teacher to each other.

Cancer—Capricorn

Both of these signs have strong defense mechanisms. Cancer's is a protective shell. Capricorn's is a cold stony wall. In a relationship, both of these defenses play off each other. Cancer shows weakness (complains, whines) as a means of getting protection, which dovetails nicely with Capricorn's need to play the authoritarian parental father figure (even when it's a female) who takes responsibility for the vulnerable child (Cancer). But if Capricorn shows vulnerability, such as a fear of not being "right," Cancer panics, becomes insecure, and erects a self-protective shell. On the other hand, if Capricorn takes over Cancer's life, this active cardinal sign gets crabby. Learning to "parent" each other and reinforce strong traditional values could be the key to happiness here.

Leo—Aquarius

Both are stubborn fixed signs with opposite points of view. Leo is "me-oriented" and does not like to share. Aquarius is "them-oriented" and identifies with others. The Leo charisma comes from projecting the self—others are there for applause, while Aquarius shines as the symbol or spokesperson of a group, which reflects self-importance. Aquarius is the talk-show host, working from the audience. Leo is the guest star, on stage. Leo is not about to become one of the Aquarius crowd (especially if the crowd includes Aquarius' ex-lovers). Aquarius will not confine interests to Leo (become an exclusive Leo fan). If Leo can learn to share and Aquarius can give one-on-one attention, these opposites could balance out.

Virgo—Pisces

In Pisces, Virgo finds someone who apparently needs their services badly. Virgo in turn is attracted to Pisces because this sign can deal with the tricky side of life that can't be organized or made to run on schedule. Sensitive Pisces seems to need Virgo's clarity, orderliness, and practicality to keep together and in line. You can see how easy it is for this to become a bargain between the helper and the apparently helpless. When Pisces gets organized and Virgo gets in touch with their own irrational side, these two could form a more solid relationship.

Will Your Romance Click or Crash? Take This Quiz to Find Out

1. How many signs away are your sun signs?
2. How many signs away are your moon signs? This reflects your emotional compatibility.
3. How many signs away are your Venus signs? This reflects compatible tastes.
4. How many signs away are your Mercury signs? This reflects the way you'll communicate.
5. How many signs away are your Mars signs? This reflects your temper and your drive.

Score

Same sign: 7
Adjacent sign: 5
Two signs away: 8
Three signs away: 4
Four signs away: 10
Five signs away: 3
Opposite your sign: 7

High scores: 55–77 Plenty of clicks! A winner. Minimum compromises, but is there enough excitement?

Medium scores: 35–55 Crashes or freezes. Be sure you are willing to compromise.

Low scores: 21–35 A maximum compromise relationship. Lots of sparks but plenty of adjustments to make.

CHAPTER 7

What Makes Your Horoscope Special—Your Rising Sign

It's often said that every horoscope is unique. But you may wonder why, since many people were born on your same birthday. Most of your high school class will have the slow-moving planets (Uranus, Neptune, Pluto) and very possibly Jupiter and Saturn in the same sign as you do. What makes you truly special is your rising sign. It's the key to your specific horoscope, since it sets up the sequence of the houses of your chart.

What is a rising sign? At the moment you were born, when you assumed an independent physical body, one of the signs of the zodiac (that is, a thirty-degree slice of the sky) was just passing over the eastern horizon. In astrology, this is called the rising sign, often referred to as the ascendant. Other babies who were born later or earlier in the day, in the same hospital as you were born, might have planets in the same signs as you do, but would have a different rising sign, because as the earth turns, a different sign rises over the horizon every two hours. Therefore the planets would be in a different place or "house" in their horoscopes, accentuating different areas of their lives.

On the circular wheel of the horoscope, the other signs follow the rising signs in sequence, rotating counterclockwise. The rising sign marks the first house, which represents your first presentation to the world, your physical body, how you come across to others. It has been called your "shop window," the first impression you give to others. After the rising sign is determined, then each "house" or area of your chart will be influenced by the signs following it.

Without a valid rising sign, your collection of planets would have no "homes." Once the rising sign is established, it becomes possible to analyze a chart accurately because the astrologer knows in which area of life (house) the planet will operate. For instance, if Mars is in Gemini and your rising sign is Taurus, then Mars will be active in the second or financial house of your chart. If your rising sign is Virgo, then Mars will energize the career portion of your horoscope. That is why many astrologers insist on knowing the exact time of a client's birth, before they analyze a chart.

Your rising sign has an important relationship with your sun sign. Some will complement the sun sign; others hide the sun under a totally different mask, as if playing an entirely different role, so it is often difficult to guess the person's sun sign from outer appearances. For example, a Leo with a conservative Capricorn ascendant would come across as much less flamboyant than a Leo with a fiery Aries or Sagittarius ascendant. The exception is when the sun sign is reinforced by other planets; then, with other planets on its side, the sun may assert its personality much more strongly, overcoming the image of a contradictory rising sign. For example, a Leo with Venus and Jupiter also in Leo might counteract the conservative image of the Capricorn ascendant, in the above example. However, in most cases, the ascendant is the ingredient most strongly reflected in the first impression you make.

Rising signs change every two hours with the Earth's rotation. Those born early in the morning when the sun was on the horizon will most likely project the image of their sun sign. These people are often called a "double Aries" or a "double Virgo," because the same sun sign and ascendant reinforce each other.

Look up your rising sign on the chart at the end of this chapter. Since rising signs change every two hours, it is important to know your birth time as close to the minute as possible. Even a few minutes difference could change the rising sign and therefore the setup of your

126

chart. If you are unsure about the exact time, but know within a few hours, check the following descriptions to see which is most like the personality you project.

Aries Rising—Fiery Emotions

You are the most aggressive version of your sun sign, with boundless energy that can be used productively. Watch a tendency to overreact emotionally and blow your top. You come across as openly competitive, a positive asset in business or sports. Be on guard against impatience, which could lead to head injuries. Your walk and bearing could have the telltale head forward Aries posture. You may wear more bright colors, especially red, than others of your sign. You may also have a tendency to drive your car faster.

Taurus Rising—The Earth Mother

You'll exude a protective nurturing quality, even if you're male, which draws those in need of TLC and support. You're slow-moving, with a beautiful (or distinctive) speaking or singing voice that can be especially soothing or melodious. You probably surround yourself with comfort, good food, luxurious surroundings, sensual pleasures, and prefer welcoming others into your home to gadding about. You may have a talent for business, especially in trading, appraising, real estate. This ascendant gives a well-padded physique that gains weight easily.

Gemini Rising—Expressive Talents

You're naturally sociable, with lighter, more ethereal mannerisms than others of your sign, especially if you're female. You love to communicate with people and express your ideas and feelings easily. You may have writing or public speaking talent. You thrive on a constantly changing scenario with many different characters, though you may be far more sympathetic and caring than you project. You will probably travel widely, changing partners and jobs several times (or juggle two at once). Physically, you should cultivate a calm, tranquil atmosphere, because your nerves are quite sensitive.

Cancer Rising—Sensitive Antenna

You easily pick up others' needs and feelings, a great gift in business, the arts, and personal relationships, but guard against overreacting or taking things too personally especially during full moon periods. Find creative outlets for your natural nurturing gifts, such as helping the less fortunate, particularly children. Your insights would be useful in psychology, your desire to feed and care for others in the restaurant, hotel, or child-care industry. You may be especially fond of wearing romantic old clothes, collecting antiques, and, of course, good food. Since your body may retain fluids, pay attention to your diet. To relax, escape to places near water.

Leo Rising—The Scene Player

You may come across as more poised than you really feel; however, you play it to the hilt, projecting a proud royal presence. This ascendant gives you a natural flair for drama. You'll also project a much more outgoing, optimistic, sunny personality than others of your sign. You take care to please your public by always projecting your best star quality, probably tossing a luxuriant mane of hair or, if you're female, dazzling with a spectacular jewelry collection. Since you may have a strong parental nature, you could well be the regal family matriarch or patriarch.

Virgo Rising—Cool and Calculating

Virgo rising masks your inner nature with a practical, analytical outer image. You seem neat, orderly, more particular than others of your sign. Others in your life may feel they must live up to your high standards.

Though at times you may be openly critical, this masks a well-meaning desire to have only the best for loved ones. Your sharp eye for details could be used in the financial world, or your literary skills could draw you to teaching or publishing. The healing arts, health care, and service-oriented professions attract many with this Virgo emphasis in their chart. Physically, you may have a very sensitive digestive system.

Libra Rising—The Charmer

Libra rising makes you appear as a charmer, more of a social, public person than others of your sign. Your private life will extend beyond your home and family to include an active social life. You may tend to avoid confrontations in relationships, preferring to smooth the way or negotiate diplomatically, rather than give in to an emotional reaction. Because you are interested in all aspects of a situation, you may be slow to reach decisions. Physically, you'll have good proportions and pleasing symmetry. You're likely to have pleasing, if not beautiful, facial features. You move gracefully, and you have a winning smile and good taste in your clothes and home decor. Legal, diplomatic, or public relations professions could draw your interest.

Scorpio Rising—Magnetic Power

You project an intriguing air of mystery when Scorpio's secretiveness and sense of underlying power combines with your sign. You can project the image of a master manipulator, always in control and moving comfortably in the world of power. Your physical look comes across as intense and many of you have remarkable eyes, with a direct, penetrating gaze. But you'll never reveal your private agenda and you tend to keep your true feelings under wraps (watch a tendency toward paranoia). You may have an interesting romantic history with secret love affairs. Many of you heighten your air of mystery by wearing black. You're happiest near water and should provide yourself with a seaside retreat.

Sagittarius Rising—The Wanderer

You travel with this ascendant. You may also be a more outdoor, sportive type, with an athletic, casual, outgoing air. Your moods are camouflaged with cheerful optimism or a philosophical attitude. Though you don't hesitate to speak your mind, you can also laugh at your troubles or crack a joke more easily than others of your sign. This ascendant can also draw you to the field of higher education or to spiritual life. You'll seem to have less attachment to things and people and may travel widely. Your strong, fast legs are a physical bonus.

Capricorn Rising—Serious Business

This rising sign makes you come across as serious, goal-oriented, disciplined, and careful with cash. You are not one of the zodiac's big spenders, though you might splurge occasionally on items with good investment value. You're the traditional, conservative type in dress and environment, and you might come across as quite formal and businesslike. You'll function well in a structured or corporate environment where you can climb to the top. (You are always aware of who's the boss.) In your personal life, you could be a loner or a single parent who is "father and mother" to your children.

Aquarius Rising—One of a Kind

You come across as less concerned about what others think and could even be a bit eccentric. You're more at ease with groups of people than others in your sign, and may be attracted to public life. Your appearance may be unique, either unconventional or unimportant to you. Those with the sun in a water sign (Cancer, Scorpio, Pisces) may exercise your nurturing qualities with a large group, an extended family, a day-care or community center.

Pisces Rising—Romantic Roles

Your creative, nurturing talents are heightened and so is your ability to project emotional drama. And your dreamy eyes and poetic air bring out the protective instinct in others. You could be attracted to the arts, especially theater, dance, film, or photography, or to psychology, spiritual, or charity work. Since you are vulnerable to up and down mood swings, it is especially important for you to find interesting, creative work where you can express your talents and boost your self-esteem. Accentuate the positive and be wary of escapist tendencies, particularly involving alcohol or drugs, to which you are supersensitive.

Rising Sign Quiz

Can You Guess the Rising Sign of These Celebrities?

1. Bill Clinton and John F. Kennedy. Their charming smiles and easy social manner charmed the ladies.
2. Marilyn Monroe. Born to take center stage.
3. Madonna. Conscious of health, diet, and exercise.
4. Paul Newman. Rejected the Hollywood scene for a quiet life in Connecticut. Looks great in gray hair.
5. Candice Bergen. A world traveler. Outspoken Murphy Brown was her best-known role.
6. Bill Gates. Acquisitive, possessive, private, a moneymaker.
7. Drew Barrymore. Light, lively, a life of changes.
8. Diana Ross. Extreme, gutsy, a survivor.
9. Robert Redford. Remote, imaginative filmmaker.
10. Audrey Hepburn. Unique appearance, crusader for a worthy cause.

11. Bette Midler. Exciting, fiery redhead, confrontational, dynamic energy, expressive face.
12. Wilt Chamberlain. "Wilt the Stilt," 7'1", powerful body image, big moneymaker, huge appetites— claimed he slept with 20,000 women.

Answers:

1. Libra
2. Leo
3. Virgo
4. Capricorn
5. Sagittarius
6. Cancer
7. Gemini
8. Scorpio
9. Pisces
10. Aquarius
11. Aries
12. Taurus

RISING SIGNS—A.M. BIRTHS

	1 AM	2 AM	3 AM	4 AM	5 AM	6 AM	7 AM	8 AM	9 AM	10 AM	11 AM	12 NOON
Jan 1	Lib	Sc	Sc	Sc	Sag	Sag	Cap	Cap	Aq	Aq	Pis	Ar
Jan 9	Lib	Sc	Sc	Sag	Sag	Sag	Cap	Cap	Aq	Pis	Ar	Tau
Jan 17	Sc	Sc	Sc	Sag	Sag	Cap	Cap	Aq	Aq	Pis	Ar	Tau
Jan 25	Sc	Sc	Sag	Sag	Sag	Cap	Cap	Aq	Pis	Ar	Tau	Tau
Feb 2	Sc	Sc	Sag	Sag	Cap	Cap	Aq	Pis	Pis	Ar	Tau	Gem
Feb 10	Sc	Sag	Sag	Sag	Cap	Cap	Aq	Pis	Ar	Tau	Tau	Gem
Feb 18	Sc	Sag	Sag	Cap	Cap	Aq	Pis	Pis	Ar	Tau	Gem	Gem
Feb 26	Sag	Sag	Sag	Cap	Aq	Aq	Pis	Ar	Tau	Tau	Gem	Gem
Mar 6	Sag	Sag	Cap	Cap	Aq	Pis	Pis	Ar	Tau	Gem	Gem	Can
Mar 14	Sag	Cap	Cap	Aq	Aq	Pis	Ar	Tau	Tau	Gem	Gem	Can
Mar 22	Sag	Cap	Cap	Aq	Pis	Ar	Ar	Tau	Gem	Gem	Can	Can
Mar 30	Cap	Cap	Aq	Pis	Pis	Ar	Tau	Tau	Gem	Can	Can	Can
Apr 7	Cap	Cap	Aq	Pis	Ar	Ar	Tau	Gem	Gem	Can	Can	Leo
Apr 14	Cap	Aq	Aq	Pis	Ar	Tau	Tau	Gem	Gem	Can	Can	Leo
Apr 22	Cap	Aq	Pis	Ar	Ar	Tau	Gem	Gem	Gem	Can	Leo	Leo
Apr 30	Aq	Aq	Pis	Ar	Tau	Tau	Gem	Can	Can	Can	Leo	Leo
May 8	Aq	Pis	Ar	Ar	Tau	Gem	Gem	Can	Can	Leo	Leo	Leo
May 16	Aq	Pis	Ar	Tau	Gem	Gem	Can	Can	Can	Leo	Leo	Vir
May 24	Pis	Ar	Ar	Tau	Gem	Gem	Can	Can	Leo	Leo	Leo	Vir
June 1	Pis	Ar	Tau	Gem	Gem	Can	Can	Can	Leo	Leo	Vir	Vir
June 9	Ar	Ar	Tau	Gem	Gem	Can	Can	Leo	Leo	Leo	Vir	Vir
June 17	Ar	Tau	Gem	Gem	Can	Can	Can	Leo	Leo	Vir	Vir	Vir
June 25	Tau	Tau	Gem	Gem	Can	Can	Leo	Leo	Leo	Vir	Vir	Lib
July 3	Tau	Gem	Gem	Can	Can	Can	Leo	Leo	Vir	Vir	Vir	Lib
July 11	Tau	Gem	Gem	Can	Can	Leo	Leo	Leo	Vir	Vir	Lib	Lib
July 18	Gem	Gem	Can	Can	Can	Leo	Leo	Vir	Vir	Vir	Lib	Lib
July 26	Gem	Gem	Can	Can	Leo	Leo	Vir	Vir	Vir	Lib	Lib	Lib
Aug 3	Gem	Can	Can	Can	Leo	Leo	Vir	Vir	Vir	Lib	Lib	Sc
Aug 11	Gem	Can	Can	Leo	Leo	Leo	Vir	Vir	Lib	Lib	Lib	Sc
Aug 18	Can	Can	Can	Leo	Leo	Vir	Vir	Vir	Lib	Lib	Sc	Sc
Aug 27	Can	Can	Leo	Leo	Leo	Vir	Vir	Lib	Lib	Lib	Sc	Sc
Sept 4	Can	Can	Leo	Leo	Leo	Vir	Vir	Vir	Lib	Lib	Sc	Sc
Sept 12	Can	Leo	Leo	Leo	Vir	Vir	Lib	Lib	Lib	Sc	Sc	Sag
Sept 20	Leo	Leo	Leo	Vir	Vir	Vir	Lib	Lib	Sc	Sc	Sc	Sag
Sept 28	Leo	Leo	Leo	Vir	Vir	Lib	Lib	Lib	Sc	Sc	Sag	Sag
Oct 6	Leo	Leo	Vir	Vir	Vir	Lib	Lib	Sc	Sc	Sc	Sag	Sag
Oct 14	Leo	Vir	Vir	Vir	Lib	Lib	Lib	Sc	Sc	Sag	Sag	Cap
Oct 22	Leo	Vir	Vir	Lib	Lib	Lib	Sc	Sc	Sc	Sag	Sag	Cap
Oct 30	Vir	Vir	Vir	Lib	Lib	Sc	Sc	Sc	Sag	Sag	Cap	Cap
Nov 7	Vir	Vir	Lib	Lib	Lib	Sc	Sc	Sc	Sag	Sag	Cap	Cap
Nov 15	Vir	Vir	Lib	Lib	Sc	Sc	Sc	Sag	Sag	Cap	Cap	Aq
Nov 23	Vir	Lib	Lib	Lib	Sc	Sc	Sag	Sag	Sag	Cap	Cap	Aq
Dec 1	Vir	Lib	Lib	Sc	Sc	Sc	Sag	Sag	Cap	Cap	Aq	Aq
Dec 9	Lib	Lib	Lib	Sc	Sc	Sag	Sag	Sag	Cap	Cap	Aq	Pis
Dec 18	Lib	Lib	Sc	Sc	Sc	Sag	Sag	Cap	Cap	Aq	Aq	Pis
Dec 28	Lib	Lib	Sc	Sc	Sag	Sag	Sag	Cap	Aq	Aq	Pis	Ar

RISING SIGNS—P.M. BIRTHS

	1 PM	2 PM	3 PM	4 PM	5 PM	6 PM	7 PM	8 PM	9 PM	10 PM	11 PM	12 MIDNIGHT
Jan 1	Tau	Gem	Gem	Can	Can	Can	Leo	Leo	Vir	Vir	Vir	Lib
Jan 9	Tau	Gem	Gem	Can	Can	Leo	Leo	Leo	Vir	Vir	Vir	Lib
Jan 17	Gem	Gem	Can	Can	Can	Leo	Leo	Vir	Vir	Vir	Lib	Lib
Jan 25	Gem	Gem	Can	Can	Leo	Leo	Leo	Vir	Vir	Lib	Lib	Lib
Feb 2	Gem	Can	Can	Can	Leo	Leo	Vir	Vir	Vir	Lib	Lib	Sc
Feb 10	Gem	Can	Can	Leo	Leo	Leo	Vir	Vir	Lib	Lib	Lib	Sc
Feb 18	Can	Can	Can	Leo	Leo	Vir	Vir	Vir	Lib	Lib	Sc	Sc
Feb 26	Can	Can	Leo	Leo	Leo	Vir	Vir	Lib	Lib	Lib	Sc	Sc
Mar 6	Can	Leo	Leo	Leo	Vir	Vir	Vir	Lib	Lib	Sc	Sc	Sc
Mar 14	Can	Leo	Leo	Vir	Vir	Vir	Lib	Lib	Lib	Sc	Sc	Sag
Mar 22	Leo	Leo	Leo	Vir	Vir	Lib	Lib	Lib	Sc	Sc	Sc	Sag
Mar 30	Leo	Leo	Vir	Vir	Vir	Lib	Lib	Sc	Sc	Sc	Sag	Sag
Apr 7	Leo	Leo	Vir	Vir	Lib	Lib	Lib	Sc	Sc	Sc	Sag	Sag
Apr 14	Leo	Vir	Vir	Vir	Lib	Lib	Sc	Sc	Sc	Sag	Sag	Cap
Apr 22	Leo	Vir	Vir	Lib	Lib	Lib	Sc	Sc	Sc	Sag	Sag	Cap
Apr 30	Vir	Vir	Vir	Lib	Lib	Sc	Sc	Sc	Sag	Sag	Cap	Cap
May 8	Vir	Vir	Lib	Lib	Lib	Sc	Sc	Sag	Sag	Sag	Cap	Cap
May 16	Vir	Vir	Lib	Lib	Sc	Sc	Sc	Sag	Sag	Cap	Cap	Aq
May 24	Vir	Lib	Lib	Lib	Sc	Sc	Sag	Sag	Sag	Cap	Cap	Aq
June 1	Vir	Lib	Lib	Sc	Sc	Sc	Sag	Sag	Cap	Cap	Aq	Aq
June 9	Lib	Lib	Lib	Sc	Sc	Sag	Sag	Sag	Cap	Cap	Aq	Pis
June 17	Lib	Lib	Sc	Sc	Sc	Sag	Sag	Cap	Cap	Aq	Aq	Pis
June 25	Lib	Lib	Sc	Sc	Sag	Sag	Sag	Cap	Cap	Aq	Pis	Ar
July 3	Lib	Sc	Sc	Sc	Sag	Sag	Cap	Cap	Aq	Aq	Pis	Ar
July 11	Lib	Sc	Sc	Sag	Sag	Sag	Cap	Cap	Aq	Pis	Ar	Tau
July 18	Sc	Sc	Sc	Sag	Sag	Cap	Cap	Aq	Aq	Pis	Ar	Tau
July 26	Sc	Sc	Sag	Sag	Sag	Cap	Cap	Aq	Pis	Ar	Tau	Tau
Aug 3	Sc	Sc	Sag	Sag	Cap	Cap	Aq	Aq	Pis	Ar	Tau	Gem
Aug 11	Sc	Sag	Sag	Sag	Cap	Cap	Aq	Pis	Ar	Tau	Tau	Gem
Aug 18	Sc	Sag	Sag	Cap	Cap	Aq	Pis	Pis	Ar	Tau	Gem	Gem
Aug 27	Sag	Sag	Sag	Cap	Cap	Aq	Pis	Ar	Tau	Tau	Gem	Gem
Sept 4	Sag	Sag	Cap	Cap	Aq	Pis	Pis	Ar	Tau	Gem	Gem	Can
Sept 12	Sag	Sag	Cap	Aq	Aq	Pis	Ar	Tau	Tau	Gem	Gem	Can
Sept 20	Sag	Cap	Cap	Aq	Pis	Pis	Ar	Tau	Gem	Gem	Can	Can
Sept 28	Cap	Cap	Aq	Aq	Pis	Ar	Tau	Tau	Gem	Gem	Can	Can
Oct 6	Cap	Cap	Aq	Pis	Ar	Ar	Tau	Gem	Gem	Can	Can	Leo
Oct 14	Cap	Aq	Aq	Pis	Ar	Tau	Tau	Gem	Gem	Can	Can	Leo
Oct 22	Cap	Aq	Pis	Ar	Ar	Tau	Gem	Gem	Can	Can	Leo	Leo
Oct 30	Aq	Aq	Pis	Ar	Tau	Tau	Gem	Can	Can	Can	Leo	Leo
Nov 7	Aq	Aq	Pis	Ar	Tau	Tau	Gem	Can	Can	Can	Leo	Leo
Nov 15	Aq	Pis	Ar	Tau	Gem	Gem	Can	Can	Can	Leo	Leo	Vir
Nov 23	Pis	Ar	Ar	Tau	Gem	Gem	Can	Can	Leo	Leo	Leo	Vir
Dec 1	Pis	Ar	Tau	Gem	Gem	Can	Can	Can	Leo	Leo	Vir	Vir
Dec 9	Ar	Tau	Tau	Gem	Gem	Can	Can	Leo	Leo	Leo	Vir	Vir
Dec 18	Ar	Tau	Gem	Gem	Can	Can	Can	Leo	Leo	Vir	Vir	Vir
Dec 28	Tau	Tau	Gem	Gem	Can	Can	Leo	Leo	Vir	Vir	Vir	Lib

CHAPTER 8

Your Axis of Action—The Secrets of Timing by the Moon

Would you like to predict your most significant trends for the months ahead, as astrologers do? You can, by using the rising sign table in this book and simply looking up at the moon!

Though it might seem obvious to some moon-watchers, many of us have never stopped to think that in each sun sign period (note: we do not mean the calendar month), the new moon will be in the same sign as the sun, while the full moon will fall in the opposite sign, creating a polarized axis. The issues governed by the houses where the moon falls will have special importance over the upcoming month. In the new moon's house are the issues that are beginning. In the full moon's house are culminations, things coming to light. Sometimes the new moon in this axis of action comes first, at other times it comes after the full moon (as it does this fall), creating a different dynamic. Once in a while there are two new or full moons in the same sign, as happens this summer, which can reverse the order of the axis.

The object here is to find the houses (or area of life) on the axis where the new moon and full moon fall in your horoscope. First, look up your rising sign in the chart in this book on pages 133–134. This is actually an approximate rising sign for you, because it is impossible to be precise without knowing your exact time of birth. The sequence of houses that follows after your rising sign will most likely have the signs on the cusp (or beginning of the house) in sequential order. For example, if your rising sign is Scorpio, the second house cusp would be Sagittarius, the third house cusp Capricorn, the fourth Aquarius, and so on. However, to be on the safe side, consult the polarity of the previous sign as well. That's because there is a possibility that the degree of your rising sign may be so far along in the sign that the moon falls in the previous house. For instance, taking the above example, if your rising sign is fifteen degrees of Scorpio and the new moon falls at ten degrees Scorpio, it would be in the previous or twelfth house, rather than the first house. (Note: If you do not know your rising sign, assume that it is the same as your sun sign. Though the forecast will not be as accurate, it will still be relevant.)

The areas of your life covered by the twelve houses are actually six pairs of polarities. For example, the first house deals with independent action (it's the "me" house) while the opposite house, the seventh, deals with relationships (it's the "you" house). The second house deals with your possessions, the income you earn by yourself, what is "mine"; the opposite, eighth house, deals with joint resources, issues of power, or control, what is "ours." Here's how they line up:

First House (Rising Sign)/Seventh House Polarity

This polarity usually brings up issues of me versus you, independence versus dependence, freedom versus closeness, solo ventures versus partnerships, as well as the ability to commit and to form a contractual relationship. This could bring up issues in your marital or partnership life. If the new moon falls in your seventh house, you may be making a new commitment or you may meet someone who becomes a marital or business partner. If the new moon falls in your first house, you'll begin an independent venture and you'll be feeling very much on your own. Legal issues (seventh house) and court cases also happen at this time.

Second House/Eighth House

This polarity deals with what you own by yourself versus what you own with others (insurance, bank loans, taxes, inheritance, joint property), and with buying and selling. This polarity also brings up issues of your physical body, which "you own" versus sexual activity, which is joint physical activity.

Third House/Ninth House

This polarity will deal with issues in your local area versus the world at large, with neighbors versus people of a different background, with students versus higher education and with writing letters versus writing books. Your immediate, outgoing communications and thoughts versus your expansive thoughts and your philosophy of life are also considered. So are hobbies, skills, and students versus higher education and teachers, as well as how your mind works in everyday matters versus how your mind receives higher ideas. You may be traveling and dealing with issues of education, writing, publishing, and religion, or you may be very much on the go in your local area, involved with relatives—the third house rules siblings.

Fourth House/Tenth House

This is the axis of your private (fourth) versus your public life (tenth). It concerns your home life versus your life outside the home (career), and the nurturing side of your life versus the authority figures. Issues of prestige and status versus domestic situations, family, and "roots" will come up.

Fifth House/Eleventh House

The fifth is your house of personal self-expression, what you create (including your children) versus the eleventh house, where you express yourself through a group. The eleventh is your clubs, your labor union, your political party, your teams, and the goals and ideals you identify

with. Your contribution to society is here as well. Vying
with those interests are your personal projects and what
you want to do to express your own interests. Here also
are your romantic love affairs (the ones that might not
lead to commitment). Along this axis, issues arise involving your love life, or what you want to do for yourself
balanced with what your group or society wants. It's
about what "I" want versus what "they" want.

Sixth House/Twelfth House

This is where you deal with the reality functions of the
material world versus situations where you leave the material world behind. The sixth house is where you organize,
maintain your body in working order, work with the world
in a structured way versus the twelfth house where you go
with the flow, surrendering, giving up something. It's an
area of order (function) versus chaos (creativity).

This is also the polarity of addiction (twelfth house)
versus codependency (sixth). It's the polarity, too, of the
conscious (sixth) versus the unconscious (twelfth). The
sixth house is where you are in situations of responsibility, where you are the caretaker, versus the twelfth
house, where you have no responsibility, where you are
taken care of (prisons, hospitals, institutions). The
twelfth house is often called the house of self-undoing,
because it is the area where you have no brakes or
boundaries. The sixth house is where you set up the
structures and boundaries that will later enable you to
function in the twelfth house . . . you must learn the
scales and techniques (sixth) before you can play the
concerto (twelfth).

The House Game

Put the following in the appropriate houses:
   A. An attractive person you're flirting with
   B. Your mate
   C. A hospital stay

D. A philosophy course
E. IRS payments
F. Making the baseball team
G. Your new boss
H. Medical checkups
I. A letter from your sister
J. A family dinner
K. Your gold necklace
L. A solo trip

Answers:

A. Fifth house
B. Seventh house
C. Twelfth house
D. Ninth house
E. Eighth house
F. Eleventh house
G. Tenth house
H. Sixth house
I. Third house
J. Fourth house
K. Second house
L. First house

If There's an Eclipse on the Axis

Eclipses tend to throw the new moon/full moon axis off balance, as if there were a temporary short circuit of the usual cyclical energy. So be prepared for the unexpected in whatever you do in that house area. (There are five eclipses this year.)

Recap—How to Find Your Lunar Axis of Action

1. Look up your rising sign in the chart on pages 133–134. Example: For the following explanations, we'll assume your rising sign is Leo.

2. Determine the sequence of the twelve houses, following the rising sign.
   Example: First house, Leo. Second house, Virgo. Third house, Libra. Fourth house, Scorpio. Fifth house, Sagittarius. Sixth house, Capricorn. Seventh house, Aquarius. Eighth house, Pisces. Ninth house, Aries. Tenth house, Taurus. Eleventh house, Gemini. Twelfth house, Cancer.
3. Determine the signs of houses that are opposite each other.
   Example: First house Leo is opposite seventh house Aquarius, second house Virgo is opposite eighth house Pisces.
4. Look up the current new and full moon in the chart at the end of this chapter.
   Example: The new moon on January 24 falls in Aquarius, the following full moon in Leo happens on February 8.
5. Determine the issues that are reflected by the new and full moon. For someone with Leo rising, the Leo/Aquarius axis would indicate issues involving the first and seventh house, personal freedom versus relationships.

New and Full Moons for 2001

(Note: these are calculated for EST)

JANUARY
Full Moon: January 9—(Lunar Eclipse) Cancer
New Moon: January 24—Aquarius
FEBRUARY
Full Moon: February 8—Leo
New Moon: February 23—Pisces
MARCH
Full Moon: March 9—Virgo
New Moon: March 24—Aries
APRIL
Full Moon: April 7—Libra
New Moon: April 23—Taurus

MAY
Full Moon: May 7—Scorpio
New Moon: May 23—Gemini
JUNE
Full Moon: June 5—Sagittarius
New Moon: June 21—(Solar Eclipse) Cancer
JULY
Full Moon: July 5—(Lunar Eclipse) Capricorn
New Moon: July 20—also in Cancer
AUGUST
Full Moon: August 4—Aquarius
New Moon: August 18—Leo
SEPTEMBER
Full Moon: September 2—Pisces
New Moon: September 17—Virgo
OCTOBER
Full Moon: October 2—Aries
New Moon: October 16—Libra
NOVEMBER
Full Moon: November 1—Taurus
New Moon: November 15—Scorpio
Full Moon: November 30—Gemini
DECEMBER
New Moon: December 14—(Solar Eclipse) Sagittarius
Full Moon: December 30—(Lunar Eclipse) Cancer

CHAPTER 9

Meet Your Astrologer! What a Personal Reading Can— and Can't—Do for You

If you're at a crossroads in your life and have been wondering whether an astrological reading could help you make the right decisions, it might be time for a personal consultation. But should you choose a telephone reading, a celebrity-endorsed astrologer, have a chat room reading on the Internet, buy a personalized computer printout that promises many pages of deep insights, or find an astrologer in your city? The dizzying variety of options available today makes choosing a reading a confusing dilemma. The following basic guidelines can help you sort out your options to find the reading that's right for you.

The One-on-One Reading

Nothing compares to a one-on-one consultation with a professional astrologer who has analyzed thousands of charts and can pinpoint the potential in yours. During your reading, you can get your specific questions answered. For instance, how to get along better with your mate or coworker. There are many astrologers who now combine their skills with training in psychology and are well suited to help you examine your alternatives.

To give you an accurate reading, an astrologer needs certain information from you. Before your reading, a reputable astrologer should ask for the date, time, and place of birth of the subject of the reading. (A horoscope can be cast about anything that has a specific time and place.) Most astrologers will then enter this information into a computer, which will calculate a chart in seconds. From the resulting chart, the astrologer will do an interpretation.

If you don't know your exact birth time, you can usually locate it at the Bureau of Vital Statistics at the city hall or county seat of the state where you were born. If you still have no success in getting your time of birth, some astrologers can estimate an approximate birth time by using past events in your life to determine the chart.

How to Find a Good Astrologer

Your first priority should be to choose a qualified astrologer. Rather than relying on word of mouth or grandiose advertising claims, do this with the same care you would choose any trusted adviser such as a doctor, lawyer, or banker. Unfortunately, anyone can claim to be an astrologer—to date, there is no licensing of astrologers or established professional criteria. However, there are nationwide organizations of serious, committed astrologers that can help you in your search.

Good places to start your investigation are organizations such as the American Federation of Astrologers or the National Council for Geocosmic Research (NCGR), which offers a program of study and certification. If you live near a major city, there is sure to be an active NCGR chapter or astrology club in your area—many are listed in astrology magazines available at your local newsstand. In response to many requests for referrals, the NCGR has compiled a directory of professional astrologers, which includes a glossary of terms and an explanation of specialties within the astrological field. Contact the NCGR headquarters (see the resource list in this book) for information.

Be Aware of When to Beware

As a potentially lucrative freelance business, astrology has always attracted self-styled experts who may not have the knowledge or the counseling experience to give a helpful reading. These astrologers can range from the well-meaning amateur to the charlatan or street-corner gypsy who has for many years given astrology a bad name. Be very wary of astrologers who claim to have occult powers or who make pretentious claims of celebrated clients or miraculous achievements. You can often tell from the initial phone conversation if the astrologer is legitimate. He or she should ask for your birthday, time and place and conduct the conversation in a professional manner. Any astrologer who gives a reading based only on your sun sign is highly suspect.

When you arrive at the reading, the astrologer should be prepared. The consultation should be conducted in a private, quiet place. The astrologer should be interested in your problems of the moment. A good reading involves feedback on your part, so if the reading is not relating to your concerns, you should let the astrologer know. You should feel free to ask questions and get clarifications of technical terms. The reading should be an interaction between two people, rather than a solo performance. The more you actively participate, rather than expecting the astrologer to carry the reading or come forth with oracular predictions, the more meaningful your experience will be. An astrologer should help you validate your current experience and be frank about possible negative happenings, but suggest a positive course of action.

In their approach to a reading, some astrologers may be more literal, others more intuitive. Those who have had counseling training may take a more psychological approach. Though some astrologers may seem to have an almost psychic ability, extrasensory perception or any other parapsychological talent is not essential. A very accurate picture can be drawn from the data in your horoscope chart.

An astrologer may do several charts for each client, including one for the time of birth and a "progressed chart," showing the evolution from birth to the present time. According to your individual needs, there are many other possibilities, such as a chart for a different location, if you are contemplating a change of place. Relationships between any two people, things, or events can be interpreted with a chart that compares one partner's horoscope with the other's. A composite chart, which uses the midpoint between planets in two individuals charts to describe the relationship, is another commonly used device.

An astrologer will be particularly interested in transits—times when planets will pass over the planets or sensitive points in your birth chart, which signal important events in your life.

Many astrologers offer tape-recorded readings, another option to consider. In this case, you'll be mailed a taped reading based on your birth chart. This type of reading is more personal than a computer printout and can give you valuable insights, but it is not equivalent to a live reading, when you can have a face-to-face dialogue with the astrologer and discuss your specific interests and issues of the moment.

Phone Readings—Real or Phony?

Telephone readings come in two varieties . . . one is a dial-in taped reading, usually by a well-known astrologer. The other is a live consultation with an "astrologer" on the other end of the line. The taped readings are general daily or weekly forecasts, applied to all members of your sign and charged by the minute. The quality depends on the astrologer. One caution: be aware that these readings can run up quite a telephone bill, especially if you get into the habit of calling every day. Be sure that you are aware of the per-minute cost of each call beforehand.

Live telephone readings also vary with the expertise of the astrologer. Ideally the astrologer at the other end of the line enters your birth data into a computer that calculates your chart. This chart will then be referred to during the consultation. The advantage of a live telephone reading is that your individual chart is used and you can ask about a specific problem. However, before you invest in any reading, be sure that your astrologer is qualified and that you fully understand in advance how much you will be charged.

About Computer Readings

Companies that offer computer programs (such as ACS, Matrix, Astrolabe) also offer a variety of computer-generated horoscope readings. These can be quite comprehensive, offering a beautiful printout of the chart plus many pages of detailed information about each planet and aspect of the chart. You can then study your chart at your convenience, since the details of the chart are interpreted in a very understandable way. Of course, the interpretations will be general, since there is no personal input from you, and may not cover your immediate concerns. Since computer-generated horoscopes are much lower in cost than live consultations, you might consider them as either a supplement or preparation for an eventual live reading. You'll then be more familiar with your chart and able to plan specific questions in advance. They also make a terrific gift for astrology fans. There are several companies in our "Yellow Pages" chapter that offer computerized readings prepared by reputable astrologers.

CHAPTER 10

The Sydney Omarr Yellow Pages

Have you caught the "astrology bug"? If so, you'll want to meet other astrology fans, attend conferences, buy a program for your computer, maybe even attend a college devoted to astrology. In this chapter, we'll give you the information you need to locate the latest products and services available, as well as the top astrology organizations that hold meetings and conferences in your area.

There are organized groups of astrologers all over the country who are dedicated to promoting the image of astrology in the most positive way. The National Council for Geocosmic Research (NCGR) is one nationwide group that is dedicated to bringing astrologers together, promoting fellowship and high-quality education. Their accredited course system promotes a systematized study of all the different facets of astrology. Whether you'd like to know more about such specialties as financial astrology or techniques for timing events, or if you'd prefer the psychological or mythological approach, you'll find the leading experts at NCGR conferences.

Your computer can be a terrific tool for connecting with other astrology fans at all levels of expertise, as we explore in the Internet chapter in this book. Even if you are using a "dinosaur" from the eighties, there are still calculation and interpretation programs available for DOS and MAC formats. They may not have all the bells and whistles or exciting graphics, but they'll get the job done!

Newcomers to astrology should learn some of the basics, including the glyphs (astrology's special shorthand language), before you invest in a complex computer program. Use the chapter in this book to help you learn the symbols easily, so you'll be able to read the charts without consulting the "help" section of your program every time. Several programs such as Astrolabe's "Solar Fire," have pop-up definitions to help you decipher the meanings of planets and aspects. Just click your mouse on a glyph or an icon on the screen and a window with an instant definition appears.

You may be pleasantly surprised that you don't have to spend a fortune to get a perfectly adequate astrology program. In fact, if you are connected to the Internet, you can download one free. Astrology software is available at all price levels, from a sophisticated free application like "Astrolog," which you can download from a Web site, to inexpensive programs for under $100 such as Halloran's "Astrology for Windows," to the more expensive astrology programs such as "Winstar," "Solar Fire," or "Io" (for the Mac), which are used by serious students and professionals. Before you make an investment, it's a good idea to download a sample from the company's Web site or order a demo disk. If you just want to have fun, investigate an inexpensive program such as Matrix Software's "Kaleidoscope," an interactive application with lots of fun graphics. If you're baffled by the variety of software available, most of the companies on our list will be happy to help you find the right application for your needs.

If you live in an out-of-the-way place or are unable to fit classes into your schedule, you have several options. There are on-line courses offered at astrology Web sites, such as *www.panplanet.com.* Some astrology teachers will send you a series of audiotapes or you can order audio-taped seminars of recent conferences; other teachers offer correspondence courses that use their workbooks or computer printouts.

Nationwide Astrology Organizations and Conferences

Contact these organizations for information on conferences, workshops, local meetings, conference tapes, or referrals:

National Council for Geocosmic Research

Educational workshops, tapes, conferences, and a directory of professional astrologers are available from this nationwide organization devoted to promoting astrological education. For a $35 annual membership fee, you get their excellent publications and newsletters, plus the opportunity to network with other astrology buffs at local chapter events (there are chapters in twenty states). For general information about NCGR, contact:

NCGR
P.O. Box 38866
Los Angeles, CA 90038
Telephone: (818) 705-0797

At this writing, the contact for new memberships is:

Linda Fei, Membership Director
1359 Sargent Ave.
St. Paul, MN 55105
E-mail: LindaFei@aol.com
Telephone: (651) 698-1691

Or visit their Web page: *http://www.geocosmic.org* for updates and local events.

American Federation of Astrologers (A.F.A.)

One of the oldest astrological organizations in the United States, established 1938. It offers conferences, conventions, and a correspondence course. It will refer you to an accredited A.F.A. astrologer.

A.F.A.
P.O. Box 22040
Tempe, AZ 85285-2040
Telephone: (480) 838-1751
Fax: (480) 838-8293

A.F.A.N. (Association for Astrological Networking)

Did you know that astrologers are still being arrested for practicing in some states? A.F.A.N. provides support, legal information, works toward improving the public image of astrology. Here are the people who will go to bat for astrology when it is attacked in the media. Everyone who cares about astrology should join!

A.F.A.N.
8306 Wilshire Blvd, Suite 537
Beverley Hills, CA 90211

ARC Directory

(Listing of Astrologers Worldwide)
2920 E. Monte Vista
Tucson, AZ 85716
Telephone: (602) 321-1114

Pegasus Tapes

(Lectures, Conference tapes)
P.O. Box 419
Santa Ysabel, CA 92070

International Society for Astrological Research

(Lectures, Workshops, Seminars)
P.O. Box 38613
Los Angeles, CA 90038

ISIS Institute

(Newsletter, Conferences, Astrology tapes, Catalog)
P.O. Box 21222
El Sobrante, CA 94820–1222
Telephone (800) 924-4747 or (510) 222-9436
Fax: (510) 222-2202

Astrology Software

Astrolabe

Box 1750–R
Brewster, MA 02631
Telephone: (800) 843-6682

Check out the latest version of their powerful "Solar Fire" software for Windows—it's a breeze to use and will grow with your increasing knowledge of astrology to the most sophisticated levels. This company also markets a variety of programs for all levels of expertise, a wide selection of computer astrology readings, and Mac programs. A good resource for innovative software as well as applications for older computers.

Matrix Software

315 Marion Ave.
Big Rapids, MI 49307
Telephone: (800) PLANETS

You'll find a wide variety of software in all price ranges, demo disks at student and advanced levels, and lots of interesting readings. Check out "Kaleidoscope," an inexpensive program with beautiful graphics, and "Winstar Plus," their powerful professional software, if you're planning to study astrology seriously.

Astro Communications Services

Dept. AF693, PO Box 34487
San Diego, CA 92163–4487
Telephone: (800) 888-9983

You'll find books, software for Mac and IBM compatibles, individual charts, and telephone readings. Also find technical astrology materials here, such as "The American Ephemeris." They will calculate charts for you if you do not have a computer.

Air Software

115 Caya Avenue
West Hartford, CT 06110
Telephone: (800) 659-1247

Powerful, creative astrology software, like their award-winning "Star Trax." For beginners, check out "Father Time," which finds your best days. Or "Nostradamus," which answers all your questions. Also, financial astrology programs for investors.

Time Cycles Research—For Mac Users!!!

375 Willets Avenue
Waterford, CT 06385
Fax: (869) 442-0626
E-mail: *astrology@timecylces.com*
Internet: *http://www.timecycles.com*

Yes, there are astrologers who use Macs! This is where they come to for astrology software that's as sophisticated as it gets. If you have a Mac, you'll love their beautiful graphic IO Series programs.

Astro-Cartography

(Charts for location changes)
Astro-Numeric Service Box 336–B
Ashland, OR 97520
Telephone: (800) MAPPING

Astrology Magazines

In addition to articles by top astrologers, most have listings of astrology conferences, events, and local happenings.

AMERICAN ASTROLOGY
475 Park Avenue South
New York, NY 10016

DELL HOROSCOPE
P.O. Box 53352
Boulder, CO 89321–3342

PLANET EARTH
The Great Bear
P.O. Box 5164
Eugene, OR 97405

THE MOUNTAIN ASTROLOGER
P.O. Box 11292
Berkeley, CA 94701

ASPECTS
Aquarius Workshops
P.O. Box 260556
Encino, CA 91426

Astrology Schools

Though there are many correspondence courses available through private teachers and astrological organizations, up until now, there has never been an accredited college of astrology. That is why the address below is so important.

The Kepler College of Astrological Arts and Sciences

Kepler College, the first institution of its kind to combine an accredited liberal arts education with extensive astrological studies, should now be in operation. A degree-granting college that is also a center of astrology has long been the dream of the astrological community and will be a giant step forward in providing credibility to the profession.
For more information:

The Kepler College of Astrological Arts and Sciences
P.O. Box 77511
Seattle, WA 98177–0511
Telephone: (206) 706-0658
or *http://www.keplercollege.org*

CHAPTER 11

The Best Clicks to Hot Astrology Spots On-line

How to Surf the Internet for Free Software, Meet Top Astrologers, and Connect with Other Astrology Fans.

Once upon a time, you had to live in a big city to find other astrology fans. Otherwise, you had to travel to conferences to study with the best teachers or buy astrology books. Now the world of astrology is just a few clicks away, if you own or have access to a computer. There's a global community of astrologers on-line with sites that offer everything from chart services to chat rooms to individual readings. Even better, many of the most exciting sites offer *free* software, *free* charts, *free* articles to download. You can virtually get an education in astrology from your computer screen, share your insights with new astrology-minded pals in a chat room or on a mailing list, later meet them in person at one of the hundreds of conferences around the world.

So if you're curious to see a copy of your chart (or someone else's), want to study astrology in depth, or chat with another astrology fan, log on!

One caveat, however: since the Internet is constantly changing and growing, some of these sites may have changed addresses or content by the time this book is published, even though this selection was chosen with an eye to longevity. Sites were also chosen for general interest among the many thousands of astrology-oriented places on the net. Most have links to other sites for further exploration.

Free Charts

Do you want to see what your chart looks like? Want to practice reading the glyphs? Or would you like to check out the chart of that cool Aquarius you've just met in Mexico. If you've got access to the Internet (or there's an Internet café nearby), just click to one of these addresses:

ASTROLABE Software at *http://www.alabe.com* distributes some of the most creative and user-friendly programs now available, like "Solar Fire," a favorite of top astrologers. Visitors are greeted with a chart of the time when you log on. They will also E-mail a copy of your chart (or anyone else's chart) to you. Though you can't read it immediately at the site, it's worth waiting for.

For an instant chart displayed on the screen, surf to this address: *http://www.astro.ch/* and check into "ASTRODIENST," also home of a world atlas that will give you the accurate longitude and latitude worldwide. After entering your birthday and place of birth, you can print out your chart in a range of chart formats. One handy feature for beginners: the planetary placement is written out in an easy-to-read list alongside the chart (a real timesaver, if you haven't yet learned to read the astrology glyphs).

Free Software

Software manufacturers on the Web are generous with free downloads of demo versions of their software. You may then calculate charts using their data. This makes sense if you're considering investing serious money in astrology software and want to see how the program works in advance. You'll find a demo preview of ASTROLABE Software programs that are favored by many professional astrologers at *http://www.alabe. com/*. Check out the latest demo version of "Solar Fire," one of the most user-friendly astrology programs available—you'll be impressed!

For a fully functional astrology program:

Walter Pullen's amazingly complete ASTROLOGY program is offered absolutely free at this site: *http://www.magitech.com/~cruiser1/astrolog.htm.*

This ultra-sophisticated program comes in versions for all formats—DOS, WINDOWS, MAC, UNIX—and has some cool features such as a revolving globe and a constellation map. A "must" for those who want to get involved with astrology, without paying big bucks for a professional caliber program. Or for those who want to add ASTROLOG's unique features to their astrology software library. This program has it all!

Another great resource for software is Astro Computing Services. Their Web site has free demos of several excellent programs. Note especially their "Electronic Astrologer," one of the most effective and reasonably priced programs on the market. Go to *http://www.astrocom.com* for ACS software, books, readings, chart services, and software demos.

Go to another *http://www.astroscan.ca* for a free program called ASTROSCAN. Stunning graphics and ease of use make this a winner. It seems too good to be free!

At Halloran Software's site, *http://www.halloran.com,* there are four levels of Windows astrology software from which to choose. The "Astrology for Windows" shareware program is available in unregistered demo form as a free download and in registered form for $26.50. The calculations in this program may be all that an astrology hobbyist needs. The price for the full-service program is certainly reasonable.

Improve Your Social Life

Join a News Group or Mailing List!

You'll never feel lonely again, but you will be very busy reading the letters that overflow your mailbox every day. Be prepared! Of the many news groups, there are several devoted to astrology. The most popular is "alt.astrology." Here's your chance to connect with astrologers worldwide, exchange information, answer some of the skeptics who frequent this news group. Your mailbox will be jammed with letters from astrologers from everywhere on the planet, sharing charts of current events, special techniques, and personal problems.

Free Screen Saver and More

The Astrology Matrix offers a way to put your sign in view with a beautifully designed graphic screen saver downloadable at this site. There are also many other diversions at this site, so spend some enjoyable hours here. If a problem's got you stumped, find the answer via a variety of oracles. After you've consulted the stars, the I Ching, the runes, and the Tarot, you'll be sure to have the answer. Then consult their almanac to help you schedule the best day to sign on the dotted line, ask for a raise, or plant your rosebush. Address: *http://thenewage.com/*.

Free Astrology Course

Schedule a long visit to: *http://www.panplanet.com/,* where you will find the Canopus Academy of Astrology, a site loaded with goodies. For the experienced astrologer there are excellent articles from top astrologers. They've done the work for you when it comes to picking the best astrology links on the Web, so be sure to check out those bestowed with the Canopus Award of Excellence.

Astrologer Linda Reid, an accomplished astrology teacher and author, offers a complete on-line curriculum for all levels of astrology study plus individual tutoring. To get your feet wet, Linda is offering an excellent biginners' course at this site. A terrific way to get well grounded in astrology.

Visit an Astro Mall

Surf to *http://www.astronet.com* for the Internet's equivalent of an Astrology Mall.

ASTRONET offers interactive fun for everyone. At this writing, there's a special area for teenage astrology fans, access to popular astrology magazines like *American Astrology,* advice to the lovelorn, plus a grab bag of horoscopes, featured guests, a shopping area for books, reports, software, even jewelry.

Find an Astrologer Here

Metalog Directory of Astrology
http://www.astrologer.com

Looking for an astrologer in your local area? Perhaps you're planning a vacation in Australia or France and would like to meet astrologers or combine your activities with an astrology conference there? Go no further than this well-maintained resource. Here is an extensive worldwide list of astrologers and astrology sites. There is also an agenda of astrology conferences and seminars all over the world.

The A.F.A. Web Site
http://www.astrologers.com

This is the interesting Web site of the prestigious American Federation of Astrologers. The A.F.A. has a very similar address to the Metalog Directory and also has a directory of astrologers, restricted to those who meet their stringent requirements. Check out their correspondence course, if you would like to study astrology in depth.

Tools Every Astrologer Needs Are On-line:

Internet Atlas
http://www.astro.ch/atlas/

Find the geographic longitude and latitude and the correct time zone for any city worldwide. You'll need this information to calculate a chart.

The Exact Time, Anywhere in the World
http://www.timeticker.com

A fun site to find the exact time anywhere in the world. Click on the world map and the correct time and zone for that place lights up.

The Zodiacal Zephyr
http://www.zodiacal.com

A great jumping-off place for an astrology tour of the Internet. There's a good selection of articles, plus tools such as a U.S. and world atlas, celebrity birth data, information on conferences, software, and tapes. The links at this site will send you off in the right direction.

Astrology World
http://astrology-world.com

Astrologer Deborah Houlding has gathered some of the finest European astrologers on this terrific Web site. Great freebies, links, and lists of conferences. A "must," especially if you're traveling to the U.K.!

Astrology Alive
http://www.astrologyalive.com/

Barbara Schermer has one of the most creative approaches to astrology. She's an innovator in the field and was one of the first astrologers to go on-line, so there's always a "cutting edge" to this site. Great list of links.

National Council for Geocosmic Research (NCGR)
http://www.geocosmic.org/

A key stop on any astrological tour of the Net. Here's where you can find local chapters in your area, get information on the NCGR testing and certification programs, get a conference schedule. You can also order lecture tapes from their nationwide conferences, or get complete lists of conference topics, to study at home. Good links to resources.

Where to Find Charts of the Famous

When the news is breaking, you can bet Lois Rodden will be the first to get accurate birthdays of the headline-makers, and put up their charts on her Web site: *www.astrodatabank.com*. Rodden's research is astrology's most reliable source for data of the famous and infamous. Her new Web site features birthdays and charts of current newsmakers, political figures, international celebrities. It's also the place where you can purchase her database of thousands of birthdays of the famous, a must for astrological researchers.

Another site with birthdays and charts of famous people to download is *http://www.astropro.com*

You can get the sun and moon signs, plus a biography of the hottest new film stars here: *www.mrshowbiz.com.*

Another good source of celebrity birthdates is *http://www.metamaze.com/bdays/*. You can find some interesting offbeat celebs here like Matt Drudge and Joey Buttafuoco.

For Astrology Books

National Clearing House for Astrology Books

A wide selection of books on all aspects of astrology, from basics to advanced. Many hard-to-find books. Surf to: *http://www.astroamerica.com*

These addresses also have a good selection of astrology books, some of which are unique to the site.

http://www.panplanet.com
http://thenewage.com
http://www.astrocom.com

Browse the huge astrology list of the on-line bookstore Amazon.com at *http:www.amazon.com/*.

Astrology Tapes

Pegasus Tapes
http://www.pegasustape.com

You can study at home with world-famous astrologers via audiocassette recordings from Pegasus Tapes. There's a great selection taped from conferences, classes, lectures, and seminars. An especially good source for astrologers who emphasize psychological and mythological themes.

Your Questions Answered

Astrology FAQ
(Frequently Asked Questions)
http://www.magitech.com/pub/astrology/info/faq.txt

Here are answers to questions that are on everyone's mind. Especially useful information, if you're countering astrology-bashers.

History and Mythology of Astrology
http://www.elore.com

Be sure to visit the astrology section of this gorgeous site, dedicated to the history and mythology of many traditions. One of the most beautifully designed sites we've seen.

The Mountain Astrologer
http://www.mountainastrologer.com/

A favorite magazine of astrology fans, *The Mountain Astrologer* has an interesting Web site featuring the latest news from an astrological point of view, plus feature articles from the magazine.

Financial Astrology

Find out how financial astrologers play the market. Here are hot picks, newsletters, specialized financial astrology software, and mutual funds run by astrology seers.

Go to *www.afund.com* or *www.alphee.com* for tips and forecasts from two top financial astrologers.

CHAPTER 12

Are You a Typical Scorpio?

"Secretive, power-hungry, sexy, vengeful, intense" . . . does that sound like you? Some of you will agree whole-heartedly with the description of your typical Scorpio Sun Sign characteristics. Others might say, "Hey, wait a minute, I'm a party animal with a great sense of humor." Or "I'm outgoing and diplomatic." What we're talking about when we say you're a "Scorpio," is the sign the sun was passing through at the time of your birth. But there are ten other planets that also color your horo-scope. For example, if only the sun was in Scorpio and the moon was passing through outgoing Gemini at the time you were born, you're likely to have a more social personality than the typical Scorpio. So, the more Scor-pio planets you have, the more likely the following de-scriptions will resemble you.

The Scorpio Man:
Undercover Operator

Though Scorpio has the reputation of being the sexiest man in the zodiac, you know there is more to life than procreation. However, you keep your thoughts and feel-ings to yourself. You're that mysterious stranger with the stony façade few can penetrate. You don't need to flex muscles to show off your masculinity; your penetrating eyes send the message to every woman.

If the truth be known, you're much more interested in issues of power and control. You're challenged by unsolved problems and mysteries of any kind. You're a natural detective who won't stop until he knows what makes things and people tick. In spite of your aloof manner, you're always aware of what is going on and who is running the show, and you're remarkably perceptive about people's true motives.

Beneath your deliberately cool surface, you may be far less secure. One of the most sensitive signs of the zodiac, you keep your vulnerability a dark secret to seal yourself off from rejection. When you do fall for someone, nothing less than total possession will do. Scorpio feels he should own the woman he loves (though he's also able to enjoy pure sex for its own sake elsewhere). In romance and elsewhere, yours is the most possessive sign, with no toleration for disloyalty.

You are single minded in pursuit of what you want, be it a job, a prize, or a person. It was with good reason that Scorpio fashion designer Calvin Klein named his fragrance "Obsession." Your great concentration, intensity, and stamina make you a formidable competitor, but your love of power can degenerate into manipulation, bullying, and even violence if you are frustrated. You harbor a grudge and seek revenge when injured—as Teddy Roosevelt said, "Speak softly, but carry a big stick."

In a Relationship

When Scorpio falls in love, you are so single minded about the object of your affection that, if you lose that love for any reason, you are devastated. Often this is the one experience that can teach Scorpio about healthy detachment and the wisdom of getting to know someone slowly and gradually for longevity's sake.

After issues of power and control are settled within the relationship, you are a loyal and devoted mate. But first you may go through a period of testing, when you are not above using emotional manipulation to gain the upper hand. You need a partner who will add rational balance and perspective to your life when you go to extremes and who will help you to look on the lighter, brighter side of life.

The Scorpio Woman: Ms. Mysterious

Like your male counterpart, the mysterious, mesmerizing Scorpio woman hides her intense emotions under a cool, controlled facade, but inside you are passionate, determined, and totally committed to everything you do. This makes you very stable and somewhat predictable. Scorpio is not one for surprises or spontaneous moves; there is usually a strategy behind every step you take. All your formidable energy is zeroed in on your goal. The Scorpio woman is rarely plagued by self-doubt—you know exactly where you are going and rarely waver from your path. Once committed, you remain loyal and dedicated, and you will patiently see your projects through to completion.

Since you are extremely vulnerable, beneath your cool controlled surface, you are deeply hurt by betrayal. When disappointed, you can strike back with lethal accuracy. The good girl–bad girl extremes of Scorpio are reflected in the controversial sex and power-charged roles celebrities often embody in the public and private lives. Scorpios such as Demi Moore, k.d. lang, and Jodie Foster have played many such roles in recent years. Scorpio singer k.d. lang won the cover a national magazine when she declared herself a lesbian. Scorpios Jodie Foster and Goldie Hawn have braved the Hollywood establishment by producing and directing their own projects. Hillary Rodham Clinton, another prime example, has faced the most public sexually charged circumstances in recent times.

Unfortunately, Scorpio's intensity frightens away many who are not ready to commit to a bond that reaches to the soul level. The Scorpio woman considers this kind of hesitation a weakness and therefore blocks out many potentially interesting relationships. It is only after a period of tempering that you learn tolerance for a more balanced and rational relationship—and learn to give your partner space to be his own person.

A Scorpio woman is not one to play around with or take lightly. You may seem very sweet and naive, but you can easily see through deception. An excellent detective, you sense immediately when something is hidden, though you yourself are never completely open about your own motives. When others question what is lurking beneath that unruffled surface, your secretiveness can backfire, causing suspicion and mistrust. Anger brings out your venomous side. Scorpio has a paranoid tendency to overreact to imaginary slights. Since you tend to see things in black and white, you can go to extremes when you're upset, when it is very difficult to coax you out of a black mood. You are more likely to seek revenge than to forgive and forget.

As a Scorpio woman, you have the ability to evoke transformation in the lives of others. Scorpio is one of the "heaviest" signs of the zodiac, so let those who skim the surface of life be forewarned. You delve deep and demand total commitment—anything less is not worthwhile. Yet you deliver an unforgettable experience—no one involved with a Scorpio woman is ever the same again.

In a Relationship

The typical Scorpio is intensely loyal and devoted to your mate. Though you may experiment before settling down, the Scorpio woman is looking for total commitment. After marriage, you can be so completely involved with your husband that you can be devastated if the marriage fails. However, once committed, your intense involvement could boomerang if you become overly demanding, possessive, and jealous, and thereby smother a more freedom-loving partner. You must learn not to give in to those negative suspicions, which can escalate into destructive paranoia.

You reach your full potential as a mate after you have learned to share yourself with your partner, rather than try to control the relationship. On the plus side, Scorpios will stay with your true mate, after he earns your trust, through the most difficult times. You are someone he can count on to support him, no matter what the sacrifice. And, in the long run, you can transform his life for the better.

Your Role in the Family

The Scorpio Parent

Scorpio's intense all-or-nothing commitment extends to their role as parent. Though you may not express your feelings openly, you are able to convey to your children the feeling of being deeply loved, and it is this strong foundation of emotional security that gives your children confidence. Trust and loyalty are unspoken givens. You'll defend your children to the maximum, keeping them out of the public eye as famous mothers Hillary Clinton, Jodie Foster, and Meg Ryan do. You'll provide them with the ways and means to live up to your high hopes, but you are a strict parent who insists on control and discipline, which could create problems with an equally strong-willed child. You may have to learn lessons of flexibility and tolerance from your children, and you will also have to learn when to let go, allowing your children to follow their own interest in the outside world. However, your children always know you will be there for them, ready to provide a life raft in the roughest waters.

The Scorpio Stepparent

As a stepparent, you'll have to develop a light touch and a sense of humor. Scorpio marriages are all-or-nothing ones, with intense one-on-one involvement, so it is especially important that you and your stepchildren get to know each other before the marriage, and that you are sincerely willing to reach out to them. Otherwise, power struggles can develop. It could also help to discuss problems openly as they occur, rather than letting anger, hurt feelings, or misunderstanding build up. Be flexible enough to allow your mate time with the children, apart from you, and have some outside activities to help diffuse your energy, so it is not overly concentrated on the family.

The Scorpio Grandparent

Grandchildren can regenerate Scorpio, providing some of the most liberating, joyful experiences of your life. At last you can show your playful, childlike side, with a fun-loving little playmate who demands nothing of you. You're free from the disciplining responsibilities of parenthood and the intense emotional commitment. You're no longer involved in power struggles or overworked, so you're free to spend happy times with the children. Grandchildren can also bring out the generosity in Scorpio, particularly when providing for their future security. You'll make a lasting impression on the youngest generation, and they'll make you feel born again!

CHAPTER 13

Live the Scorpio Way Every Day!

Your sun sign influences the styles that suit you best, the colors and sounds that lift your mood, even the places you might enjoy visiting. So try putting more of your Scorpio sun sign in your daily life and see the happy difference.

At Home with Scorpio

Your decor may be very posh and sensual, with plenty of dark woods, rich tapestry colors, sensual sink-in upholstery, brocade walls, luxurious leather or suede-like upholstery, and Oriental rugs. Or you'll go to the opposite extreme, paring down to the bare essentials, with a stark, minimal, almost monastic look, and sticking to one or two colors, often black and white or neutral beiges. The latter kind of Scorpio may be so focused on other aspects of your life that you ignore your surroundings entirely. Then you might live in a virtually unfurnished apartment, simply because you're not involved enough to decorate.

For those who *do* care, marine motifs, sensual nudes, and dramatic artifacts are likely appeal to you. Or you may go for the Victorian look, with dark carved wood furniture. You'll be sure to have a sensual bedroom, perhaps pulling out all the stops with satin sheets, mirrored walls, and sensational lighting effects.

Sounds for Scorpio

Scorpios go for power in music, expressed in great symphonies and dramatic operas, with life-and-death themes. But they also love sexy tangos, sensual cello sounds, Paul Simon, Bonnie Raitt, and Joni Mitchell. More avant-garde Scorpios go for intense heavy-metal sounds, with a driving beat and an undercurrent of danger. The black leather and biker paraphernalia side of the rock scene is pure Scorpio. Gospel music stirs your soul, while the New Age sounds of Yanni calm your mind.

The Scorpio Vacation Guide

Scorpios relax and unwind near the sea, so a great beach location is always a winner for you. You'll discover one that's away from the crowd, one that feels like yours alone, such as the deserted beaches of Martha's Vineyard, Baja California, or the Caribbean in the off-season. You will never go to a place because it's "in" (at least, not for a vacation). You'll also respond to a vacation with a built-in challenge—a difficult mountain to scale, great fishing or skiing, unexplored terrain.

Australia, Brazil, Morocco, Norway, or China are exotic Scorpio destinations. You'll also enjoy exploring the ruins of Greece, Mexico, and Peru, and the erotically decorated temples of India.

Scorpios can travel with the minimum luggage and are usually expert packers. Invest in some leather carry-on bags so you can skip the baggage claim and avoid lost luggage. Combination locks should keep your possessions secure, though you might want to get a hidden money belt or a waist pack to store your vital items, as well as waterproof containers so that credit cards and cash can "swim" with you. Scorpios who are truly concerned with security can even find clothes hangers with secret compartments to store valuables. (In fact, hidden pockets or compartments of any kind are very much a Scorpio thing.)

Credit cards are ruled by Scorpio, so before you go, check which cards are accepted and how much cash you'll need. Investigate travel insurance and any special travel deal provided by your credit card company and carry traveler's checks instead of cash whenever possible. Finally, stash photocopies of all important credit cards and ID's in a safe place, just in case.

Your Scorpio Colors

No-color black and deep, rich burgundy are traditional Scorpio-friendly colors. But some Scorpios, particularly if they are blondes, prefer off-white tones or elegant neutrals.

Scorpio Fashion Tips

Scorpios make an unforgettable statement, whatever their style. Like other fixed signs, they usually stick to their trademark look, be it a sporty pared-down style like Jodie Foster; the cool, classic look, like Maria Shriver and Jane Pauley; or the ultra-feminine style of Winona Ryder. Vogue editor Anna Wintour is known for her classic bob hairdo and dark glasses worn at all times. Many Scorpio women prefer the androgynous man-tailored look. Scorpios love to wear black, particularly black velvet or black leather, and will use intense makeup or none at all to play up strong bone structure and mesmerizing eyes.

Your Fashion Role Models

Calvin Klein's style is pure Scorpio, with its uncluttered, sexy look from head to toe. Leave it to a Scorpio to put a woman in man-styled underwear and name a perfume

"Obsession." Rae Kawaikubo, the trendsetting designer of Comme des Garcons, is also a Scorpio. She goes to another extreme, making a severe avant-garde statement with stark, futuristic shapes that transform the body.

The Scorpio Food Fan

Scorpio usually finds a favorite restaurant and sticks with it. You are a creature of habit who has strong likes and dislikes. Good seafood is usually a favorite, especially lobster or the spare elegance of Japanese cuisine, which features raw fish. Dark publike restaurants with paneled walls are your kind of lair. You might have an offbeat, secret place where you can hide out with someone special. Any restaurant near the ocean, or on a boat, is a sure winner.

CHAPTER 14

The Scorpio Way
to Good Health

Your sign rules the regenerative and eliminative organs, so sexual activity can be a source of good or ill health for Scorpio. It is important to examine your attitudes about sex, and to follow safe sexual practices. Though you have a strong constitution that can literally rise from the ashes of extreme illness or injury, don't take this for granted or abuse it with self destructive habits. Try to curb excessive tendencies in any area of your life, since going to extremes is one of Scorpio's health dangers. You are often challenged by testing that famous Scorpio willpower by living too close to the edge.

Yo-yo dieting, with its extreme ups and downs can be another Scorpio problem. This sign often works transformation on yourself, by going from extreme heaviness to thinness and back again. Since you can obsess about food and diet, try to diffuse this energy into other areas of your life.

It's no accident that Scorpio's month is football season, which reminds us that sports are a very healthy way to diffuse emotions. If you enjoy winter sports, be sure to prepare ahead of time for the ski slopes or ice skating. Scorpio loves intense life or death competition, so be sure your muscles are warmed up before going all out.

CHAPTER 15

Scoping Out Scorpio on the Job

Scorpios usually know exactly what you want and will endure grueling training to prepare for a top position. You are capable of getting and keeping major responsibility, though others may underestimate your quiet demeanor, mistaking it for shyness at first. However your focused drive and sense of direction will soon make its presence felt. For a prime example of a quiet Scorpio who became a self-made success look no further than Bill Gates, chairman of Microsoft, at this writing the richest man in the world.

Scorpio-type talents often work best within a structured organization rather than in a freelance situation. Large companies give you a wide scope and plenty of potential power. Higher-ups soon notice how you stay cool in a crisis and keep your job well under control.

As the zodiac's super-sleuth, you shine in detective, research, or troubleshooting spots. Your concentration and focus shine in life-or-death fields like medicine and in high-pressure television spots (Pat Sajak, Jane Pauley, Morley Safer, Walter Cronkite, and Dick Cavett are Scorpios), where you'll be the steady anchor. Handling other people's money can be trusted to Scorpio accountants, financial planners, investment bankers, and brokers. Your sharp perception works for you in psychology, psychotherapy, or the theater. Both the fashion world (Calvin Klein) and fine arts (Pablo Picasso) appreciate your strong statements. Stay away from jobs that have a dead end, that are in risky, fly-by-night businesses, or that require on-the-spot improvisation rather than steady discipline.

Scorpio in Charge

You hire your staff with a keen perception of everyone's needs and motives. You are totally in command of all that happens in your domain and will rarely hand over the reins, even temporarily. Since you do not trust easily, you may be hesitant to delegate and therefore will take on too much responsibility yourself. Your suspiciousness could even degenerate into paranoia, when you think of others in black-and-white terms—either for you or against you. But because you care intensely about your work, you can be generous with others who are equally dedicated. Though you can be a lethal player of power games, you are extremely supportive of anyone who gives you the proper respect and loyalty.

Scorpio Teamwork

Since you aim for total control of your job, you will always have a motive behind your moves. You like work where there is a challenge and a chance to wield power, whether it's a weapon, a big machine, or a company checkbook. Sometimes, Scorpio will work overtime to make yourself indispensable, simply for the power of being so needed! You are always aware of what is happening in the office and of who's doing what to whom. You are particularly good at assessing the weak points of others (or of the organization), and using this to your advantage. When you're interested in your work, you have unbeatable stamina, tolerating working conditions and hours that would make others rebel! You are very steady and stable on the job, rarely getting sidetracked to another profession or seduced by another organization.

To Get Ahead Fast

Pick a job where there is a weakness you can correct or chaos you can order—and then take over! Play up your best characteristics.

- Cool control
- Stamina
- Perception
- Concentration
- Ability to handle pressure
- Steadiness
- Drive

Scorpio Career Role Models

Study the success stories of these highly successful Scorpio entrepreneurs. (Biographies of Bill Gates and Ted Turner should be on your reading list.) You might get some useful tips for moving ahead on the fast track.

- Bill Gates
- Ted Turner
- Hillary Rodham Clinton
- Christie Hefner
- Calvin Klein
- Milton Bradley
- Averell Harriman
- Christiaan Barnard, heart transplant surgeon
- Anna Wintour, editor, *Vogue*

CHAPTER 16

The Scorpio Hall of Fame

We're fascinated by reading tabloids and tattletales about the rich, famous, and infamous in the post-Millennium, but astrology can tell you more about your heroes than most magazine articles. Like what really turns them on (check their Venus). Or what makes them rattled (scope their Saturn). Compare similarities and differences between the celebrities who embody the typical Scorpio sun-sign traits and those who seem untypical. Then look up other planets in the horoscope of your favorites, using the charts in this book, to see how other planets influence the horoscope. It's a fun way to get your education in astrology.

Scorpio Celebrities

Kevin Kline (10/24/47)
Pablo Picasso (10/25/1881)
Tracy Nelson (10/25/63)
Pat Sajak (10/26/46)
Jaclyn Smith (10/26/47)
Hillary Rodham Clinton (10/26/47)
John Cleese (10/27/39)
Simon LeBon (10/27/58)
Marla Maples (10/27/63)
Evelyn Waugh (10/28/03)
Dennis Franz (10/28/44)
Annie Potts (10/28/52)
Bill Gates (Microsoft) (10/28/55)

Lauren Holley (10/28/66)
Julia Roberts (10/28/67)
Richard Dreyfus (10/29/47)
Kate Jackson (10/29/48)
Winona Ryder (10/29/70)
Louis Malle (10/30/32)
Grace Slick (10/30/39)
Dale Evans (10/31/12)
Diedre Hall (10/31/49)
Jane Pauley (10/31/50)
Harry Hamlin (10/31/51)
Barbara Basson (11/1/29)
Lyle Lovett (11/1/57)
Jenny McCarthy (11/1/72)
Daniel Boone (11/2/1754)
Stefanie Powers (11/2/42)
k.d. lang (11/2/61)
Charles Bronson (11/3/22)
Roseanne (11/3/52)
Pauline Trigere (11/4/12)
Yanni (11/4/22)
Matthew McConaughey (11/4/69)
Roy Rogers (11/5/12)
Ike Turner (11/5/31)
Sam Shepard (11/5/43)
Tatum O'Neal (11/5/63)
Mike Nichols (11/6/31)
Maria Shriver (11/6/55)
Ethan Hawke (11/6/70)
Billy Graham (11/7/18)
Bonnie Raitt (11/8/49)
Carl Sagan (11/9/34)
Richard Burton (11/10/25)
Roy Scheider (11/10/32)
Demi Moore (11/11/62)
Leonardo DiCaprio (11/11/74)
Grace Kelly (11/12/29)
Richard Mulligan (11/13/32)
Whoopi Goldberg (11/13/55)
Aaron Copeland (11/14/1900)

Prince Charles (11/14/48)
Ed Asner (11/15/29)
Bo Derek (11/16/56)
Lauren Hutton (11/17/43)
Danny DeVito (11/17/44)
Linda Evans (11/18/42)
Ted Turner (11/19/38)
Ahmad Rashad (11/19/49)
Meg Ryan (11/19/61)
Jodie Foster (11/19/62)
Sean Young (11/20/59)
Marlo Thomas (11/21/38)
Goldie Hawn (11/21/45)
Nicolette Sheridan (11/21/63)
Mariel Hemingway (11/21/61)
Rodney Dangerfield (11/22/21)
Harpo Marx (11/23/1893)

CHAPTER 17

Scorpio Partnership Potential:

How You Get Along with Every Other Sign

Are you thinking about teaming up with someone either romantically or professionally? Here are the pluses and minuses of every combination, so you'll know what to expect before you commit. Look up your lover, your boss, your potential roommate. But bear in mind that we're all a combination of many different planets, most likely in other signs, so be tolerant of your choices. There could be another planet in the picture that will make a big difference in how well (or not) you get along.

Scorpio/Aries

PLUSES:
One of the zodiac's challenging pairs, your Mars-ruled chemistry could ignite with frequent battles of the sexes. You both love a dare! Neither of you gives in, but you'll never bore each other (though you might wear each other out). Aries' direct, uncomplicated forcefulness especially intrigues Scorpio, who's caught off guard, for once.

MINUSES:
You could play so hard to get that you never really connect! Aries never quite trusts secretive Scorpio, while Scorpio's intrigues and power plays can fizzle under di-

rect Aries fire. You are both jealous and controlling, but this dynamic duo can work if you focus on high ideals and mutual respect.

Scorpio/Taurus

PLUSES:
Many marriages happen when these opposites attract. Taurus has a calming effect on Scorpio's innate paranoia. And Taurus responds to Scorpio's intensity and fascinating air of mystery. Together, these signs have the perfect complement of sensuality and sexuality.

MINUSES:
Problems of control are inevitable when you both want to run the show. Avoid long and bitter battles or silent standoffs by drawing territorial lines from the start.

Scorpio/Gemini

PLUSES:
You're a fascinating mystery to each other. Gemini is immune from Scorpio paranoia, laughs away dark moods, and matches wits in power games. Scorpio's intensity, focus, and sexual magnetism draws Gemini like a moth to a flame.

MINUSES:
Scorpio gets "heavy," possessive, and jealous, which Gemini doesn't take seriously. To make this one last, Gemini needs to treat Scorpio like the one and only, while Scorpio must use a light touch and learn not to take Gemini's flirtations to heart.

Scorpio/Cancer

PLUSES:
Cancer actually enjoys Scorpio's intensity and possessiveness—it shows how much they care! And, like Prince Charles and Camilla Parker-Bowles (and Princess Diana), this pair cares deeply about those they love. Strong emotions are a great bond which can survive heavy storms.

MINUSES:
Scorpio's mysterious melancholy moods can leave Cancer feeling isolated and insecure. And the more Cancer clings, the more Scorpio withdraws. Outside interests can lighten the mood—or provide a means of escape.

Scorpio/Leo

PLUSES:
Scorpio's innate power and Leo's confidence and authority can make a fascinating high-profile combination like Leo Arnold Schwarzenegger and Scorpio Maria Shriver or Hillary and Bill Clinton. There is great mutual respect and loyalty here, as well as sexual dynamite. You two magnetic, unconquerable heroes offer each other enough challenges to keep the sparks flying.

MINUSES:
Scorpio's natural secretiveness and Leo's openness could conflict, especially if Scorpio reveals a powerful will and need for control from under a deceptively quiet facade. And Leo is often surprised by the sheer intensity of Scorpio's drive and willpower. Though Scorpio won't fight for the spotlight, they will often control behind the scenes. When these two intense, stubborn, demanding signs collide, it's a no-win siltation.

Scorpio/Virgo

PLUSES:
With Scorpio, Virgo encounters intense feelings too powerful to intellectualize or analyze. This could be a grand passion, especially when Scorpio is challenged to uncover Virgo's earthy, sensual side. Your penetrating minds are sympatico and so is your dedication to meaningful work (here is a fellow healer). Virgo provides the stability and structure that keeps Scorpio on the right track.

MINUSES:
Virgo may cool off if Scorpio goes to extremes or plays manipulative games, while Scorpio could find Virgo's perfectionism irritating and approach to sex too limited.

Scorpio/Libra

PLUSES:
The interplay of Scorpio intensity and cool Libran objectivity makes an exciting cat-and-mouse game. Libran intellect and flair balances out Scorpio's powerful charisma, while Scorpio adds warmth and substance to Libra.

MINUSES:
Libras must learn to handle Scorpio's sensitive feelings with velvet gloves. When not taken seriously, Scorpio retaliates with a force that could send the Libran scales swinging off balance. On the other hand, Scorpio must give Libra room to exercise his or her mental and social skills.

Scorpio/Scorpio

PLUSES:
The list of legendary Scorpio–Scorpio couples here reads like a historical who's who—from Abigail and John

Adams and Marie and Pierre Curie, to Dale Evans and Roy Rogers. You'll match each other's intensity and commitment, know instinctively where to tread with caution.

MINUSES:
Since you both like to be in control, power struggles are always on the menu. Share some of your secrets and air your grievances immediately, rather than letting them fester.

Scorpio/Sagittarius

PLUSES:
Sagittarius sees an erotic adventure in Scorpio—and doesn't mind playing with fire. Scorpio is impressed with Sagittarius' high ideals, energy, and competitive spirit. Sagittarian humor diffuses Scorpio intensity, while Scorpio provides the focus for Sagittarius to reach those goals.

MINUSES:
Scorpio sees through schemes and won't fall for a sales pitch unless it has substance. Sagittarius may object to Scorpio's drive for power, rather than for higher goals, and will flee from Scorpio possessiveness or heavy-handed, controlling tactics.

Scorpio/Capricorn

PLUSES:
Sexy Scorpio takes Capricorn's mind off business. Though you could get wrapped up in each other, you are also turned on by power and position, and you'll join forces to scale the heights.

MINUSES:
Capricorn has no patience for intrigue or hidden agendas. Scorpio will find this sign focused on his or her

own goals and won't be easily diverted, even if this means leaving Scorpio's emotional needs—and ego—in the backseat.

Scorpio/Aquarius

PLUSES:
Both of you respect each other's uncompromising position and mental focus. You will probably have an unconventional relationship—spiced up by sexual experimentation and the element of surprise.

MINUSES:
Scorpio could feel that Aquarius is a loose cannon who is liable to sink the ship. Or both fixed signs could come to a stubborn stand off. Aquarius tunes out Scorpio possessiveness; Scorpio looks elsewhere for intimacy and intensity.

Scorpio/Pisces

PLUSES:
When these two signs click, nothing gets in their way. Pisces' desire to merge completely with his beloved is just the all-or-nothing message Scorpio has been waiting for. These two will play it to the hilt, often shedding previous spouses or bucking public opinion (like Liz Taylor and Richard Burton once did).

MINUSES:
Both signs are possessive, yet neither likes to be possessed. Scorpio could easily mistake Piscean vulnerability for weakness—a big mistake. Both signs fuel each other's escapist tendencies when dark moods hit. Learning to merge without submerging one's identity is an important lesson for this couple.

CHAPTER 18

Astrological Outlook for Scorpio in 2001

If single, you are likely to marry this year. Facts that evaded you in the recent past will be discovered and acted on this year, too. If married, you rediscover your mate mentally, emotionally, and physically.

You'll have more to do with food than in previous years. Could it be restaurant management?

Cancer and Capricorn will play important roles in your life. There's also much activity in connection with real estate as well as the possibility of going into business for yourself.

To say the least, this year will be eventful for you. With a Cancer, you have much to do with housing, where to live—and whether or not to live with each other. A love spark ignites with Capricorn; together you make a fresh start in a new direction.

These numbers will appear more often than could be coincidence: 3, 5, and 8.

You will be having unusual relationships beginning in late April. You may be encouraged to write articles about recipes or food. It is likely that you will gain an inheritance before the beginning of May.

Uranus and Neptune in your fourth house creates extreme activity to do with land, property, real estate, and long-term relationships. A situation you thought settled will prove to be the opposite. Domestic adjustments will be necessary—some of them surprising and controversial.

During January, your popularity will be on the rise, but you will have to remember resolutions about diet and nutrition. The social whirl will not permit you to get a foothold on what is happening in your life. Be especially wary on the 5th, 14th, and 23rd.

Your most memorable month this year is apt to be May, when questions must be answered about your marital state.

By following your daily guides, you can make this a banner year. There will be drama, humor, and romance for you, but at times you might have trouble keeping track of where you are and where you will be going.

Let us begin by turning the page. These guides provide your diary in advance.

CHAPTER 19

Eighteen Months of Day-by-Day Predictions—July 2000 to December 2001

JULY 2000

Saturday, July 1 (Moon in Cancer) Lucky lottery: 9, 12, 24, 13, 7, 1. The new moon and solar eclipse in that part of your horoscope is associated with publishing, travel, the higher mind. You will be with people who are bright, original thinkers. Remind them, "Today is the birthday of the U.S. postage stamp."

Sunday, July 2 (Moon in Cancer to Leo 10:39 p.m.) Your display of knowledge amazes. A Cancer asserts, "You are incredible. Where do you store that information?" Respond in a modest way, without being obsequious. An excellent day to start a project, make necessary contacts in connection with funding. Your lucky number is 1.

Monday, July 3 (Moon in Leo) What began as a dream is being transformed into reality—even as you read these words. The spotlight is on where you live, food, music, flowers, and dealings with members of the opposite sex who think you are just great. A family member returns from a journey, and announces a legal mission is completed.

Tuesday, July 4 (Moon in Leo to Virgo 11:20 p.m.) On this holiday, be grateful for survival, knowledge, for the vibrancy you exude. An excellent time for social activity and exploration of a political situation. Gemini and Sagittarius will play outstanding roles, making this a holiday you won't soon forget. Have luck with number 3.

Wednesday, July 5 (Moon in Virgo)   The Virgo moon is very favorable, spotlighting finance, romance, the ability to win friends and influence people among the high and mighty. Don't be shy about displaying knowledge, about analyzing international situations, as well as political leaders. Taurus and another Scorpio will play dynamic roles, and have these letters in their names—D, M, V.

Thursday, July 6 (Moon in Virgo)   People who claim you are behind the times will be embarrassed. Once again, your knowledge is sparkling, the information produced is stunning. The Mercury keynote is practically gilding the lily. The emphasis is on reading, writing, advertising, interpreting dreams, and reading palms.

Friday, July 7 (Moon in Virgo to Libra 2:48 a.m.) There are many Venus aspects. Attention will focus on being nice to people. Some suggest, "You should run for political office!" The emphasis is also on legal agreements, discovering your soul mate. In answer to a question about marriage, it is affirmative. Diplomacy is required and just a little more money.

Saturday, July 8 (Moon in Libra)   This Saturday finds you feeling moody. Be with someone who understands, comprehends, and appreciates great literature and music. You'll feel as if, "I am in love, but do not quite know what to do about it." Pisces and Virgo play unusual roles, and have these letters or initials in their names—G, P, Y.

Sunday, July 9 (Moon in Libra to Scorpio 9:49 a.m.) Within 24 hours, the cycle takes an abrupt turn in your favor. Tonight, learn more about what has been kept

189

secret. The spotlight is on power, intimidation, extra responsibility, the necessity for meeting and beating a deadline. This is a Sunday when people praise you, but at the same time, they can be bitter and envious.

Monday, July 10 (Moon in Scorpio)   The moon is in your sign, therefore your cycle is high. You will be in a position to call the shots. Stress universal appeal, study languages. The good news is that you overcome obstacles created by long distances. Romance is highlighted. A temporary separation lends spice because the reunion will be hot and heavy.

Tuesday, July 11 (Moon in Scorpio to Sagittarius 8:06 p.m.)   Trust a hunch. Your intuition is razor sharp. Wear dark green; make personal appearances and appeals. A love relationship is scorching. If you expected this to be an ordinary Tuesday, with calm waters, you will be disappointed. This Tuesday will be filled with drama, controversy, and romance.

Wednesday, July 12 (Moon in Sagittarius)   The Sagittarian moon relates to payments, collections, a reward for finding a lost article. A Cancer declares, "You need spiritual sustenance, as well as material gain—let us start with me inviting you to dinner tonight!" Accept the invitation; realize that you will make important contacts.

Thursday, July 13 (Moon in Sagittarius)   A former football star, currently a political leader, shares this day with you in a way—it's Jack Kemp's birthday! For you, popularity zooms. People compliment you on your ability to transform humor into profundity. Gemini and Sagittarius will play outstanding roles. Your lucky number is 3.

Friday, July 14 (Moon in Sagittarius to Capricorn 8:28 a.m.)   Within 24 hours, you'll receive the news that a relative in a distant city plans to visit. The question will be asked, "How did you know?" It's best to leave it a mystery—don't tell all. On this Friday, you learn where you stand in connection with your community, a special project, a love relationship. Taurus is represented.

Saturday, July 15 (Moon in Capricorn)   A flirtation is featured, and it lends spice. There's much joy, but know when to insist, "Enough is enough!" An excellent day for teaching, reading, writing, publishing, and advertising. Gemini, Virgo, and Sagittarius play outstanding roles, and have these letters in their names: E, N, W. Have luck with number 5.

Sunday, July 16 (Moon in Capricorn to Aquarius 9:27 p.m.)   The full moon, lunar eclipse falls in Capricorn. Discourage a relative from making a long journey. As for you, take special care in traffic. People tend to take leave of their senses, possibly involving you in an accident. Attention revolves around your home, security, music, and marital status.

Monday, July 17 (Moon in Aquarius)   This need not be a Blue Monday. Fight a tendency to be captured by sledgehammer words. Time is on your side, so define your terms. Find out exactly what is expected of you and what you might receive in return. Pisces and Virgo play substantial roles, and will have these initials in their names—G, P, Y.

Tuesday, July 18 (Moon in Aquarius)   For racing luck, try these selections at all tracks: Post position special—number 8 p.p. in the fourth race. Pick six: 8, 5, 1, 8, 2, 2. Look for these letters or initials in the names of potential winning horses or jockeys: H, Q, Z. Hot daily doubles: 8 and 5, 4 and 3, 4 and 4. Capricorn jockeys give beautiful rides, and will be in the winner's circle.

Wednesday, July 19 (Moon in Aquarius to Pisces 9:45 a.m.)   This cycle highlights foreign money exchanges, the romance of the highway, the possibility of a cruise during which you could meet your future soul mate.

Within 24 hours, your physical attractiveness will be enhanced. This scenario gets livelier by the hour with children, challenge, change, variety, a flirtation. Aries is involved.

Thursday, July 20 (Moon in Pisces)   Make personal appearances; be willing to travel, to take risks in connection with romance. Some people might object, "Act your age!" Your response: "Mine is the age of eternal youth!" However unlikely it might appear, this cycle reveals you could "discover gold."

Friday, July 21 (Moon in Pisces to Aries 8:10 p.m.) You'll be asking, "Is this déjà vu?" Today's scenario highlights familiar places and faces. It seems as if you are repeating a serious relationship, including marriage. Find out where you stand and with whom; do not put too much faith in a fantasy. Cancer and Capricorn play leading roles, and have these letters in their names—B, K, T.

Saturday, July 22 (Moon in Aries)   On this Saturday, what had been in disarray will fall into place. Family members cooperate, some reluctantly state, "You are right. You know what you are doing; we will do things your way!" Gemini and Sagittarius play outstanding roles, and have these letters in their names: C, L, U. Your lucky number is 3.

Sunday, July 23 (Moon in Aries)   Suddenly, the opposition indicates it is ready to melt. Take nothing for granted, especially promises. Heed this saying, "Get it in writing!" Also remember, "A verbal contract is not worth the paper it's written on!" Taurus and another Scorpio play triumphant roles.

Monday, July 24 (Moon in Aries to Taurus 3:45 a.m.) Explore, examine, and give full play to your intellectual curiosity. Ideas could come quickly. There's hardly time to take a second breath. Take notes about dreams, impressions, and psychic feelings. The Taurus moon relates to special agreements, deep feelings, your marital status. Virgo plays a flashy role.

Tuesday, July 25 (Moon in Taurus) Be patient and diplomatic. A Taurus is on your side, and will help obtain a payment long overdue. Agree to make a public appearance. Tell all about how it feels to be passionate, instead of indifferent. A major part of today's scenario will be concerned with music, flowers, and entertainment.

Wednesday, July 26 (Moon in Taurus to Gemini 8:03 a.m.) On this Wednesday, you no longer will be "pressed" about alliances, or your marital status. Play the waiting game. Refuse to be cajoled into making premature decisions. Money matters remain important, but do not dominate. Pisces figures in this scenario.

Thursday, July 27 (Moon in Gemini) Get ready for action! The lunar position emphasizes mystery, intrigue, an accounting error that leaves you short, unless immediate action is taken. Don't be cajoled by someone who says, "This could happen to anyone!" Capricorn and Cancer figure in today's remarkable scenario, and have these letters or initials in their names—H, Q, Z.

Friday, July 28 (Moon in Gemini to Cancer 9:31 a.m.) On this Friday, you'll complete a task. Your ideals will be fulfilled, if you keep the faith. This is not mere talk. This cycle and its aspects point to achievement, progress, advancement, and applause. What a Friday! It's the precursor to a lively, fun-filled weekend. An Aries figures prominently.

Saturday, July 29 (Moon in Cancer) People talk to you about name changes. Your opinion is sought about commercial products, how to boost sales. Consider carefully; don't underrate your own worth or the value of your time. A different approach for an overseas market is necessary. Lucky lottery: 12, 19, 18, 7, 6, 40.

193

Sunday, July 30 (Moon in Cancer to Leo 9:24 a.m.)
Focus on your family, children, challenge, a variety of experiences. Distance plays a major role—including how far to go. Imprint your style. Don't follow others; set the pace and decide where the action will be. Someone of the opposite sex tells you in a discreet way: "You are much more attractive than you realize."

Monday, July 31 (Moon in Leo) On this last day of July, a second full moon appears, a blue moon. This will be in Leo, along with a solar eclipse. A business agreement is settled. Gemini and Sagittarius will be involved. Be alert not for deceptions put forth by others, but for possible mistakes of your own. Your lucky number is 3.

AUGUST 2000

Tuesday, August 1 (Moon in Leo to Virgo 9:28 a.m.)
Today's lunation highlights your career, prestige, and conferences with community leaders. Make a fresh start in a new direction. Let it be known, "Like it or not, there are two ways to do things—the right way and my way!" Leo and Aquarius figure in today's dynamic scenario, and will have these initials in their names—A, S, J.

Wednesday, August 2 (Moon in Virgo) What a surprise! The Virgo moon relates to your hopes, wishes, and desires, the start of a winning streak. Your passions are released. Love will play an outstanding role. You'll give and receive. Your creative juices are on the move. Capricorn and Cancer play memorable roles, and could have these letters or initials in their names—B, K, T.

Thursday, August 3 (Moon in Virgo to Libra 11:32 a.m.) An acquaintance made months ago in a different city or country will pay dividends. What was a chance meeting will grow into a meaningful relationship. An excellent day for entertaining and being entertained. You'll be asking, "What did I do right, so that I can do it again?" Have luck with number 3.

Friday, August 4 (Moon in Libra) The Libra moon coincides with "I hear beautiful music!" Much that happens is in secret. The emphasis is on theater, institutions, and museums. Ask questions, and give full play to your intellectual curiosity. It's necessary to overcome distance and language obstacles. You will do so with aplomb.

Saturday, August 5 (Moon in Libra to Scorpio 5:05 p.m.) Words and music—you will write, speak, teach, and communicate. People express confidence in your abilities. You'll thank them, although no thanks are required. A flirtation figures prominently, which leads to a clash of ideas and then to physical attraction. Lucky lottery: 5, 50, 10, 12, 18, 19.

Sunday, August 6 (Moon in Scorpio) In your high cycle, previous disturbances can be blotted out. Emphasize your personality, special appeal that includes physical beauty and handsomeness. Attention revolves around your home and family, expressions of dissent blended with love. Taurus and Libra will play outstanding roles.

Monday, August 7 (Moon in Scorpio) Slow down! Trust your judgment, or a hunch. Nothing will really move until you say, "Go ahead." It is just that kind of cycle. You emit an aura of mystery and power. Someone who previously opposed you will now plead, "Can I come aboard?" Pisces and Virgo are in the picture, and have these initials in their names—G, P, Y.

Tuesday, August 8 (Moon in Scorpio to Sagittarius 2:31 a.m.) You have obtained your second emotional wind. By tomorrow, you'll gain from contacts made during the past three weeks. Some will plead with you, "Can't we have one final fling?" The moon is leaving your sign; you'll know more about money within 24 hours—whether or not it is obtainable.

195

Wednesday, August 9 (Moon in Sagittarius) News of your progress travels quickly. You will be offered a consulting role. On a personal level, the emphasis is on romance, desirability, and passion. Travel is in the cards. At first, you will be hesitant. Finally, you will be talked into it. Aries plays a major role.

Thursday, August 10 (Moon in Sagittarius to Capricorn 2:45 p.m.) For racing luck, try these selections at all tracks. Post position special—number 7 p.p. in the third race. Pick six: 1, 4, 7, 2, 6, 6. Watch for these letters or initials in the names of potential winning horses or jockeys: A, S, J. Hot daily doubles: 1 and 4, 6 and 7, 3 and 3. Brash Leo jockeys set records. Winners pay longshot prices.

Friday, August 11 (Moon in Capricorn) The Capricorn moon relates to relatives who take trips and report findings. Your popularity increases; what had been withheld will be revealed to your advantage. There's gourmet dining tonight. Show your appreciation of the cook's talent. Capricorn is involved.

Saturday, August 12 (Moon in Capricorn) This could be a lively Saturday night. Don't take yourself too seriously. Laugh at your own foibles. Favorable comments are made about your fashion sense. Give full play to your intellectual curiosity. Accept legitimate answers, not evasions. Have luck with number 3.

Sunday, August 13 (Moon in Capricorn to Aquarius 3:44 a.m.) Those who claim you are nit-picking will soon change their attitude. You as an individual or your group or both will receive honors. Thoroughness in approach played an important role in achieving success. Taurus, Leo, and another Scorpio figure in this dynamic scenario, with these initials in their names—D, M, V.

Monday, August 14 (Moon in Aquarius) You might be musing, "August must be my lucky month!" You are on solid ground, despite objections from those who lack faith, talent, and inspiration. Do things your way; it is the right way. Disregard those who have nothing better to do than to voice foolish criticisms.

Tuesday, August 15 (Moon in Aquarius to Pisces 3:42 p.m.)   The full moon in Aquarius relates to your home and property. A courtship has lasted long enough. You'll be asked to volunteer for a charity–political project. It could be a chance to show off your writing skills. Keep plans flexible; turn on the Scorpio charm and power. Taurus figures in this scenario.

Wednesday, August 16 (Moon in Pisces)   For racing luck, try these selections at all tracks: Post position special—number 1 p.p. in the sixth race. Pick six: 5, 7, 3, 4, 8, 1. Watch for these letters or initials in the names of potential winning horses or jockeys—G, P, Y. Hot daily doubles: 5 and 7, 3 and 7, 8 and 4. There could be muddy tracks, with long-shot winners, Pisces jockeys shine.

Thursday, August 17 (Moon in Pisces)   You'll be called upon to bring together those with opposing ideas. Accept the challenge, Be gracious, charming, and adorable. Under those conditions, who could say no to you? An older person is hungry for praise and affection. A Cancer is involved.

Friday, August 18 (Moon in Pisces to Aries 1:45 a.m.)   You come to terms with a question or problem previously ignored. Someone of the opposite sex confesses love but also needs money and cannot wait any longer! Look beyond the immediate; remain idealistic. Circumstances move topsy-turvy, but you will be in position to stand tall and, if you so choose, to be haughty.

Saturday, August 19 (Moon in Aries)   You'll be musing, "What a Saturday. I feel as if I drank from the Fountain of Youth!" The key is to make a fresh start in a new direction, to maintain your creative control. Let it be known, "There are two ways to do things—the right way and my way." Leo and Aquarius play dramatic roles. Your lucky number is 1.

Sunday, August 20 (Moon in Aries to Taurus 9:32 a.m.)   You'll contemplate, "So much happened last night, I will be grateful for a rest today!" Focus on your home, family, the restoration of faith in yourself. The spotlight is also on direction, motivation, the need to keep valuables under lock and key. A Cancer is involved.

Monday, August 21 (Moon in Taurus)   Welcome the fact that the moon is in Taurus! This relates to publicity, public appearances, style, a clash of ideas that stirs your creative juices. Attention revolves around legal decisions and marriage. An excellent dining experience tonight; a love relationship reignites. A Sagittarian is in the picture.

Tuesday, August 22 (Moon in Taurus to Gemini 2:56 p.m.)   Go slow. If you don't know what to do, do nothing! Mechanical problems require attention—pronto. Take special care with electrical outlets, in your automobile and home. Taurus and another Scorpio play significant roles, and have these letters or initials in their names—D, M, V.

Wednesday, August 23 (Moon in Gemini)   For racing luck, try these selections at all tracks: Post position special—number 3 p.p. in the second race. Pick six: 6, 3, 6, 1, 4, 2. Watch for these letters or initials in the names of potential winning horses or jockeys: E, N, W. Hot daily doubles: 6 and 3, 5 and 5, 7 and 7. Speed horses win. A Gemini jockey sets a record.

Thursday, August 24 (Moon in Gemini to Cancer 6 p.m.)   The moon in Gemini relates to fabulous luck. You'll enter areas previously closed. A unique welcome is prepared for you. Focus on your home, family, and security. There's music in your life. Taurus, Libra, and another Scorpio will play top roles, and have these letters or initials in their names—F, O, X.

Friday, August 25 (Moon in Cancer)   Your creative juices stir. A family member comments, "You seem to be so much more alive today!" Be gallant; return the compliment without any hint of sarcasm. This scenario highlights children, challenge, change, variety, and personal magnetism. Virgo plays a role.

Saturday, August 26 (Moon in Cancer to Leo 7:17 p.m.)   People talk to you about names and numbers. In a humorous way, reply, "Don't worry, I've got your number!" The Cancer moon relates to sensuality, creativity, plans for higher education associated with a journey. Capricorn and Cancer play stimulating roles. Your lucky number is 8.

Sunday, August 27 (Moon in Leo)   The Leo moon relates to your standing in the community, conferences with people who hold executive positions. Display showmanship, use words to get your message across in a dramatic and entertaining way. Aries and Libra figure in this dynamic scenario, and have these letters in their names—I and R.

Monday, August 28 (Moon in Leo to Virgo 7:56 p.m.)   The answer to your constant question: affirmative. There will be love in your life, perhaps more than you originally anticipated. Leo and Aquarius will figure in today's exciting scenario. Look for these letters or initials in their names: A, S, J. No heavy lifting!

Tuesday, August 29 (Moon in Virgo)   The new moon in Virgo wipes the slate clean of worry, brooding, hitting yourself with sledgehammer words. You'll have an excellent perspective on the future. This could be the start of a winning streak! Your finances improve. Money comes from a surprise source. An Aquarian plays a role.

Wednesday, August 30 (Moon in Virgo to Libra 9:34 p.m.)   The lunar position continues to activate your ability to pick winners. You also will win friends and influence people in a way that brings ultimate success and perhaps fame and fortune. Published material figures prominently. A Sagittarian promises, "No matter what, I will save the day!" Your lucky number is 3.

Thursday, August 31 (Moon in Libra)   Your last chance! The moon is getting ready to move from your eleventh house, the section of your horoscope associated with luck, speculation, and sex appeal. Don't hesitate! Grab the brass ring and hold tight! Taurus, Leo, and another Scorpio play colorful roles, and could have these letters or initials in their names—D, M, V.

SEPTEMBER 2000

Friday, September 1 (Moon in Libra)   People you meet today seem to be almost at opposite ends politically, emotionally, and intellectually. Keep your equilibrium; enjoy a clash of ideas among people who are intelligent enough not to permit disagreements to get too personal. Leo plays a top role.

Saturday, September 2 (Moon in Libra to Scorpio 1:56 a.m.)   For racing luck, try these selections at all tracks: Post position special—number 5 p.p. in the seventh race. Pick six: 3, 3, 2, 5, 1, 1. Watch for these letters or initials in the names of potential winning horses or jockeys: C, L, U. Hot daily doubles: 3 and 3, 7 and 2, 2 and 5. Big prices! Gemini and Sagittarian jockeys ride long shots to the winner's circle.

Sunday, September 3 (Moon in Scorpio)   The moon in your sign coincides with your high cycle. Take the initiative, stress independence, and be original. You'll exude an aura of personal magnetism, sensuality, and sex appeal. An envious individual could throw a monkey wrench into your plans. You will overcome it!

Monday, September 4 (Moon in Scorpio to Sagittarius 10:10 a.m.) Within 24 hours, you could hit the financial jackpot. As your cycle continues high, some people claim, "You have all the luck in the world!" Don't bother to answer; merely smile. The emphasis is on reading, writing, and teaching. A flirtation lends spice, and will involve a Sagittarian.

Tuesday, September 5 (Moon in Sagittarius) Suddenly, your past efforts seem to take wing. There are no more delays. You get the action you crave. Beautify your surroundings. Get ready to entertain important guests at home. You'll surprise yourself with your cooking skill. Taurus, Libra, and another Scorpio play major roles, and have these letters or initials in their names—F, O, X.

Wednesday, September 6 (Moon in Sagittarius to Capricorn 10:10 a.m.) Much that happens is shrouded in mystery. Play a behind-the-scenes role. Don't tell all; play your cards close to the chest. A financial deal is better than most, not as good as some. Your response: "I want to get it over with without any more delay!" Pisces is in this picture.

Thursday, September 7 (Moon in Capricorn) What was lost two days ago will be discovered, the manner of recovery somewhat embarrassing. Tonight define terms, outline boundaries, and let it be known that there is a deadline and it must be met. Focus on responsibility, pressure, an intense attraction that could ultimately lead to marriage.

Friday, September 8 (Moon in Capricorn) For racing luck, try these selections at all tracks: Post position special—number 8 p.p. in the first race. Pick six: 8, 4, 5, 2, 6, 1. Be alert for these letters or initials in the names of potential winning horses or jockeys: I and R. Hot daily doubles: 8 and 4, 7 and 7, 1 and 3. Horses and jockeys from foreign lands turn in sterling performances, paying good prices.

Saturday, September 9 (Moon in Capricorn to Aquarius 10:46 a.m.)   You will not be cold on this Saturday! Focus on affection, declarations of love, a fresh start in a new direction. Within 24 hours you'll be on more solid ground, dealing with an eccentric individual who will have your best interests at heart. Your lucky number is 1.

Sunday, September 10 (Moon in Aquarius)   You have two choices—to select someone who is not necessarily attractive, but very efficient, or to choose an attractive and dynamic person with little business sense. The spotlight is on direction, motivation, your marital status. A Cancer plays an important role.

Monday, September 11 (Moon in Aquarius to Pisces 10:35 p.m.)   Trust your intuitive intellect. Stick with the unusual. Create your own tradition. An Aquarian declares, "Business or not, I want to be with you. Do not let us be ships that pass in the night!" Gemini and Sagittarius play fascinating roles, and have these initials in their names—C, L, U.

Tuesday, September 12 (Moon in Pisces)   The Pisces moon relates to your fifth house, that section of the horoscope associated with creativity, challenge, variety, and sex appeal. People are drawn to you. Some will admit, "At times, I can hardly keep my hands off you!" Another Scorpio is involved.

Wednesday, September 13 (Moon in Pisces)   Today's scenario features challenge, change, the need to keep plans flexible. The full moon relates to a serious romantic interlude. If you're merely playing games, look out! People take you seriously and you should not make promises that you do not intend to fulfill. Gemini is involved.

Thursday, September 14 (Moon in Pisces to Aries 8:01 a.m.) What seemed always to be out of order will be fixed, much to your relief. An Aries enters the picture, helps you get organized. This relationship, however, is tense, so watch your words and your step. Taurus, Libra, and another Scorpio play fascinating roles, and have these letters in their names—F, O, X.

Friday, September 15 (Moon in Aries) A Pisces attracts you and the feeling is mutual. Attend to business first, including the repair of mechanical objects. The Pisces person is sensitive, psychic, but requires "careful handling." A Virgo also enters the picture, playing the role of critic. Have luck with number 7.

Saturday, September 16 (Moon in Aries to Taurus 3:06 p.m.) More headstrong young people will be in trouble; take special care in traffic. Avoid confrontations. You'll be regarded as a role model. The emphasis is on overtime, meeting and beating a deadline. If single, you give serious thought to partnership and marriage. Your lucky number is 8.

Sunday, September 17 (Moon in Taurus) It's your kind of day! Discussions involve literature, travel, sociology, and theology. Look beyond the obvious. Break free from stifling rules and regulations. People who previously showed no interest will now be at your doorstep. Aries plays a role.

Monday, September 18 (Moon in Taurus to Gemini 8:23 p.m.) People say, "You could get away with murder!" Response: "You take care of your business and I'll take care of mine!" Make a fresh start. Welcome a different kind of love. The lunar position highlights public relations, legal rights, and marriage. Money will be involved.

Tuesday, September 19 (Moon in Gemini) Do not jump from one project to another—finish what you start.

A well-meaning Gemini is confused, restless, needs to be told, "Calm down; get yourself together!" You are being pulled in two directions; the family says this way, friends and lovers say the other way.

Wednesday, September 20 (Moon in Gemini to Cancer 12:16 p.m.)   Focus on entertainment, a night of love and laughter. Delve deep into a mystery, the answers are found in arcane literature. A friend who suffered an emotional breakdown will recover and prove once again to be your important ally. Gemini and Sagittarius figure in this dynamic scenario.

Thursday, September 21 (Moon in Cancer)   For racing luck, try these selections at all tracks: Post position special—number 4 p.p. in the forth race. Pick six: 2, 5, 8, 4, 3, 2. Watch for these letters or initials in the names of potential winning horses or jockeys: D, M, V. Hot daily doubles: 2 and 5, 8 and 2, 6 and 4. A big favorite disappoints, will be out of the money.

Friday, September 22 (Moon in Cancer)   What a Friday! You look good and you feel good. Someone you are attracted to could go for you in a big way! Caution: don't take everything you hear seriously! Take notes; perhaps you should start a diary. Gemini, Virgo, and Sagittarius will play leading roles.

Saturday, September 23 (Moon in Cancer to Leo 3:01 a.m.)   Attention revolves around romance, style, panache, a domestic adjustment that could affect where you live and with whom. Beautify your surroundings, pay attention to household pets and plants. A Libran declares, "I didn't know you had it in you!" Lucky lottery: 12, 40, 6, 13, 18, 24.

Sunday, September 24 (Moon in Leo)   Pay attention to spiritual matters. Challenge a Leo to define terms. The emphasis is on your career, prestige, knowing who you are and why you are here. Some people assert, "Come down off your high horse!" Respond: "You stay down there. I will remain up here!"

Monday, September 25 (Moon in Leo to Virgo 5:03 a.m.)   Results! You achieve your goal; An important person asks, "Where have you been? We need people like you!" Answer: "Right here, thank you!" A development that is important to your career and general happiness is taking place. Capricorn and Cancer figure in this dramatic scenario, and have these letters in their names—H, Q, Z.

Tuesday, September 26 (Moon in Virgo)   Suddenly, you find yourself holding a cornucopia of plenty. Win friends and influence people; show that you are lucky in speculative ventures. You could also be lucky in love if you can keep your emotional equilibrium. Libra plays a role.

Wednesday, September 27 (Moon in Virgo to Libra 7:23 a.m.)   The new moon in your twelfth house throws light on areas previously dark. A clandestine relationship is featured; take care not to step on too many toes! Your Scorpio vim and vigor will be very much in evidence. Observe the sun in the sky and realize your place is at the top. Don't mess it up! Your lucky number is 1.

Thursday, September 28 (Moon in Libra)   Attention revolves around your home, large household products, decisions related to your budget in connection with enlarging your living quarters. The emphasis is also on food, cooking, repaying debts for recent favors. Cancer and Capricorn come up with creative solutions to your problems.

Friday, September 29 (Moon in Libra to Scorpio 11:31 a.m.)   Within 24 hours, the moon will be in your sign. Joy replaces gloom. Take the initiative, wear bright colors. Don't burn your bridges. A farewell party on your behalf is being arranged even as you read these words.

It is possible you might not be going anyplace, but the atmosphere will be such as to say, "Don't stay away too long!" Have luck with number 3.

Saturday, September 30 (Moon in Scorpio) The Scorpio moon represents a time when you call the shots. Take leave without being arrogant. Assert yourself; don't let others grab the spotlight. A love relationship heats up, and could get too hot not to cool down. Be aware of possible complications; enjoy yourself, without losing your sense of responsibility. Another Scorpio is involved.

OCTOBER 2000

Sunday, October 1 (Moon in Scorpio to Sagittarius 6:51 p.m.) You'll have reason to celebrate. In your high cycle, highlight diversity, versatility, read and write about fashions. Special: if you want to keep your figure, remember resolutions about exercise, diet, and nutrition. Gemini and Sagittarius figure in this scenario, and have these letters or initials in their names—C, L, U.

Monday, October 2 (Moon in Sagittarius) Sleepers awake! What a Monday—you'll be in rhythm with Wall Street; your stock selections are profitable. Stress original thinking. Have the courage of your convictions. Speak from sincerity and from your heart. A very important person confides in you; you will have the privilege of inside information.

Tuesday, October 3 (Moon in Sagittarius) Today, puzzle pieces fall into place. You will muse, "This is one Tuesday I won't soon forget!" Some people accuse you of holding back important information. Turn on your charm and style, to diffuse their curiosity.

Wednesday, October 4 (Moon in Sagittarius to Capricorn 5:44 a.m.) There's peace once again at home. A Capricorn, usually recalcitrant, moves over to your side of an argument. Siblings are involved. Forces that were scattered will settle down. Today's scenario highlights flowers, music, gifts representing tokens of affection and love. Your lucky number is 6.

Thursday, October 5 (Moon in Capricorn)   Stick to familiar ground and subjects. Some people seem intent on embarrassing you. Insist on a definition of terms and let it be known that you did not recently fall off a turnip truck. Pisces and Virgo play meaningful roles, and have these letters or initials in their names—G, P, Y.

Friday, October 6 (Moon in Capricorn to Aquarius 6:34 p.m.)   Within 24 hours, attention will revolve around property, sales, purchases, and long-term negotiations. Tonight, the spotlight is on financial maneuvers, the pressure of a deadline, an intense love relationship. Capricorn and Cancer play astonishing roles, and could have these letters in their names—H, Q, Z.

Saturday, October 7 (Moon in Aquarius)   For racing luck, try these selections at all tracks: Post position special—number 8 p.p. in the first race. Pick six: 8, 2, 1, 7, 5, 4. Watch for these letters or initials in the names of potential winning horses or jockeys: I and R. Hot daily doubles: 8 and 2, 7 and 7, 5 and 5. A loveable jockey, an Aries, wins in a photo finish and pays a big price.

Sunday, October 8 (Moon in Aquarius)   Your spiritual values surface. Leo and Aquarius encourage you to speak your mind. Stress originality and the courage of your convictions. It would appear that you have a gift of prophesy. Neither encourage nor discourage it. Let the facts speak for themselves. You will discover a shiny object.

Monday, October 9 (Moon in Aquarius to Pisces 6:37 a.m.)   The subject of partnership and marriage looms large. The Pisces moon relates to creativity, style, romance, and children. Give full play to your intellectual curiosity, and get your ideas on paper. Strive to remember your dreams and to write them. A flirtation lends spice, and could be more significant than you originally anticipated.

Tuesday, October 10 (Moon in Pisces)   After a sharp reaction to your lovemaking effort, find out where you stand and proceed accordingly. Do not wear your heart on your sleeve. If you immediately tell everything, the person you are interested in will lose interest in you! Gemini and Sagittarius figure in this scenario, and have these letters or initials in their names—C, L, U.

Wednesday, October 11 (Moon in Pisces to Aries 3:52 p.m.)   Lucky lottery: 4, 40, 11, 12, 22, 18. A roadblock is temporary, and will eventually serve as a stepping-stone toward your ultimate goal. Don't neglect your children; keep your promises. The emphasis is on entertainment, creativity, and style. Taurus, Leo, and another Scorpio play outstanding roles.

Thursday, October 12 (Moon in Aries)   Health matters dominate. Obtain a fitness report. A recent warning about your blood pressure should not be taken lightly. You are vital, dynamic, romantic, and everything would be just great if you keep your resolutions about exercise, diet, and nutrition. Your lucky number is 5.

Friday, October 13 (Moon in Aries to Taurus 10:06 p.m.)   Watch your step! It is Friday the 13th and there is a full moon. People act in aggressive, overly-emotional ways. The Venus keynote blends with your Pluto. Where love is concerned, it will be exciting, controversial and possibly more expensive than you planned. Libra is involved.

Saturday, October 14 (Moon in Taurus)   This is one Saturday night during which you should play a quiet role. The Taurus moon relates to commitments, both legal and otherwise. If single, you receive proposals that include marriage. Pisces and Virgo dominate this scenario, and will have these letters or initials in their names—G, P, Y.

Sunday, October 15 (Moon in Taurus)   Romance blends with legal affairs. Questions about partnership and marriage loom large. A frank discussion could clear the air with someone you trust. If the truth is told, you will extricate yourself from an embarrassing situation. Capricorn and Cancer will play instrumental roles.

Monday, October 16 (Moon in Taurus to Gemini 2:19 a.m.)   There's a possible deception with bank figures, very likely a computer error. Nevertheless, insist on a review of the tabulations. Learn more about tax and license requirements. Aries and Libra will play leading roles, and have these letters or initials in their names—I and R.

Tuesday, October 17 (Moon in Gemini)   Assert yourself. Focus on being original, daring, having the courage of your convictions. A new kind of love is featured; don't turn away from an exciting opportunity to present new material. Puzzle pieces fall into place in connection with what many regard as the occult. Your lucky number is 1.

Wednesday, October 18 (Moon in Gemini to Cancer 5:38 a.m.)   A situation or condition that kept you at home will be removed. You'll have the opportunity to travel, to write and publish, to express your love. Some people will comment, "You get all the breaks, how come?" Either ignore it, or respond, "I earn everything I get!"

Thursday, October 19 (Moon in Cancer)   A Cancer is involved in planning a social activity that will bring together people who share your interests. This includes charity, politics, and literature. Travel arrangements are featured. Be cooperative, without making commitments that throw your own agenda off-track. Sagittarius is involved.

Friday, October 20 (Moon in Cancer to Leo 8:43 a.m.)   An apparent slowdown provides the opportunity to get your second emotional wind. Be aware of the details, minor chinks in your armor. Taurus, Leo, and another Scorpio play significant roles, and could have these letters or initials in their names—D, M, V. Proofreading is necessary.

Saturday, October 21 (Moon in Leo)   The moon in Leo relates to your career, prestige, a conference with community leaders. You have plenty of power, so don't waste it. Emphasize freedom of thought and action—write your views. Gemini, Virgo, and Sagittarius will play fascinating roles. Lucky lottery: 5, 50, 15, 24, 7, 18.

Sunday, October 22 (Moon in Leo to Virgo 11:54 a.m.)   Attention revolves around your home, music, a family reunion. Sensitive subject involves your budget, money and how it gets that way. Deal gingerly with a Taurus who appears to be aching for a fight. A long-distance call strengthens your viewpoint about international affairs.

Monday October 23 (Moon in Virgo)   Suddenly, the light shines brighter. The moon in your eleventh house coincides with friends, hopes, wishes, the start of a winning streak. You will have luck in matters of speculation, but don't go overboard. This means keep your emotional equilibrium and use common sense.

Tuesday, October 24 (Moon in Virgo to Libra 3:31 p.m.)   Strength continues, the Saturn keynote blends reality into what is becoming a fantastic situation. People begin to sense that something unusual is going on, and they want to get in on it. Capricorn and Cancer figure in this mysterious scenario, and are likely to have these letters in their names—H, Q, Z.

Wednesday, October 25 (Moon in Libra)   Accent an aura of mystery and intrigue. The music background helps encourage illusion and romance. Someone who seldom speaks up will be on a talking streak. Be patiently amused. The focus is on recognition, romance, an invitation to travel. An Aries figures prominently.

Thursday, October 26 (Moon in Libra to Scorpio 8:25 p.m.)   People move around freely. Some choose you as arbitor of their disputes and problems. Go along with this for a little while, then announce, "It has been very interesting, but now I must find someone to help solve *my* problems!" Leo dominates this scenario.

Friday, October 27 (Moon in Scorpio)   The new moon in Scorpio emphasizes elements of timing and luck. You'll be right up there in front, so take a position of leadership. A relationship could become serious enough for marriage. The spotlight is also on a division of property, a business relationship that could develop into a solid partnership.

Saturday, October 28 (Moon in Scorpio)   The moon in your sign emphasizes your personality, inventiveness, creativity, sex appeal. Accept the challenge of new products, a unique advertising–publicity campaign. Emphasize humor; overcome distance, language barriers. A fashion note should be injected into a variety of programs. Your lucky number is 3.

Sunday, October 29—Eastern Standard Time (Moon in Scorpio to Sagittarius 2:42 a.m.)   There's plenty of romance today. You'll extricate yourself creatively from a boring routine. Money is coming in. A lost article can be located. Circumstances now move in your favor. Your motto will be, "You get what you pay for!" Taurus, Leo, and another Scorpio figure in this scenario.

Monday, October 30 (Moon in Sagittarius)   Today you will know that your position is solid, that a recent advancement was not just pure luck. Wake up singing! People will enjoy your company and let you know it.

Gemini, Virgo, and Sagittarius dominate this exciting scenario.

Tuesday, October 31 (Moon in Sagittarius to Capricorn 1:03 p.m.)   It's National Magic Day! It is also Halloween, but magicians celebrate the memory of the remarkable Harry Houdini. There could be a blend of magic tricks along with Halloween pranks. Stick close to home, be diplomatic, and praise those who come up with original costumes. Taurus plays a fantastic role.

NOVEMBER 2000

Wednesday, November 1 (Moon in Capricorn)   Lucky lottery: 4, 10, 11, 22, 32, 16. The lunar position emphasizes bright ideas. A well-meaning relative pokes his nose where it does not belong, causes a delay in negotiations. Taurus, Leo, and another Scorpio figure in this dramatic scenario, and could have these letters or initials in their names—D, M, V.

Thursday, November 2 (Moon in Capricorn)   Take notes. This applies especially to your diary or dreams. You will exude an aura of sensuality and sex appeal. What begins as a flirtation could descend into a complicated situation. Gemini, Virgo, and Sagittarius play leading roles, and have these initials in their names— E, N, W.

Friday, November 3 (Moon in Capricorn to Aquarius 1:41 a.m.)   For racing luck, try these selections at all tracks: Post position special—number 2 p.p. in the fourth race. Pick six: 1, 2, 3, 2, 5, 5. Watch for these letters or initials in the names of potential winning horses or jockeys: F, O, X. Hot daily doubles: 1 and 2, 6 and 6, 2 and 4. An apprentice jockey, possibly a Libran, steals the show, brings in a long shot.

Saturday, November 4 (Moon in Aquarius) A double-play could become a double-cross. An element of deception is present. Keep your guard up, and protect yourself in emotional clinches. A chance exists tonight to perfect techniques and streamline procedures. Pisces and Virgo insist on having their way.

Sunday, November 5 (Moon in Aquarius to Pisces 2:15 p.m.) Within 24 hours, the creative surge enables you to hold tight to your principles, to stay in control. Before the moon takes over for the sun, your goal will be in sight. A Capricorn becomes your ally, opens doors previously shut tight.

Monday, November 6 (Moon in Pisces) This could be the beginning or the end of a situation or relationship. What once set you on fire could now have a freezing effect. Follow your instincts in knowing when to let go. Aries and Libra play dramatic roles, and could have these letters or initials in their names—I and R.

Tuesday, November 7 (Moon in Pisces) Answer to question: yes, there's no time to waste. Assert yourself, stress originality, take a risk. Yes, a new love is on the horizon. Leo and Aquarius figure in today's dynamic scenario, and could have these letters or initials in their names: A, S, J. Your lucky number is 1.

Wednesday, November 8 (Moon in Pisces to Aries 12:03 a.m.) Lucky lottery: 2, 29, 9, 1, 50, 13. A family member cooperates in putting forth a proposal that requires an investment. Be careful not to oversell. Ride with the tide. You are doing the right thing and will be at the right place. A Cancer says, "I am all for you!"

Thursday, November 9 (Moon in Aries) Diversify, stress versatility, but avoid scattering your forces. The Aries moon relates to fitness, getting the job done, relating positively to coworkers. A Sagittarian speaks frankly, but has your best interests at heart. Have luck with number 3.

Friday, November 10 (Moon in Aries to Taurus 6:13 a.m.)   On this Friday, you will say, "Perhaps it is time for me to make a definite decision about legal affairs, partnership, and marriage. A situation that previously you ignored as being fantasy will now have a different kind of appeal. Another Scorpio is involved.

Saturday, November 11 (Moon in Taurus)   The full moon in Taurus highlights public relations, romance in connection with marriage. Married or single, no matter what your chronological age, the full moon will stimulate a creative process that could coincide with falling madly in love. Your lucky number is 5.

Sunday, November 12 (Moon in Taurus to Gemini 9:29 a.m.)   On this Sunday, you'll resolve, "From now on, I'm going to take more time to appreciate family life!" Within 24 hours the moon position will emphasize mystery, the occult, discovering hidden wealth. Taurus, Libra, and another Scorpio will play fascinating roles.

Monday, November 13 (Moon in Gemini)   Discover in which direction you intend to proceed. You'll be helped along this line by an ambitious Gemini who declares, "Let's take this show on the road!" Keep your equilibrium. Praise restless Gemini, but finally insist, "My way will be the only way!"

Tuesday, November 14 (Moon in Gemini to Cancer 11:22 a.m.)   Previous efforts pay dividends. You'll obtain the desired results. Whatever you do in the near future is likely to be right for you, despite objections from some family members. Refuse to be "touted" off track—you're doing the right thing, meeting and beating a deadline.

Wednesday, November 15 (Moon in Cancer)   Focus on universal appeal, overcoming obstacles that include language and distance. The moon in its own sign coincides with travel, publishing, renewed interest in theology. Aries and Cancer announce, "We are a team now, how do you like it?"

Thursday, November 16 (Moon in Cancer to Leo 1:20 p.m.)   For racing luck, try these selections at all tracks: Post position special—number 7 p.p. in the third race. Pick six: 2, 1, 7, 4, 3, 8. Watch for these letters or initials in the names of potential winning horses or jockeys: A, S, J. Hot daily doubles: 2 and 1, 3 and 3, 4 and 6. Leo jockeys shine, and receive rave notices.

Friday, November 17 (Moon in Leo)   Focus on your ability to fit in with various groups, or people. A Cancer declares, "No doubt about it, you inspire me!" The Leo moon represents your career, promotion and production, falling in love with someone who holds an executive position. The question of marriage looms large.

Saturday, November 18 (Moon in Leo to Virgo 4:17 p.m.)   For racing luck, try these selections at all tracks: Post position special—number 5 p.p. in the seventh race. Pick six: 3, 5, 2, 7, 1, 8. Watch for these letters or initials in the names of potential winning horses or jockeys: C, L, U. Hot daily doubles: 3 and 5, 7 and 1, 2 and 2. Gemini and Sagittarius ride long shots to the winner's circle.

Sunday, November 19 (Moon in Virgo)   On this Sunday, you will look upward, wondering, "I didn't realize it before, but now I feel that someone up there likes me!" The moon in your eleventh house represents the fulfillment of hopes, wishes, desires, good fortune in matters of speculation. Taurus is in this picture.

Monday, November 20 (Moon in Virgo to Libra 8:36 p.m.)   Get ready for a swift change of plans. Someone

215

who was to map the itinerary falls out. The fickle finger of fate now points to you. Take notes, write the program, exude personal magnetism, and do not reject someone of the opposite sex who is strongly attracted to you.

Tuesday, November 21 (Moon in Libra)   The emphasis is on where you live, flowers, music, the aroma of good cooking. The spotlight falls on decisions relating to close associations, partnership, and marriage. You'll receive a gift tonight representing love—celebrate it! Another Scorpio is in the picture!

Wednesday, November 22 (Moon in Libra)   On this Wednesday, you will be musing, "Life sure can be mysterious!" Focus on intrigue, deception, the tendency to cover up the facts and substitute fallacies. You'll be with people who are sensitive, psychic, and difficult to deal with if you are ultra-temperamental. Pisces and Virgo dominate this scenario. Have luck with number 7.

Thursday, November 23 (Moon in Libra to Scorpio 2:34 a.m.)   It's Thanksgiving and the moon is in your sign. Passionate revelations blend with the traditional turkey dinner. Your position is strong; people rely on you. Many confide family and financial problems. Be understanding. Offer tea and sympathy; let it be known, "I can just about survive my own problems!"

Friday, November 24 (Moon in Scorpio)   Your cycle continues high. State terms; be finished with a relationship that found you being taken for granted. Make room for a new love, for travel and exploration, for writing and publishing. Aries and Libra play fascinating roles, and have these letters in their names—I and R.

Saturday, November 25 (Moon in Scorpio to Sagittarius 10:34 a.m.)   On this Saturday, the new moon relates to your ability to locate lost articles, to improve your income potential. Make a fresh start, imprint your style, and do not follow others. Special: don't lift heavy objects!

A very bright Leo will be in your life and will transform many of your previous concepts and ideas. Your lucky number is 1.

Sunday, November 26 (Moon in Sagittarius)   A family gathering is in order—perhaps an accountant should be present, too. Discussions revolve around the sale or purchase of a building, home economics, a budget that must be adhered to by everyone. Cancer and Capricorn will play domineering roles, and have these initials in their names—B, K, T.

Monday, November 27 (Moon in Sagittarius to Capricorn 8:58 p.m.)   What previously was fuel for an argument is transformed into an invitation for a constructive clash of ideas. Comments are made about fashion, your appearance, where you intend to go for dining and entertaining. A Gemini figures prominently.

Tuesday, November 28 (Moon in Capricorn)   You will long remember this Tuesday! You'll be encouraged to express ideas. You gain a bright, prosperous Capricorn as an ally. Yet, you'll also be able to declare, "I did things my way!" Taurus, Leo, and another Scorpio play outstanding roles, and will have these initials in their names—D, M, V.

Wednesday, November 29 (Moon in Capricorn)   There's much discussion about names—whether or not to change them. Focus on trips, visits, communication with a relative who has been out of town. You will be called upon to cheer someone who has been down in the emotional dumps. You'll do it, too! Lucky lottery: 3, 5, 18, 22, 9, 7.

Thursday, November 30 (Moon in Capricorn to Aquarius 9:27 a.m.)   On this last day of November, you will be inspired to submit concepts, formats, and ideas. Some people raise eyebrows, declaring, "Where have you been hiding all this time?" Response: "Guess I've been too shy to warrant your notice." A Libra figures in this scenario.

DECEMBER 2000

Friday, December 1 (Moon in Aquarius)   All in all, a money month! Today you get a hint of potential, which is tremendous! Focus on words that are spoken or written. A family member provides valuable information about durable goods. Gemini, Virgo, and Sagittarius figure in this scenario, and have these letters or initials in their names—E, N, W.

Saturday, December 2 (Moon in Aquarius to Pisces 10:24 p.m.)   Attention revolves around your home, design, color coordination, renewed interest in plant life. To some, you might appear to be too generous. Your response: "That is the way it is, at least for today!" A relative is seriously considering where to live, marital status, and architectural design.

Sunday, December 3 (Moon in Pisces)   The Pisces moon relates to creativity, style, the adventure of discovery. Don't wait for others to express opinions; do what you "feel." Answer: affirmative, expand your horizons, display your product and talent. Pisces and Virgo figure in this dynamic, exciting scenario.

Monday, December 4 (Moon in Pisces)   Make this announcement: "Play square with me, or else!" Some people require a reminder. Give it to them straight! Focus on children, challenge, change, and variety. Capricorn and Cancer will play leading roles and have these initials in their names—H, Q, Z.

Tuesday, December 5 (Moon in Pisces to Aries 9:19 a.m.) Within 24 hours, people and events that evaded you will be available—to your advantage. Focus on universal appeal, letting people know that you appreciate and respect

218

their customs and language. A very delicate situation! Aries and Libra will play dramatic roles.

Wednesday, December 6 (Moon in Aries) The Aries moon relates to a job that must be done, a deadline. Don't wait for a couch potato—be up and at them—display leadership, let the chips fall where they may. Spotlight showmanship, colorful ornaments, displays that attract attention. A Leo figures prominently.

Thursday, December 7 (Moon in Aries to Taurus 4:28 p.m.) For racing luck, try these selections at all tracks: Post position special—number 1 p.p. in the sixth race. Pick six: 1, 4, 5, 3, 2, 1. Look for these letters or initials in the names of potential winning horses or jockeys: B, K, T. Hot daily doubles: 1 and 4, 6 and 3, 1 and 7. Cancer jockeys ride favorites, bring them in the money.

Friday, December 8 (Moon in Taurus) Ask questions, make inquiries, give full rein to your intellectual curiosity. On this Friday, the emphasis is placed on cooperation, an ability to bring together people whose ideas clash. The spotlight will also be on legal affairs, your reputation, credibility, and marriage.

Saturday, December 9 (Moon in Taurus to Gemini 7:52 p.m.) Stick to practical affairs. Focus on payments and collections, income potential. A Taurus who seems pugilistic is secretly an admirer, and will fight for your cause. Read between the lines, discover the hidden clause in a legal document. Your lucky number is 4.

Sunday, December 10 (Moon in Gemini) The moon moves to Gemini, your eighth house, which relates to interest in the occult, the savings account of your partner or mate. Someone who attempts to deceive will be caught red-handed. Read and write, respect the power of the word. A publishing contact!

Monday, December 11 (Moon in Gemini to Cancer 8:50 p.m.)   The full moon in your eighth house relates to intense romantic activity, sex appeal. Venus is involved, so you'll be saying, "Perhaps I should not have shown my hand—I made it look too easy to 'conquer.' " Taurus and Libra play leading roles.

Tuesday, December 12 (Moon in Cancer)   The imagination can do funny things—for you today, it will do marvelous things. Hold on to your sense of wonder. Enjoy being fooled by a clever magician. Look beyond the immediate; be aware of potential; refuse to be discouraged by those who lack talent or inspiration.

Wednesday, December 13 (Moon in Cancer to Leo 9:10 p.m.)   Power play! You make the correct moves at the right time. People you contacted three months ago will prove to be your valuable allies. Stress humor, versatility, the ability to make do with the material at hand. A Capricorn says, "I am here to stay!" Your lucky number is 8.

Thursday, December 14 (Moon in Leo)   A project is completed. You'll receive credit long deserved. The lunar position highlights promotion, prestige, dealings with the high and mighty. You'll ask yourself, "What took me so long?" Aries and Libra figure prominently, and could have these letters in their names—I and R.

Friday, December 15 (Moon in Leo to Virgo 10:31 p.m.)   Accent showmanship, colorful wrappings, and displays. Wear combinations of yellow and gold. Your reputation as a great lover will be challenged. Say this: "My ability at lovemaking depends upon my energy level!" People will adore your frankness. An Aquarian is involved.

Saturday, December 16 (Moon in Virgo)   On this Saturday, you get your way. Ah, there's the rub! What is your way? The Virgo moon in your eleventh house means your sense of discrimination is razor sharp. Don't settle for second best; insist on obtaining the best, and you will. Capricorn is involved.

Sunday, December 17 (Moon in Virgo)   Social activities accelerate. Discussions will range from astrology to fashion to international affairs. Gemini and Sagittarius will dominate in an enjoyable way. Examine a variety of publications; make a decision about a publication of your own.

Monday, December 18 (Moon in Virgo to Libra 2:02 a.m.)   People engage you in scientific discussions. The Libra moon relates to hospitals, institutions, theaters, museums. Secrets are exposed, mainly to your advantage. Some will state, "You yourself are a big secret!" Regard this as a joke.

Tuesday, December 19 (Moon in Libra)   A discussion with a Sagittarian revolves around economics. Let it be known, "I am not going to give up something for nothing!" The emphasis is on words, flirtation, a range of feelings, and experiences. Virgo will play a sensational role.

Wednesday, December 20 (Moon in Libra to Scorpio 8:13 a.m.)   Lucky lottery: 6, 51, 7, 8, 15, 1. As your cycle moves up, within 24 hours you'll have the pick of the litter. Attention revolves around design, comfortable living, taking steps to protect your valuables. Taurus and Libra play outstanding roles.

Thursday, December 21 (Moon in Scorpio)   With the moon in your sign, you'll exude an aura of confidence and sex appeal. Don't take orders—give them! Designate where the action will be. Participate in an artistic project. Pisces and Virgo are very much in the picture, and have these initials in their names—G, P, Y.

Friday, December 22 (Moon in Scorpio to Sagittarius 4:58 p.m.)   You will call this "my lucky Friday!" Elements of timing and surprise ride with you, highlighting glamour, intrigue, a variety of color combinations. Some will comment, "You certainly know how to attract attention—and sell!" A Cancer is involved.

Saturday, December 23 (Moon in Sagittarius)   On this Saturday, you'll be in contact with someone who left for a foreign country, could be overstaying a visit. The moon position indicates the need to keep track of foreign exchange rates. Make inquiries, check with a knowledgeable person who knows the meaning of money.

Sunday, December 24 (Moon in Sagittarius)   It's Christmas Eve. Visitors from far away will bring unique gifts. Sincere resolutions are also part of this dynamic scenario. You'll display amazing skill in picking winners. When asked how you do it, reply, "Just lucky, I guess!" A Leo figures prominently.

Monday, December 25 (Moon in Sagittarius to Capricorn 3:55 a.m.)   There's a new moon and solar eclipse in Capricorn, the perfect setup for this holiday! The spotlight is on family, many gifts relating to cookbooks, restaurants, and food. Take special care in traffic. Give the right of way, rather than become involved in an argument.

Tuesday, December 26 (Moon in Capricorn)   Social activities accelerate. Exchange ideas, to say nothing of gifts! Keep your sense of humor. Ask questions which, if answered honestly, will result in embarrassed laughter. Gemini and Sagittarius are represented, and have these letters in their names—C, L, U.

Wednesday, December 27 (Moon in Capricorn to Aquarius 4:27 p.m.)   Check the list of people you will be involved with on New Year's Eve. Do not wait until the last minute before making reservations or formulating other plans. Restrictions are now lifted, as the moon leaves Capricorn, so you'll have more freedom of thought and action. Another Scorpio is in this picture.

Thursday, December 28 (Moon in Aquarius) The Aquarian moon relates to an unsettled domestic position. There is no bitterness, however. A clash of ideas revolves around astrology and the zodiac. Scholarship exists to prove that Sir Isaac Newton, a Capricorn, believed deeply in alchemy and astrology.

Friday, December 29 (Moon in Aquarius) Attention revolves around beautifying your surroundings, testing recipes, a domestic adjustment that could include a possible change of your residence or marital status. A special member of the opposite sex will declare, "You certainly are a smooth worker!"

Saturday, December 30 (Moon in Aquarius to Pisces 5:29 p.m.) Put things in order, including decorations for a party. The Pisces moon relates to excitement, thrills, a physical attraction. Pisces and Virgo will play dynamic, dramatic roles and will have these letters or initials in their names—G, P, Y. Your lucky number is 7.

Sunday, December 31 (Moon in Pisces) New Year's Eve: this is one Sunday you won't soon forget! Both lunar and numerical cycles relate to creativity, style, and original forms of entertainment. You'll exude an aura of sex appeal. Words flow such as, "Love you forever!" Capricorn plays a dominant role.

Happy New Year!

JANUARY 2001

Monday, January 1 (Moon in Pisces to Aries 5:13 p.m.) You will find it necessary to go slow on alcoholic beverages on this first day of the year 2001. Check the details, including proofreading—even if you don't feel like it on this holiday. Leo and Aquarius play memorable roles in your personal scenario.

Tuesday, January 2 (Moon in Aries)   What you previously took for granted needs attention. Focus on reading, writing, teaching, and making a decision about a current romance. A lost article is found—just where you left it! Gemini, Virgo, and Sagittarius will play outstanding roles.

Wednesday, January 3 (Moon in Aries)   For racing luck, try these selections at all tracks: Post position special—number 2 p.p. in the fourth race. Pick six: 6, 2, 4, 2, 3, 1. Watch for these letters in the names of potential winning horses or jockeys: F, O, X. Hot daily doubles: 6 and 2, 1 and 4, 3 and 5. Hometown favorites win; Taurus jockeys will be in the money.

Thursday, January 4 (Moon in Aries to Taurus 1:54 a.m.)   In a relatively short time your cycle moves up—but meanwhile you lie low, play the waiting game. You might feel as if the world is standing still—patience is required. In a way, the entire world is adjusting to new conditions. You and almost everyone else are being tested.

Friday, January 5 (Moon in Taurus)   The Taurus moon relates to a clash of ideas, especially with those who previously were in full agreement. The spotlight is on a partnership, marriage, and the need for legal counsel. What gets out of hand will be brought back into proper position. You're going places and the path will be smoother as the result of a special study.

Saturday, January 6 (Moon in Taurus to Gemini 6:43 a.m.)   Lucky lottery: 6, 12, 9, 3, 18, 7. Correspondence results in a possible invitation to travel overseas. People who took you for granted will tip their hats and bow.

You exude a quality of universal appeal; someone from a foreign land makes a serious proposal.

Sunday, January 7 (Moon in Gemini) You could take part in an animal rights activity. Your viewpoint will change. Make a fresh start in a new direction; be willing to take a chance on romance. Leo and Aquarius will play memorable roles today. Expect to have luck with the number 1.

Monday, January 8 (Moon in Gemini to Cancer 8:07 a.m.) You will be pulled in two directions simultaneously. There could be debate between two family members. In this case, an elder Cancer is on the right track. A love relationship that fizzled will once again sizzle. A Capricorn who once wanted nothing more to do with you is back!

Tuesday, January 9 (Moon in Cancer—Lunar Eclipse) The full moon, lunar eclipse in your ninth house, places the emphasis on travel, philosophy, and theology, highlights your ability to foretell the future. Social activities are plentiful; the key is to be selective. Gemini and Sagittarius, who could dominate this scenario, have these letters in their names—C, L, U.

Wednesday, January 10 (Moon in Cancer to Leo 7:43 a.m.) Lucky lottery: 4, 10, 32, 18, 12, 9. You will be dealing with an idealistic person whose ideas are grand, but who lacks the necessary funding. A roadblock that deterred progress could be transformed into a stepping-stone toward your ultimate goal. Another Scorpio is involved.

Thursday, January 11 (Moon in Leo) Start writing! Take note of your dreams—tonight's will be prophetic! A flirtation that begins mildly today could become too hot not to cool down. The key is to know when to say, "Enough is enough!" A relative inveigles you into joining in a short trip relating to missing legal papers.

Friday, January 12 (Moon in Leo to Virgo 7:25 a.m.)
Attention revolves around your home, your community, your income potential, and your marital status. You receive a gift today of a valuable stone. You are being courted! Before accepting, be sure you are aware of the consequences. Taurus, Libra, and another Scorpio command dominant roles.

Saturday, January 13 (Moon in Virgo) For racing luck, try these selections at all tracks: Post position special—number 1 p.p. in the seventh race. Pick six: 1, 4, 2, 5, 1, 1. Watch for these letters in the names of potential winning horses or jockeys: H, Q, Z. Hot daily doubles: 1 and 4, 2 and 5, 7 and 7. Underdogs win and pay longshot prices. Horses that run well in mud will excel.

Sunday, January 14 (Moon in Virgo to Libra 9:05 a.m.) A powerful Sunday for you! People will be drawn to you for advice and entertainment. The moon in your eleventh sector coincides with your ability to win friends and influence people, and you can expect to have good fortune in finance and romance. Cancer and Capricorn, who assert their views, will play major roles today.

Monday, January 15 (Moon in Libra) A friend you left behind some time ago will make a surprise appearance. Talk will consist mainly of memories, money, and marriage. Do not commit yourself to a proposition of living together. What has ended has really ended—know it and respond accordingly. Aries plays an intense role.

Tuesday, January 16 (Moon in Libra to Scorpio 2:03 p.m.) Make up for lost time! Let the world know where you stand and what you intend to do about it. The focus is on independence, originality, and a willingness to make room for a new love. Leo and Aquarius, who will play dominating roles, could have these letters in their names—A, S, J.

Wednesday, January 17 (Moon in Scorpio)   For racing luck, try these selections at all tracks: Post position special—number 6 p.p. in the fifth race. Pick six: 4, 2, 1, 5, 6, 8. Watch for these letters in the names of potential winning horses or jockeys: B, K, T. Hot daily doubles: 4 and 2, 1 and 3, 4 and 8. Favorites come in third. Winners will be ridden by Cancer-born jockeys.

Thursday, January 18 (Moon in Scorpio to Sagittarius 10:36 p.m.)   When the moon is in your sign, your cycle is high and you will be where the action is. Circumstances turn in your favor, so be selective. Stress independence, creativity, and originality. Gemini and Sagittarius, who figure in today's scenario, have these letters in their names—C, L, U. Your lucky number is 3.

Friday, January 19 (Moon in Sagittarius)   Be willing to revamp and revise, and to tear down in order to rebuild. What had been a burden rather than a blessing will be eliminated within 24 hours. Let others know how you feel; don't leave it to guesswork. You learn more about the practical side of romance, including how much a ring will cost.

Saturday, January 20 (Moon in Sagittarius)   For racing luck, try these selections are all tracks: Post position special—number 3 p.p. in the second race. Pick six: 2, 3, 4, 8, 2, 2. Watch for these letters in the names of potential winning horses or jockeys—E, N, W. Hot daily doubles: 2 and 3, 5 and 5, 1 and 2. Speed horses get out in front and will be in the money.

Sunday, January 21 (Moon in Sagittarius to Capricorn 9:56 a.m.)   Questions about money arise—you will get your fair share! You'll be invited to dinner by a Libra. Dining will be accompanied by music and an elaborate scheme or scenario. Before this evening is over, you'll find out what this is all about!

Monday, January 22 (Moon in Capricorn)   Do your best, but do not expect miracles. The current cycle relates to illusion, delusion, and a tendency toward self-deception. It would be easy to be frustrated on a day such as this, but don't let it happen. You will understand that time is on your side—do not equate delay with defeat!

Tuesday, January 23 (Moon in Capricorn to Aquarius 10:42 p.m.)   You make a remarkable comeback following yesterday's tendency toward gloom. The pressure of responsibility remains, but this time you can do something about it. You'll be dealing with supervisors and important people. You'll handle complicated assignments with aplomb.

Wednesday, January 24 (Moon in Aquarius)   The new moon in Aquarius relates to your fourth house, which means greater desire for security and the safety of your family. A long-distance call verifies your views. Plan ahead for a possible trip to another country. Aries and Libra play meaningful roles, and have these initials in their names—I and R.

Thursday, January 25 (Moon in Aquarius)   Make a fresh start in a new direction, emphasizing independence of thought and action. It's an excellent day for changing the appearance of your home. Stress originality, as well as the willingness to tear down in order to rebuild. Leo and Aquarius will play dominant roles. Your lucky number is 1.

Friday, January 26 (Moon in Aquarius to Pisces 11:37 a.m.)   Today you recover your sense of direction and motivation. Within 24 hours, the moon will be in Pisces, your fifth house, that section of your horoscope having to do with children, challenge, change, and sex appeal. Cancer and Capricorn, who play leading roles, have these initials in their names—B, K, T.

Saturday, January 27 (Moon in Pisces)   On this Saturday, social activities accelerate. The Pisces moon heightens your personal magnetism, as well as your aura of sensuality and sex appeal. Gemini and Sagittarius, who play outstanding roles, have these letters in their names—C, L, U. Lucky lottery: 32, 51, 4, 5, 8, 22.

Sunday, January 28 (Moon in Pisces to Aries 11:33 p.m.)   What a Sunday! You will not be alone. Children will gravitate toward you. If single, a member of the opposite sex will say, "I love being with you!" Talk about and share your spiritual values. Taurus, Leo, and another Scorpio, who play outstanding roles, have these initials in their names—D, M, V.

Monday, January 29 (Moon in Aries)   Your health improves. You'll be in greater control of your own destiny. It's an excellent day for writing, taking notes, and tapping into your creative potential. You do have writing ability. Virgo and Sagittarius will play memorable roles.

Tuesday, January 30 (Moon in Aries)   Attention revolves around your home, music, security, basic issues, diet, and nutrition. You'll be musing, "On this Tuesday, I find out that I am not alone, and that I cannot continue to break the rules of health." The spotlight is on employment, with special attention on getting along with coworkers.

Wednesday, January 31 (Moon in Aries to Taurus 9:19 a.m.)   On this last day of January, the pace slows as you go through a period of self-revelation. A family member asks, "Have you been keeping up with your health rules?" You can honestly answer, "I do my best and I feel my best is good enough!" Pisces is in this picture.

Thursday, February 1 (Moon in Taurus)   You're back down to earth! Practical matters dominate, including the sale or purchase of a home or other property. A flirtation begins mildly, but soon could get too hot not to cool down. Gemini, Virgo, and Sagittarius, who play leading roles, could have these initials in their names— E, N, W.

Friday, February 2 (Moon in Taurus to Gemini 3:54 p.m.)   Attention revolves around where you live, basic domestic issues, and your income potential. Beautify your surroundings, because you soon will have an important, surprise guest. Taurus, Leo, and another Scorpio, who play significant roles, have these letters in their names—F, O, X.

Saturday, February 3 (Moon in Gemini)   Lie low and play the waiting game. Review accounting figures—your bank account could appear to go haywire. A glamorous member of the opposite sex declares, "I don't care about your past; I'm crazy about you!" Pisces and Virgo play magnificent roles today. Your lucky number is 7.

Sunday, February 4 (Moon in Gemini to Cancer 6:59 p.m.)   A power play day! The Gemini moon relates to your eighth house, which means mystery and intrigue. Your answer to most questions today should be, "That's for me to know and for you to find out!" Some will accuse you of being in the playground of the occult.

Monday, February 5 (Moon in Cancer)   Everything points to your popularity—you could be persuaded to travel to another country. You will overcome distance and language barriers. It will be fun to be with you. People compete for the privilege of wining and dining you.

Tuesday, February 6 (Moon in Cancer to Leo 7:20 p.m.) This is the time to make a fresh start in a new direction. New love is on the horizon, so be ready! Leo and Aquarius, who will play dynamic roles today, could have these letters in their names—A, S, J. Display your pioneering spirit; accent showmanship and color coordination.

Wednesday, February 7 (Moon in Leo) For racing luck, try these selections at all tracks: Post position special—number 1 p.p. in the sixth race. Pick six: 8, 2, 1, 3, 5, 1. Watch for these letters in the names of potential winning horses or jockeys—B, K, T. Hot daily doubles: 8 and 2, 6 and 5, 3 and 3. Home-grown jockeys will be in the winner's circle.

Thursday, February 8 (Moon in Leo to Virgo 6:34 p.m.) The full moon in Leo equates to your career, promotion, and production, as well as your ability to attract followers. The Jupiter keynote means that elements of timing and luck ride with you. Gemini and Sagittarius, who will play important roles in your life today, have these letters in their names—C, L, U.

Friday, February 9 (Moon in Virgo) The lunar position coincides with your ability to win friends and influence people. Today you have good fortune in finance and romance. People who say you are stubborn are envious. Reminder: Don't ask for more than you can handle, because you are liable to get it! Taurus is represented.

Saturday, February 10 (Moon in Virgo to Libra 6:45 p.m.) Lucky lottery: 10, 50, 6, 5, 11, 7. Make a fresh start. Be independent; do not follow others—let them follow you, if they so desire. Be ready for change, travel, and a variety of sensations and experiences. Gemini, Virgo, and Sagittarius play memorable roles today.

Sunday, February 11 (Moon in Libra) On this Sunday, there will be a reunion with a family member who has been trying to make amends for having misspoken. There's music in your life tonight, so dance to your own tune. Spiritual values surface, as published material provides the key to what you have been seeking.

Monday, February 12 (Moon in Libra to Scorpio 9:52 p.m.)   Play the waiting game and don't commit yourself to any definite course of action. Pisces and Virgo, who play roles in your life today, could have these letters in their names—G, P, Y. It is time to emerge from your emotional shell. Be sure others know that you have feelings, too.

Tuesday, February 13 (Moon in Scorpio)   Within 24 hours, when the moon will be in Scorpio, your cycle will be on the rise. You will be able to pick and choose and to select quality. Tonight, with Saturn playing a significant role, you'll agree to more responsibility and more money. A Cancer is involved.

Wednesday, February 14 (Moon in Scorpio)   You receive more Valentine's Day cards than in previous years. A fanatical member of the opposite sex threatens to self-inflict harm unless you give and receive love. This is a repeat of neurotic behavior—be careful! Lucky lottery: 36, 19, 12, 40, 42, 50.

Thursday, February 15 (Moon in Scorpio to Sagittarius 5:02 a.m.)   Refuse to be the subject of a drug experiment. Break free from those who take you for granted. Highlight originality and a fresh start in a new direction. Avoid lifting heavy objects, if possible. The emphasis is on your back and heart. Tonight, go easy on alcoholic beverages.

Friday, February 16 (Moon in Sagittarius)   Move away from standard procedures, creating your own style and techniques. The focus is also on areas of partnership and marriage. You're due for a sensational seafood dinner tonight! The menu will include broiled lobster. A

Cancer does the inviting and will be the chef. Your lucky number is 2.

Saturday, February 17 (Moon in Sagittarius to Capricorn 3:58 p.m.)   For racing luck, try these selections at all tracks: Post position special—number 5 p.p. in the seventh race. Pick six: 2, 7, 1, 4, 3, 5. Watch for these letters in the names of potential winning horses or jockeys—C, L, U. Hot daily doubles: 2 and 7, 4 and 4, 1 and 1. Longshot horses will be in the money; Sagittarian jockeys will be in the winner's circle.

Sunday, February 18 (Moon in Capricorn)   A short trip involves a relative and some legal documents. You are going places, but be sure you don't get involved in a wild-goose chase. A relative, likely another Scorpio, is highly nervous at this time and slightly confused. Do plenty of proofreading, check details, bypass bureaucrats, and go right to the top.

Monday, February 19 (Moon in Capricorn)   On this first workday of the week, you will be restless, dynamic, and ready for a variety of experiences. You'll exude personal magnetism, along with an aura of sensuality and sex appeal. Some people will promise you anything, but ask them to put it in writing!

Tuesday, February 20 (Moon in Capricorn to Aquarius 4:53 a.m.)   A deal involving property is pending—don't upset the applecart! A Capricorn who is leaving town wants to have one last big night with you. Go easy on the alcohol. There is another day tomorrow and you will be a large part of it. Libra figures in this scenario.

Wednesday, February 21 (Moon in Aquarius)   Lucky lottery: 7, 11, 18, 27, 51, 1. Define your terms, outline your boundaries, and pay close attention to a real estate transaction. A relationship that started three weeks ago is coming to fruition. This scenario highlights mystery, intrigue, and hidden values. Pisces will set the pace.

Thursday, February 22 (Moon in Aquarius to Pisces 5:44 p.m.)   Use the element of time, including timing requests and the setting of an appointment that could result in much profit for you. Capricorn and Cancer persons who play leading roles, could have these letters in their names—H, Q, Z. A passionate member of the opposite sex claims, "I can't live without you!"

Friday, February 23 (Moon in Pisces)   The Pisces new moon relates to change, travel, a variety of sensations, and sex appeal. You will have good fortune in matters of speculation by sticking with the number 9. A relationship that was supposed to get started is over before it has a chance to breathe. Aries is in the picture.

Saturday, February 24 (Moon in Pisces)   You get a rare opportunity to make a fresh start in a different direction. Think with your head as well as your heart— basing actions now on pure impulse will prove costly. Make personal appearances, wearing bright colors and letting people know, "I am here and I am at liberty!"

Sunday, February 25 (Moon in Pisces to Aries 5:19 a.m.)   You receive numerous proposals, including those relating to partnership and marriage. If married, you rediscover your mate emotionally, mentally, and physically. Overcome a tendency to brood via meditation. A perplexing money problem will be solved—you will wake up with the answer.

Monday, February 26 (Moon in Aries)   Keep your plans flexible, following the general health rules. Make peace with a coworker. Social activities accelerate; your popularity is on the rise; you will receive a gift that adds to your wardrobe. You'll hear these comments: "You look especially good today—did you do something to your hair?"

Tuesday, February 27 (Moon in Aries to Taurus 3:04 p.m.)   The emphasis today will be on keeping promises to yourself about work and health. Taurus, Leo, and another Scorpio, who figure prominently, could have these letters in their names—D, M, V. You are on solid ground, but in getting there you pushed aside some creative plans. Use your imagination!

Wednesday, February 28 (Moon in Taurus) The emphasis is on legal agreements, public relations, a clash of ideas, and your marital status. Some people remind you of what Napoleon is quoted as saying: "Impossible is an adjective used by fools!" On this last day of the month, get your thoughts, ideas, concepts, and formats in writing. Your lucky number is 5.

MARCH 2001

Thursday, March 1 (Moon in Taurus to Gemini 10:34 p.m.) You start off the month with the moon in Taurus, your opposite sign. Thus, the emphasis will be on ideas, legal areas of your life, public relations, and marriage. Attention revolves around your home and a major domestic adjustment that could include a change of residence or marital status.

Friday, March 2 (Moon in Taurus to Gemini 10:34 p.m.) Within 24 hours, the moon will be in Gemini, your eighth house, which will relate to accounting, mystery, and the occult. Today and tonight, however, the emphasis continues on the way you look to others and the way you feel inside. Questions about marriage continue to loom large.

Saturday, March 3 (Moon in Gemini) Focus on power, authority, promotion, and production. A relationship is intense, and it could be too hot not to cool down. Capricorn and Cancer, who will play outstanding roles, could have these letters in their names—H, Q, Z. An older person offers to lend the benefit of experience. Your lucky number is 8.

Sunday, March 4 (Moon in Gemini to Cancer 3:23 a.m.)
Spiritual values surface. It could be a matter of "I will
help you if you in return will help me." Finish what you
start, letting go of petty complaints and minor disputes.
The solution to a mystery comes during the late after-
noon. Reward yourself with a fine dinner tonight.

Monday, March 5 (Moon in Cancer)   The spotlight
is on travel, so reach beyond your present situation. You
could receive favorable reviews and good publicity. It's
an excellent day for distribution, publishing, and advertising. Stress innovation and inventiveness as you make a
fresh start in a new direction—and that could include
romance!

Tuesday, March 6 (Moon in Cancer to Leo 5:29 a.m.)
Once again, you could be in a quandary over your marital status. The emphasis will be on food, survival, fun,
love, romance, and marriage. You gain a sense of direction and motivation. Cancer and Capricorn, who play
sensitive roles, could have these letters in their names—
B, K, T.

Wednesday, March 7 (Moon in Leo)   For racing luck,
try these selections at all tracks: Post position special—
number 5 p.p. in the second race. Pick six: 1, 5, 3, 7, 2,
4. Watch for these letters in the names of potential wining horses or jockeys—C, L, U. Hot daily doubles: 1 and
5, 3 and 3, 6 and 6. A Sagittarian jockey rides a record-
breaking long-shot winner.

Thursday, March 8 (Moon in Leo to Virgo 5:43 a.m.)
Show off your product in an imaginative, colorful way.
You hurdle obstacles today; many are in awe at an ability
you might have been hiding up to now. Explain: "Being
a Scorpio, with a Pluto ruler, I don't pull punches or
hide. You get what you see!" Another Scorpio is
involved.

Friday, March 9 (Moon in Virgo)   A break from tradition is indicated, to your advantage. The full moon in your eleventh house brings a shower of good luck. People will be drawn to you; you can obtain funding for a unique project. Gemini, Virgo, and Sagittarius, who play roles, have these letters in their names—E, N, W.

Saturday, March 10 (Moon in Virgo to Libra 5:46 a.m.)   A family member announces, "I've got a wonderful Saturday plan, and you are going to join me!" The emphasis is on art, music, and luxury. Show your appreciation without being obsequious. If you don't like something, say that, too—but be polite. You will have luck with the number 6.

Sunday, March 11 (Moon in Libra)   This could be termed a perfect Sunday. It's an excellent day for worshiping, meditating, and defining terms in your own mind. Pisces and Virgo, who play important roles, could have these initials in their names—G, P, Y. See relationships and people as they exist, not merely as you wish they were.

Monday, March 12 (Moon in Libra to Scorpio 7:42 a.m.) The moon in your twelfth house in Libra tells of activity behind the scenes, as well as visits to friends confined to home and hospital. Soothing words and music are involved, so be cooperative and form a mutual admiration society. Capricorn and Cancer will play meaningful roles.

Tuesday, March 13 (Moon in Scorpio)   Your cycle moves up as circumstances turn in your favor. Be selective—choose the best, for nothing else will do. Imprint your style, leading the way and refusing to follow others. Aries and Libra, who play sensational roles, have these letters in their names—I and R. Your lucky number is 9.

Wednesday, March 14 (Moon in Scorpio to Sagittarius 1:17 p.m.)   Lucky lottery: 1, 12, 18, 33, 45, 51. You'll meet a temperamental Leo whose charm offsets his temper. A new and different kind of love is upcoming, causing you to decide that life can be beautiful after all! A member of the opposite sex declares, "I can hardly keep my hands off you!"

Thursday, March 15 (Moon in Sagittarius) Debts are collected, as you receive money you thought you might never see again. Focus on your home, family, security, and marital status. A Thursday-night dinner out would be just what the doctor ordered. Cancer and Capricorn, who play important roles today, have these initials in their names—B, K, T.

Friday, March 16 (Moon in Sagittarius to Capricorn 11:02 p.m.) In the purchase of stocks, diversify. Ask questions, make inquiries, giving full rein to your intellectual curiosity. For a change of pace, buy novelty items for gifts. Gemini and Sagittarius, who play outstanding roles, have these letters in their names—C, L, U. Your lucky number is 3.

Saturday, March 17 (Moon in Capricorn) On this St. Patrick's Day, have fun, but practice restraint when it comes to alcohol. Taurus, Leo, and another Scorpio figure prominently. You'll know them because of these letters in their names—D, M, V. Within 24 hours, you'll hear from a relative in transit, and an invitation to dinner follows.

Sunday, March 18 (Moon in Capricorn) A tour of a museum or attendance at a movie would be moving in the rhythm of the current cycle. The Mercury keynote relates to reading, writing, and learning through the process of teaching. Gemini, Virgo, and Sagittarius, who play interesting roles, will have these initials in their names— E, N, W.

Monday, March 19 (Moon in Capricorn to Aquarius 11:35 a.m.) Expect a blend today of Venus with Saturn. Properly interpreted, this means a bittersweet combination of laughter and tears. Strive to keep your emotional equilibrium. The spotlight is on a possible change of residence or marital status. Taurus, Libra, and another Scorpio are in the picture.

Tuesday, March 20 (Moon in Aquarius)   Play the waiting game, for time is on your side. Ignore a panicky individual who wants you to rush, trip, and fall. You learn secrets and, when you expound on them, people will think you are psychic. Don't tell all—keep them guessing. Pisces and Virgo play amazing roles.

Wednesday, March 21 (Moon in Aquarius)   For racing luck, try these selections at all tracks: Post position special—number 2 p.p. in the sixth race. Pick six: 1, 1, 2, 4, 5, 2. Watch for these letters in the names of potential winning horses or jockeys—H, Q, Z. Hot daily doubles: 1 and 1, 3 and 5, 2 and 8. Favorites will be in the money; Capricorn jockeys ride winners.

Thursday, March 22 (Moon in Aquarius to Pisces 12:27 a.m.)   Within 24 hours, the world will look brighter for you, for the moon will be in Pisces, your fifth house, that section of your horoscope relating to creative endeavors, a love relationship, and sex appeal. Reach beyond the immediate. You will be in full capacity when the stars favor you for success.

Friday, March 23 (Moon in Pisces)   On this Friday, you get what you have been asking for—a fair shake. Show off, paying attention to color coordination and showmanship. On a personal level, you will ooze sex appeal. Leo and Aquarius play sensational roles. Your lucky number is 1.

Saturday, March 24 (Moon in Pisces to Aries 11:42 a.m.)
What a Saturday night! You receive many proposals of business, partnership, and marriage. You'll experience more freedom of thought and action, so pursue creative projects. Let the right people be aware that you are

239

eager, talented, and sexual. Lucky lottery: 50, 7, 12, 18, 1, 19.

Sunday, March 25 (Moon in Aries)   Combine social activity with studies and interpretations of spiritual matters. Tonight, entertain and be entertained. Remember: To get a smile, give a smile! You should be in good humor, since earlier you received wonderful news. Gemini and Sagittarius play unorthodox roles.

Monday, March 26 (Moon in Aries to Taurus 8:49 p.m.)   The job gets done with invaluable help from Aries. Be generous in giving thanks! Taurus, Leo, and another Scorpio are also part of this exciting scenario. The puzzle pieces fall into place. The key is to properly interpret the pattern. An obstacle course will be cleared!

Tuesday, March 27 (Moon in Taurus)   The focus will be on change as you experience a variety of sensations and events. Your general health report is good, so keep resolutions about exercise, diet, and nutrition. A flirtation starts out as fun, but could become a burden. You might exclaim, "After all, it is time to say enough is enough!" Virgo is involved.

Wednesday, March 28 (Moon in Taurus)   The emphasis is on harmony, music, rhythm, and style. You will be dancing to your own tune and receiving compliments about your appearance and voice. A Libra declares, "You must come out of your emotional shell and show us the better side of your nature!" Your lucky number is 6.

Thursday, March 29 (Moon in Taurus to Gemini 4 a.m.)   Go slow, striving to make Taurus a friend, rather than a combatant. The spotlight is on publicity, public relations, legal affairs, and marriage. Pisces and Virgo, who play memorable roles today, have these letters in their names—G, P, Y. People comment, "There is something magical about you today!"

240

Friday, March 30 (Moon in Gemini)   Check facts and figures; proofread. Delve deep into mysteries. The answers will be found. You are back, and you're steady on your feet. A love relationship is rocky, but you will learn by tonight whether it is time to say, "Enough is enough!" Money is involved; indications are that you will successfully invest it.

Saturday, March 31 (Moon in Gemini to Cancer 9:21 a.m.)   On this Saturday, you meet someone who is steeped in the mantic arts and sciences, including astrology. Keep an open mind without being gullible. Your creative energy will be expressed, and you will be happy as a result. Aries is in the picture.

APRIL 2001

Sunday, April 1—Daylight Savings Time Begins (Moon in Cancer)   It might not be easy for others to fool you, but you could fall victim to self-deception. See people, places, and relationships as they exist, not merely as you wish they could be. Pisces and Virgo, who will play distinctive roles today, have these letters in their names—G, P, Y.

Monday, April 2 (Moon in Cancer to Leo 1:52 p.m.) There's plenty of contrast between today and yesterday. Your current cycle relates to business, career, and production, along with extra responsibility and more money. Cancer and Capricorn, who play astounding roles, could have these initials in their names—H, Q, Z. You'll have luck with the number 8.

Tuesday, April 3 (Moon in Leo)   For racing luck, try these selections at all tracks: Post position special— number 2 p.p. in the seventh race. Pick six: 5, 2, 8, 3, 4, 1. Watch for these letters in the names of potential winning horses or jockeys: I and R. Hot daily doubles: 5 and 2,

3 and 2, 1 and 4. Foreign jockeys and horses will be in the money.

Wednesday, April 4 (Moon in Leo to Virgo 3:45 p.m.)
Lucky lottery: 1, 4, 5, 22, 18, 40. What you aim for is achieved. You get to the heart of matters as you fall madly in love. A Leo is likely to be involved. Make a fresh start; dressing up your product and grabbing the publicity spotlight. Highlight your individuality over all else.

Thursday, April 5 (Moon in Virgo)   Questions and answers relate to marriage. Control your temper as you give serious thought to a variety of proposals. Take special care with your diet—what tastes extraordinarily good might not be good for you! Cancer and Capricorn try to play leading roles—and they will.

Friday, April 6 (Moon in Virgo to Libra 4:56 a.m.)
A celebration is due tonight. You win friends and influence due to the moon in your eleventh house. The Jupiter keynote helps things along, and when you get your way, it will be the right way. Elements of timing and luck ride with you. In matters of speculation, stick with the number 3.

Saturday, April 7 (Moon in Libra)   You are not neurotic! Someone has been following you, but they mean no harm. Taurus, Leo, another Scorpio, who figure prominently, could have these letters in their names—D, M, V. A very shy Libran approaches you, confessing, "I have been following you because I must talk to you!"

Sunday, April 8 (Moon in Libra to Scorpio 7:01 p.m.)
With the full moon in your twelfth house, you will find what the mystery is all about—and it turns out to be not as serious as it sounds. The spotlight is on the written word, short trips, visits, and a relative who is short of cash. Gemini and Virgo are very much in the picture.

Monday, April 9 (Moon in Scorpio)   On this Monday, you make peace with a family member. A gift presented to you is an art object or a special book. Express gratitude without being obsequious. You might wonder, "What now is expected from me?" The key is to be diplomatic and kind, making an intelligent concession without giving up your principles.

Tuesday, April 10 (Moon in Scorpio to Sagittarius 11:47 p.m.)   Time is on your side, so play the waiting game, refusing to equate delay with defeat. Use extra time to streamline your procedures and perfect your methods. Pisces and Virgo, who will play outstanding roles, have these letters in their names—G, P, Y. You will exude an aura of sex appeal.

Wednesday, April 11 (Moon in Sagittarius)   Lucky lottery: 8, 9, 17, 25, 26, 37. Within 24 hours, you learn that you have earned more than you originally anticipated—you could call this good news day! Things will appear to be changing all around you, including relationships. Capricorn plays a role.

Thursday, April 12 (Moon in Sagittarius)   The highlight of the day—you locate a valuable lost article! You receive a communication from someone residing in a foreign land. Blend a vacation journey with a business transaction. You'll be participating in an environmental conference. Aries and Libra will play amazing roles.

Friday, April 13 (Moon in Sagittarius to Capricorn 8:20 a.m.)   Your luck will improve; lost money will be found. Cash recently won can be used to multiply your winnings. Strive for an original approach, making personal appearances, wearing bright colors, and maintaining creative control. Leo is in this scenario.

Saturday, April 14 (Moon in Capricorn)   The emphasis is on partnership, cooperative efforts, and your marital status. A Cancer declares, "You need me in your life!" Don't take literally everything you hear. A stimulating clash of ideas takes place with Capricorn, but don't let it ruin your friendship. Your lucky number is 2.

Sunday, April 15 (Moon in Capricorn to Aquarius 8:10 p.m.) Spiritual values surface. Be open minded, not gullible. Experiment, explore, and strive to put across a variety of points that are not orthodox. Give full play to your intellectual curiosity without scattering your efforts. Add to your wardrobe and be sure to keep your resolutions about diet and exercise.

Monday, April 16 (Moon in Aquarius) On this Monday, you might find it difficult to get started. A relative appears determined not to let you sleep—go along with it because there probably is nothing else you can do. Taurus, Leo, and Capricorn, who figure in this scenario, have these initials in their names—D, M, V.

Tuesday, April 17 (Moon in Aquarius) The Aquarian moon relates to your fourth house, which means you'll be dealing with property and with sales and purchases. You recently displeased someone who has a long memory, and today you will hear about it. Be calm; keep your emotional equilibrium. Written material helps.

Wednesday, April 18 (Moon in Aquarius to Pisces 8:59 a.m.) For racing luck, try these selections at all tracks: Post position special—number 2 p.p. in the fourth race. Pick six: 2, 1, 3, 2, 5, 5. Watch for these letters in the names of potential winning horses or jockeys: F, O, X. Hot daily doubles: 2 and 1, 4 and 1, 3 and 3. Away from the track, you'll be concerned with domestic issues, including marriage and paychecks.

Thursday, April 19 (Moon in Pisces) The pace slows, but don't worry. Keep an aura of mystery and intrigue and refuse to tell all. Remember: Discretion is the better part of valor. You'll be told by someone who is usually shy, "You are so sexy that at times I have difficulty keeping my hands off you!"

Friday, April 20 (Moon in Pisces to Aries 8:16 p.m.)
The luck of Pisces will rub off on you. Practice restraint, Scorpio. Some people claim they are afraid of you because of your overly aggressive actions. Get ready for quick changes; keep your plans flexible. A different kind of love is on the horizon. A Cancer is involved.

Saturday, April 21 (Moon in Aries) The lunar position represents the beginning or ending of a serious relationship. It might be best to get away for a while—absence could cause the heart to grow fonder. A bit of abstinance would not hurt, either! Aries and Libra play featured roles. Your lucky number is 9.

Sunday, April 22 (Moon in Aries) The spotlight is on experimentation, so get in touch with yourself and prepare to make a fresh start in a new direction. You will at last know where you are going and what to do when you arrive at your destination. Leo and Aquarius figure in this scenario. Stick with the number 1.

Monday, April 23 (Moon in Aries to Taurus 4:55 a.m.)
The new moon is in your seventh house, which means there will be emphasis on cooperative efforts, partnership, and marriage. You reach a crossroads where your family pulls you one way while a love relationship pulls you in the other. As a Scorpio, you'll finally make up your own mind.

Tuesday, April 24 (Moon in Taurus) Today's scenario will include a clash of ideas, as well as signed agreements relating to your partnership and marital status. A Taurus says, "I don't always agree with you, but I love being with you!" Gemini and Sagittarius are also in this picture. Your fortunate number is 3.

Wednesday, April 25 (Moon in Taurus to Gemini 11:10 a.m.) Lie low and play the waiting game. You make a surprise discovery relating to money and your mate or partner. Taurus, Leo, and another Scorpio figure in this dramatic scenario. You will be playing a role you adore—a spy in the house of love.

Thursday, April 26 (Moon in Gemini) Check accounting. A computer might go haywire in your bank and mistakes may not be in your favor. Get ready for change, travel, and variety, and expect a sexual attraction to a coworker. Gemini, Virgo, and Sagittarius play instrumental roles.

Friday, April 27 (Moon in Gemini to Cancer 3:48 p.m.) Attention revolves around your home, family, music, and the purchase of a luxury item. A domestic adjustment relates to your income potential and your marital status. People you admire will say, "I like the sound of your voice!" A Libra declares, "You do have what it takes!" Your lucky number is 6.

Saturday, April 28 (Moon in Cancer) Pull away from those who take you for granted. Let go of a losing proposition. If you use your natural psychic instincts to read between the lines, a long-distance call will verify your beliefs. Serious discussions take place about life after death. Pisces is involved.

Sunday, April 29 (Moon in Cancer to Leo 7:24 p.m.) This is your power-play day! Your dream last night will prove prophetic, so take notes because tonight's dream will be even more so. An Aries does have your best interests at heart, but does not always show it. Capricorn and Cancer will also play major roles.

Monday, April 30 (Moon in Leo) Review yesterday's lessons and apply them tonight. You'll be musing, "I don't remember a Monday like this one!" You will be at the right place at a crucial moment, prompting some people to ask, "Why are you so lucky?" Your response: "I don't know all the answers, but astrology sure helps me!"

MAY 2001

Tuesday, May 1 (Moon in Leo to Virgo 10:15 p.m.) You'll be taking charge of your own fate as others depend on your veracity, leadership, and talents. People in high places will rely on your ability to get things done! On a personal level, a relationship that once sizzled will fizzle—but not for good. Capricorn is involved.

Wednesday, May 2 (Moon in Virgo)   Lucky lottery: 9, 5, 6, 20, 22, 19. Events are changing, even as you observe. Let people know, "I am here to stay, and I won't leave until I reach my goal." Reach beyond the immediate, opening the lines of communication and dealing gingerly with a foreign visitor.

Thursday, May 3 (Moon in Virgo)   On this Thursday, you meet new people. You yourself are physically attractive and your heart could be captured by someone of the opposite sex who has "come-hither" eyes. Leo and Aquarius, who play memorable roles, could have these letters in their names—A, S, J.

Friday, May 4 (Moon in Virgo to Libra 12:49 a.m.) The Virgo moon relates to your eleventh house, so you will have good fortune in finance and romance. It's a Friday to remember, as you prove successful at gaining funding for a unique project. Capricorn and Cancer, who play outstanding roles, have these initials in their names—B, K, T.

Saturday, May 5 (Moon in Libra)   Your social life accelerates—what a Saturday night! The Libra moon relates to your twelfth house, which is associated with glamour, intrigue, and deception. What was missing will

247

be located in an enclosed area, perhaps a closet. Your lucky number is 3.

Sunday, May 6 (Moon in Libra to Scorpio 4 a.m.)
Attention revolves around your home, living quarters, working space, earning power, and marital status. On this Sunday, you will find that Taurus, Leo, and another Scorpio, who play major roles, have these initials in their names—D, M, V. Suddenly, it will seem you are more skillful at solving crossword puzzles than in the recent past.

Monday, May 7 (Moon in Scorpio) It is a full moon in your sign. An important project is completed and you get the credit that in the past was denied to you. A flirtation is involved—be sure you know when to say, "Enough is enough." Gemini plays a top role.

Tuesday, May 8 (Moon in Scorpio to Sagittarius 9:05 a.m.) Attention revolves around your lifestyle, your home, your marital status, and your income potential. The cycle is such that you can be selective, choosing only the best. The moon appears to be smiling on you—where previously you failed, you now can succeed. A Taurus figures prominently.

Wednesday, May 9 (Moon in Sagittarius) Avoid self-deception. A male heartthrob is very much in the picture, acting in a seductive way. Make it plain who you are and what you do not intend to do. Pisces and Virgo, who figure in this scenario, could have these letters in their names—G, P, Y.

Thursday, May 10 (Moon in Sagittarius to Capricorn 5:09 p.m.) It's a powerful Thursday for you! The money seems to be rolling in! The Sagittarius moon is in your money house, enabling you to locate lost articles and to definitely improve your income potential. A Cancer will be involved.

Friday, May 11 (Moon in Capricorn) A short trip will involve a relative, bringing much talk about travel and foreign exchange rates. A journey could be tiring but stimulating. An Aries insists on being part of the scenario, apparently not believing that two is company and three is a crowd.

Saturday, May 12 (Moon in Capricorn) This could be a most romantic Saturday! A relative introduces you to someone who captivates you. Make a fresh start in a new direction, stressing originality and a spirit of adventure. Special note: Avoid heavy lifting. Leo and Aquarius figure in this scenario. Your lucky number is 1.

Sunday, May 13 (Moon in Capricorn to Aquarius 4:19 a.m.) On this Sunday, getting together with your family would be an excellent idea. To avoid fruitless arguments, make intelligent concessions but don't abandon your principles. Capricorn and Cancer, who play scintillating roles, have these letters in their names—B, K, T.

Monday, May 14 (Moon in Aquarius) Your popularity is on the rise. Today's scenario features entertaining and being entertained. Gemini and Sagittarius, who play meaningful roles, could have these initials in their names—C, L, U. Special: Remember resolutions about exercise, diet, and nutrition.

Tuesday, May 15 (Moon in Aquarius to Pisces 5 p.m.) You overcome numerous obstacles and test the solidity of goods. Attention will revolve around real estate, property, and sales and purchases. Check details, reading proofs and demonstrating that you can be thorough as well as passionate. Taurus, Leo, and another Scorpio make this a day you won't soon forget.

Wednesday, May 16 (Moon in Pisces) For racing luck, try these selections at all tracks: Post position special—number 3 p.p. in the second race. Pick six: 5, 3, 2, 2, 1, 8. Be alert for these letters in the names of potential winning horses or jockeys: E, N, W. Hot daily doubles: 5 and 3, 6 and 4, 1 and 8. Speed horses get out in front and stay there, paying longshot prices.

Thursday, May 17 (Moon in Pisces)   A gift is received—an art object or a luxury item. This helps beautify your surroundings, making your home more inviting. There's music in your life today; tonight, you dance to your own tune. The moon in Pisces in your fifth house equates to romance, sex, and love. Libra plays a role.

Friday, May 18 (Moon in Pisces to Aries 4:40 a.m.) You can afford to have your head in the clouds this Friday. The lunar position equates to thrills, excitement, creativity, and whispers of love! You might be asking, "Should I believe everything I hear, whispers or not?" You are shrewd enough, Scorpio, to decide for yourself.

Saturday, May 19 (Moon in Aries)   Come down to Earth! You will have more responsibility and will be financially rewarded as a result. Capricorn and Cancer will distinguish themselves in your life. Some people insist, "We know what is best for you!" If the truth be known, only you know what is best, so act accordingly.

Sunday, May 20 (Moon in Aries to Taurus 1:27 p.m.) The moon in Aries relates to your house of work, cooperation, basic issues, and health. Your spiritual values surface. A relationship is on the verge of ending, or a new one could be beginning. Give some time to the study of a foreign language.

Monday, May 21 (Moon in Taurus)   What a way to start a Monday! Put forth creative ideas, highlighting originality and studying love techniques. Leo and Aquarius, who figure prominently, could have these letters in their names—A, S, J. Leo helps you get ahead in your career. Aquarius reveals a secret.

Tuesday, May 22 (Moon in Taurus to Gemini 7:11 p.m.) A Cancer complains, "Lately, you never seem to have time for me!" Reply, "I parcel out my time as best I can!" The spotlight is on your home, security, and the serious consideration of your marital status. A Capricorn declares, "We have not taken a trip lately, so why not today?"

Wednesday, May 23 (Moon in Gemini) The new moon in Gemini relates to your eighth sector, which has much to do with accounting procedures, as well property to be divided between you and your partner or mate. Your interest in the occult will accelerate as you hunger for more knowledge. You'll have luck with the number 3.

Thursday, May 24 (Moon in Gemini to Cancer 10:41 p.m.) Avoid scattering forces—what you seek will be found, once you relieve the pressure on yourself. Another Scorpio, quite quixotic, enters your life and makes it more interesting. A Taurus engages you in a clash of ideas—very healthy! Leo is also in the picture.

Friday, May 25 (Moon in Cancer) Be aware of these keywords—change, travel, and variety. Your ego soars after a flirtation with someone you thought was unattainable. The written word is very important, so start a diary or write a love letter. Learn through the process of teaching others. Virgo is involved.

Saturday, May 26 (Moon in Cancer) Lucky lottery: 6, 16, 4, 40, 12, 18. Stick close to home, if possible. If you go away, as might be planned, you will be called back. Focus on art, literature, music, and moonlight. Taurus, Libra, and another Scorpio, who figure prominently, have these initials in their names—F, O, X.

Sunday, May 27 (Moon in Cancer to Leo 1:11 a.m.) Overcome a tendency to brood. Instead, transform this moody feeling into positive meditation. You will reflect on this Sunday as you look back and say,

"I'm glad I listened to my astrological guide; it would have done me no good to brood." Pisces is in the picture.

Monday, May 28 (Moon in Leo)   A big business deal is in the offing, so wash your face, brush your teeth, and get ready to play an instrumental role. Cancer and Capricorn, who figure in this scenario, have these letters in their names—H, Q, Z. The Cancer makes illuminating statements about foreign countries and how to break into their markets.

Tuesday, May 29 (Moon in Leo to Virgo 3:37 a.m.) Add showmanship and color coordination to your products. People in other lands are aware of you and your product, and they are willing to represent you. Don't stand still! You have not yet reached your potential. Aries and Libra will play dominating roles.

Wednesday, May 30 (Moon in Virgo)   Make a new start—renovate, rebuild, redecorate, and remodel. Wear bright colors, including yellow and gold and make personal appearances as you emerge from your recent emotional shell. Leo and Aquarius, who play outstanding roles, have these initials in their names—A, S, J. You will have luck with the number 1.

Thursday, May 31 (Moon in Virgo to Libra 6:40 a.m.) Join forces with Libra, Cancer, and Capricorn. Possessions are worth more than you originally anticipated. Don't permit Capricorn or Cancer to become jealous of each other—fair play is your best policy. In matters of speculation, stick with the number 2.

JUNE 2001

Friday, June 1 (Moon in Libra)   On this Friday, you get a premonition about a member of the opposite sex you will meet during a Saturday celebration. Someone, even as you read these words, could be arranging a blind date. Reach beyond the immediate; your life may be just beginning! Libra is in this picture.

Saturday, June 2 (Moon in Libra to Scorpio 10:56 a.m.) More attention needs to be given to your diet. Make a fresh start; take a chance on romance! Originality pays dividends, so be yourself, refusing to follow others. Avoid heavy lifting. Be receptive to gestures of friendship—give and receive smiles. Lucky lottery: 50, 12, 13, 14, 1, 17.

Sunday, June 3 (Moon in Scorpio) The moon in your sign coincides with elevation of spiritual values. Your judgment, intuition are on target. A family member suggests that prayer gets the results you seek. The emphasis is on food and survival. Share constructive thoughts over dinner with a Cancer. Capricorn will not be left out!

Monday, June 4 (Moon in Scorpio to Sagittarius 4:57 p.m.) Elements of timing and luck ride with you. You'll be musing, "I never thought Monday would be lucky for me, but it is!" Expect fun and frolic tonight, giving full play to your intellectual curiosity. You will meet a charming person with a marvelous sense of humor. Sagittarius is represented.

Tuesday, June 5 (Moon in Sagittarius) Be willing to tear down in order to rebuild. An invitation to travel is valid, so overcome obstacles relating to distance and language. Your natural intelligence and charm will surface. Taurus, Leo, and another Scorpio figure in today's fascinating scenario.

Wednesday, June 6 (Moon in Sagittarius) For racing luck, try these selections at all tracks: Post position special—number 2 p.p. in the second race. Pick six: 2, 2, 4, 3, 1, 8. Be alert for these letters in the names of potential winning horses or jockeys: E, N, W. Hot daily doubles: 2 and 2, 4 and 6, 1 and 7. Horses that get out in front will be in the money.

Thursday, June 7 (Moon in Sagittarius to Capricorn 1:23 a.m.) Attention revolves around decorating, remodeling, and even a possible change of residence. Listen to music, and try to learn more about the lives of legendary composers. Someone who flatters you wants something in exchange. Respond accordingly—you get nothing for nothing!

Friday, June 8 (Moon in Capricorn) The best-laid plans go awry, so have alternatives at hand. The element of deception is present—you were persuaded to sign an agreement that could be fraudulent on the face of it. Yell out for your rights! Pisces and Virgo play intimate roles. Your wishes will be fulfilled, so act accordingly.

Saturday, June 9 (Moon in Capricorn to Aquarius 12:19 p.m.) A powerful Saturday night! The Capricorn moon in your third house means dealings with relatives, trips, and a flirtation that is more serious than might be imagined. The word "responsibility" will pop up numerous times, and your career and business activities accelerate. Your lucky number is 8.

Sunday, June 10 (Moon in Aquarius) June is one-third over and you'll be thinking, "I certainly have made the most of this month!" Aries and Libra, who will play outstanding roles today, have these letters in their names—I and R. You will participate in political or charitable projects.

Monday, June 11 (Moon in Aquarius) A new deal is presented in connection with real estate, regarding the sale or purchase of property. Emphasize independence, originality, and courage. You will cut a dashing figure, and people will tell you so. A romantic interlude will prove to be much more. Leo plays a dramatic role.

Tuesday, June 12 (Moon in Aquarius to Pisces 12:52 a.m.) A crossroads! Decide whether to remain or to change the pattern of your life. An Aquarian is in the picture and, despite circumstances, will not leave. Joining Aquarius will be Cancer and Capricorn—you will need all the help you can get! A family get-together will bring positive results—and good food!

Wednesday, June 13 (Moon in Pisces) The Pisces moon relates to your fifth house, relating to children, challenge, change, variety, and sex appeal. You'll be saying, "Well, thirteen is turning out to be lucky for me!" Gemini and Sagittarius, who figure prominently, have these letters in their names—C, L, U.

Thursday, June 14 (Moon in Pisces to Aries 1:01 p.m.) You'll be saying, "I wish today could be like yesterday!" There are problems to face, but eventually, prior to the moon taking over for the sun, you will solve them. Taurus, Leo, and another Scorpio, who figure in this scenario, will have these initials in their names— D, M, V.

Friday, June 15 (Moon in Aries) Your health report is generally good. Focus on your work methods, and make a point of getting along with people who share your problems and efforts. Be ready for a change of plans. A member of the opposite sex, who intrigues you, says, "You fascinate me and I would do anything for you—and I mean *anything*!" Gemini is represented.

Saturday, June 16 (Moon in Aries to Taurus 10:37 p.m.) After the storm, expect calm, as you regain your emotional equilibrium. Like the weather, remain calm and you will be financially rewarded. Attend to that discomfort in your neck and head. Recall resolutions about exercise, diet, and nutrition—and go easy on alcohol. Lucky lottery: 14, 15, 3, 12, 6, 16.

Sunday, June 17 (Moon in Taurus) A marvelous Sunday! You are close to partnership and marriage. Within 24 hours, you'll be free to make creative decisions and to be selfish on your own behalf. Pisces and Virgo,

255

who will play significant roles, could have these letters in their names: G, P, Y.

Monday, June 18 (Moon in Taurus)   You'll make a remarkable comeback as you begin once again to realize your own strength. An older Capricorn declares, "You can be on my team anytime!" Your romantic life is regenerated—you muse, "Life can be beautiful after all!" Plant seeds that could grow into a successful enterprise.

Tuesday, June 19 (Moon in Taurus to Gemini 4:41 a.m.)   On this Tuesday, you could have luck with the number 19. If necessary, save it for tomorrow's lottery. Life takes a different turn for you; you will find that debts owed will be repaid and that favors you did will be returned threefold. Generosity is reciprocated.

Wednesday, June 20 (Moon in Gemini)   For racing luck, try these selections at all tracks: Post position special—number 7 p.p. in the third race. Pick six: 2, 3, 7, 4, 1, 9. Watch for these letters in the names of potential winning horses or jockeys: A, S, J. Hot daily doubles: 2 and 3, 4 and 6, 7 and 7. Leo jockeys have field day, winning photo finishes.

Thursday, June 21—Solar Eclipse (Moon in Gemini to Cancer 7:39 a.m.)   The new moon, solar eclipse, falls in Gemini, your eighth house. There's an abundance of activity in connection with hidden resources, mystery subjects, and sexual attraction. Expect anything but routine! Cancer and Capricorn, who play unusual roles, have these letters in their names—B, K, T.

Friday, June 22 (Moon in Cancer)   The light touch wins, and people will say you cannot win unless you put more into it. In fact, you are doing the right thing and adhering to your own Scorpio style. A Sagittarian is involved. In matters of speculation, these numbers will prove lucky for you: 3, 33, 19.

Saturday, June 23 (Moon in Cancer to Leo 8:54 p.m.)   The ninth-house influence equates to special studies, theology, and plans for a possible journey. Be cognizant of details, read proofs, revise, review, and rebuild. Another Scorpio impinges on your thoughts by declaring, "We do not need help from anyone!" Deception is involved.

Sunday, June 24 (Moon in Leo)   The focus is on authority, law, and leadership. Read and write; learn by teaching. What begins as a mild flirtation turns out to be more serious than you thought possible. Gemini, Virgo, and Sagittarius, who play outstanding roles, have these initials in their names—E, N, W.

Monday, June 25 (Moon in Leo to Virgo 9:57 a.m.) A thought that has been provoking challenge will be part of this fascinating Monday. You get results through writing. A telephone call will not do! A family member says, "I want to help you if you so permit!" Taurus, Libra, and another Scorpio figure in this exciting scenario.

Tuesday, June 26 (Moon in Virgo)   Slow your pace. Play the waiting game, for the first offer is absurdly low. Pisces and Virgo, who will play memorable roles, could have these letters in their names—G, P, Y. You're drawn in two directions, one involving fantasy and the other ultra-materialism. Your ship comes in!

Wednesday, June 27 (Moon in Virgo to Libra 12:10 p.m.)   The Virgo moon relates to your eleventh house, which in turn is associated with the fulfillment of your hopes and wishes. You'll be rewarded for what you wrote as you receive critical applause from many areas. This can be a rewarding, marvelous, creative, and profitable day for you. Your lucky number is 8.

Thursday, June 28 (Moon in Libra)   Your cycle will be completed, perhaps to your advantage. Someone is sneaking up on you, so be alert, aware, and ready to fight if the cause is right. The moon in your twelfth house relates to hospitals, institutions, and secret plans. Visit a friend who has been incarcerated. All a mistake!

Friday, June 29 (Moon in Libra to Scorpio 4:28 p.m.)   Elements of luck ride with you. What had been dark will receive the benefit of more light. Imprint your style, letting others follow you and refusing to follow them. Avoid heavy lifting and don't break too many hearts! Make personal appearances as you emerge from your emotional shell. Wear blends of yellow and gold.

Saturday, June 30 (Moon in Scorpio)   On this last day of June, the moon will be in your sign for luck, timing, and reward! Designate where the action will be; follow through on your hunches. You might be psychic—things come true just as you predict them. Cancer and Capricorn play exciting roles. Your fortunate number is 2.

JULY 2001

Sunday, July 1 (Moon in Scorpio to Sagittarius 11:13 p.m.)   What a Sunday! The moon is in your sign and it's a number-one cycle. Stress independence and the courage of your convictions. Leo and Aquarius, who play sensational roles in your life today, could have these letters in their names—A, S, J. Special: Avoid heavy lifting, if possible.

Monday, July 2 (Moon in Sagittarius)   A family get-together on this Monday! Arguments concerning money will be peaceably settled. Be receptive, making intelligent concessions without abandoning your principles. Capricorn and Cancer, who play meaningful roles, have these letters in their names—B, K, T.

Tuesday, July 3 (Moon in Sagittarius)   Fun and frolic are featured! You obviously have something to celebrate—something that makes you happy. The moon will be in your money house, so you feel a heavy burden has been lifted. Use your common sense about the stock market. Your lucky number is 3.

Wednesday, July 4 (Moon in Sagittarius to Capricorn 8:21 a.m.)   Open the lines of communication! You will receive more calls than during June. Taurus, Leo, and another Scorpio will be with you to celebrate the holiday. Compared to past holidays celebrating the nation's birthday, this year's will be very special.

Thursday, July 5—Lunar Eclipse (Moon in Capricorn) The full moon, lunar eclipse in Capricorn, is in your third house. Relatives who have been squabbling over petty issues will rely on you to settle the dispute. Avoid traveling in traffic if possible. Danger from firecrackers left over from yesterday will figure prominently.

Friday, July 6 (Moon in Capricorn to Aquarius 7:32 p.m.)   A stubborn Capricorn relative will pay you meaningful compliments. Do not sugar-coat the truth— say what you mean and mean what you say. Career questions will arise. Attention revolves around your family, home, and a possible change of residence or marital status.

Saturday, July 7 (Moon in Aquarius)   Go slow; play the waiting game. See people, places, and relationships in a realistic light. Define your terms, using extrasensory perception to serve as a reliable guide. Keep writing material at your bedside to write down your dreams as soon as you awake. Pisces plays a significant role.

Sunday, July 8 (Moon in Aquarius)   This will be like no other Sunday! Your residence could be the center of a family gathering. Discussions revolve around the sale or purchase of property, security, or insurance. Capricorn and Cancer, who will play leading roles, have these letters in their names—H, Q, Z.

Monday, July 9 (Moon in Aquarius to Pisces 8:04 a.m.)   The moon is leaving Aquarius and will enter Pisces tomorrow. Meantime, be receptive to a new, different kind of love. If you are single, you could meet your soulmate. If you're married, you rediscover your spouse in mental, emotional, and sexual ways. Aries plays the top role.

Tuesday, July 10 (Moon in Pisces)   You have been waiting for this day! If you focus on creativity and style, you will exude personal magnetism, an aura of sensuality, and sex appeal. Don't break too many hearts! Keep your plans flexible and be ready for change, travel, and a variety of sensations and experiences.

Wednesday, July 11 (Moon in Pisces to Aries 8:34 p.m.)   For racing luck, try these selections at all tracks: Post position special—number 6 p.p. in the fifth race. Pick six: 4, 8, 2, 2, 6, 4. Be alert for these letters in the names of potential winning horses or jockeys: B, K, T. Hot daily doubles: 4 and 8, 3 and 3, 2 and 6. Local jockeys born under Cancer will win photo finishes.

Thursday, July 12 (Moon in Aries)   Highlight diversity, versatility, and intellectual curiosity. A flirtation that became too hot to handle will fade. Gemini and Sagittarius, who play unusual roles, have these letters in their names—C, L, U. An invitation from a Sagittarian is intended to serve as a peace offering.

Friday, July 13 (Moon in Aries)   This could be a lucky day for you! Someone who turned down an offer you made five days ago will now gladly accept. You will muse, "Well, Friday the thirteenth has not been a jinx for me—it actually has turned around my luck and I feel very good about it!"

Saturday, July 14 (Moon in Aries to Taurus 7:12 a.m.) Lucky lottery: 5, 1, 9, 15, 16, 47. A good health report will come your way. Working conditions improve. You'll meet someone of the opposite sex who provides inspiration. Gemini, Virgo, and Sagittarius, who play roles, will have these letters in their names—E, N, W.

Sunday, July 15 (Moon in Taurus)   Focus on harmony and domestic tranquility. Serious discussions will revolve around partnership, legal agreements, public relations, and marriage. A Taurus with money will state, "With you, all things could be bright, and all you have to do is say yes."

Monday, July 16 (Moon in Taurus to Gemini 2:23 p.m.)   At a big sporting event, you are asked to pick winner. Choose a boxer or team with these letters in their names—G, P, Y. Some will accuse you of being psychic. Respond: "I am not psychic; I am just a good judge of horseflesh, boxers, and teams!"

Tuesday, July 17 (Moon in Gemini)   An exciting day! A mystery is solved and you get the credit you deserve. Check computers; some might go out of order, which is reflected in your bank account and credit card costs. Capricorn and Cancer will play prominent roles today.

Wednesday, July 18 (Moon in Gemini to Cancer 5:55 p.m.)   Lucky lottery: 15, 9, 24, 35, 44, 16. Strive for universal appeal; learn at least the rudiments of a foreign language. Find out more about the country you could visit in the near future. Aries and Libra, who will play stunning roles, have these initials in their names— I and R.

Thursday, July 19 (Moon in Cancer)   Literature received encourages you to visit Australia or Ireland—or both. Reach beyond the immediate to find that your assets and debits coincide universally with people in other lands. Leo and Aquarius play dominant roles. Your lucky number is 1.

Friday, July 20 (Moon in Cancer to Leo 6:42 p.m.)
The new moon in Cancer represents your house of learning. Be generous, willing to make intelligent concessions in any dispute. Capricorn and Cancer, who play roles, could have these letters in their names—B, K, T. Money owed to you will be paid.

Saturday, July 21 (Moon in Leo)   For racing luck, try these selections at all tracks: Post position special—number 5 p.p. in the seventh race. Pick six: 5, 2, 3, 1, 8, 6. Watch for these letters in the names of potential winning horses or jockeys: C, L, U. Hot daily doubles: 5 and 2, 6 and 6, 3 and 7. Upset winners with Sagittarian jockeys aboard will pay long-shot prices.

Sunday, July 22 (Moon in Leo to Virgo 6:28 p.m.)   A canceled appointment will ultimately work to your advantage. Improve your presentations, blending humor with the hard facts of life. At least two people will ask you how to improve their lovemaking. Make it clear that instructions in lovemaking are not your forte. Taurus is involved.

Monday, July 23 (Moon in Virgo)   Give full play to your curiosity to help you uncover a kink and remove it. An expression of gratitude could come in the form of a bonus. You'll reflect, "This is one Monday I won't soon forget!" Gemini, Virgo, and Sagittarius play astonishing roles.

Tuesday, July 24 (Moon in Virgo to Libra 7:07 p.m.)
What had been mixed up will fall into place, bringing happiness and emotional equilibrium. Attention revolves around your home, security, and music. Taurus, Libra, and another Scorpio, who play exciting roles, have these letters in their names—F, O, X.

Wednesday, July 25 (Moon in Libra)   Lucky lottery: 7, 14, 6, 12, 13, 18. If you're patient, you win, just by waiting for your selection to show up. Define your terms and outline your boundaries. A real estate transaction could be profitable for you. A secret is revealed; keep it to yourself! Discretion is truly the better part of valor.

Thursday, July 26 (Moon in Libra to Scorpio 10:17 p.m.)   Your cycle gradually moves up—today, plant the seeds of a project that could grow big-time. Focus on production, promotion, and funding. Capricorn and Cancer, who play outstanding roles, could have these letters in their names—H, Q, Z. Your lucky number is 8.

Friday, July 27 (Moon in Scorpio)   The aphorism will be proven that two is company and three is a crowd. Find privacy with a loved one, so that you can whisper sweet nothings. The moon is in your sign and you can specify where the action will be. Aries is involved.

Saturday, July 28 (Moon in Scorpio to Sagittarius 4:44 a.m.)   Your cycle is high, so take the initiative, displaying the courage of your convictions. Inventions are featured and the funding you need can be obtained if you clearly write your objectives and your plans for promotion. Avoid heavy lifting if possible. You could hear these words: "Your lovemaking has shown marked improvement!"

Sunday, July 29 (Moon in Sagittarius)   The puzzle pieces fall into place, especially regarding your family, home, or a business enterprise. A Cancer takes the lead in becoming a valuable ally. A long-distance communication verifies your views. Dinner tonight will be sumptuous. You'll say, "This is superb!"

Monday, July 30 (Moon in Sagittarius)   This could be your lucky day! Pick winners, discarding losers. Maintain your high standards as you follow your intuition. A librarian proves helpful and is physically attracted to you. Gemini and Sagittarius figure in this scenario. Your fortunate number is 3.

Tuesday, July 31 (Moon in Sagittarius to Capricorn 2:16 p.m.)   The last day of July! You locate lost articles and find ways to increase your income potential. Don't force issues—what you seek and need will be handed you on a silver platter! Taurus, Leo, and another Scorpio, who play meaningful roles, have these initials in their names—D, M, V.

AUGUST 2001

Wednesday, August 1 (Moon in Capricorn)   Get started on a new enterprise or creative endeavor. You will be dealing with temperamental people who are original thinkers. Cancer and Capricorn, who play instrumental roles in your life today, could have these letters in their names—B, K, T.

Thursday, August 2 (Moon in Capricorn)   Diversify, highlighting your versatility and intellectual curiosity, and gaining greater knowledge about exercise, diet, and nutrition. Questions about a partnership or marriage loom large. Social activities on this Thursday provide surprises and inspiration. You will hear many compliments.

Friday, August 3 (Moon in Capricorn to Aquarius 1:52 a.m.)   The moon is leaving Capricorn and, within 24 hours, will be in Aquarius, your fourth house. This relates to property value, building material, and a chance to meet the right people. Taurus, Leo, and another Scorpio, who figure prominently, have these letters in their names—D, M, V.

Saturday, August 4 (Moon in Aquarius)   The full moon is tonight. A property transaction could be completed. It's a very romantic night, if you are with the right person—and Gemini, Virgo, and Sagittarius will be among the right persons. It's an excellent day for teaching, reading, writing, and expressing your feelings. Your lucky number is 5.

Sunday, August 5 (Moon in Aquarius to Pisces 2:29 p.m.)   Look back to events that happened 24 hours ago for a valuable hint. Attention revolves around your home, domestic issues, the protection of your family, and the expansion of your interests. People comment on your voice, encouraging you to proceed with lessons.

Monday, August 6 (Moon in Pisces)   Monday gets off to slow start, but later in the day, you receive news that acts as a stimulus. You will experience mystery and sexual intrigue. A young person will confess an indiscretion. Give your opinion and counsel without appearing to be a know-it-all.

Tuesday, August 7 (Moon in Pisces)   What a Tuesday! Today's cycle features children, challenge, variety, and the opportunity for big money. Capricorn and Cancer, who play leading roles, will have these letters in their names—H, Q, Z. In matters of speculation, stick with the number 8.

Wednesday, August 8 (Moon in Pisces to Aries 3:03 a.m.)   For racing luck, try these selections at all tracks: Post position special—number 1 p.p. in the eighth race. Pick six: 8, 7, 1, 4, 3, 5. Watch for these letters in the names of potential winning horses or jockeys: I and R. Hot daily doubles: 8 and 7, 7 and 1, 1 and 1. A foreign horse does very well, especially with a Leo jockey aboard.

Thursday, August 9 (Moon in Aries)   Make a fresh start in a new direction, looking into prices and other details concerning your journey abroad. Events today could make you a celebrity. Leo and Aquarius, who play meaningful roles, could have these initials in their names—A, S, J. Your lucky number is 1.

Friday, August 10 (Moon in Aries to Taurus 2:21 p.m.)   On this Friday, relatives might seem to be popping up out of nowhere! Either stay home with them or take them with you on your Friday-night adventure. Capricorn and Cancer, who play prominent roles, have these letters in their names—B, K, T.

Saturday, August 11 (Moon in Taurus) Whatever you do this Saturday night, be careful what you start, because you will be around at the finish, facing the consequences. Gemini and Sagittarius, who play outstanding roles, have these letters in their names—C, L, U. Expect to have luck with the number 3.

Sunday, August 12 (Moon in Taurus to Gemini 10:56 p.m.) On this Sunday, expect a change of routine. Humor will dominate any gathering. People comment on your appearance and the additions to your wardrobe. Forces tend to be scattered, as you tear down in order to rebuild. Taurus, Leo, and another Scorpio are involved.

Monday, August 13 (Moon in Gemini) On this Monday, before the moon takes over from the sun, you receive many proposals—mostly relating to business and career partnership and to your marital status. Get ready for change, travel, and variety, and expect to have luck with the number 5. Within 24 hours, many pressures will be relieved.

Tuesday, August 14 (Moon in Gemini) Maintain an aura of mystery, remembering that discretion truly is the better part of valor. The focus will be on accounting, budgeting, and bank accounts. If something goes wrong with your computer, you have a perfect right to ask questions. Some people accuse you of being in the playground of the occult.

Wednesday, August 15 (Moon in Gemini to Cancer 3:53 a.m.) Lucky lottery: 15, 6, 5, 25, 13, 12. Money plays an important role, so discuss business practices with a Gemini who seeks your hand in partnership. Don't attempt to skirt the law, because this is not a particularly good day for doing that. Follow the rules!

Thursday, August 16 (Moon in Cancer) On this Thursday, you will know exactly where you are and how far you are from your ultimate goal. Make inquiries, giving full play to your intellectual curiosity. Travel is involved. Financial investments are due to pay dividends. If you're interested in the stock market, look for steel to make a comeback.

Friday, August 17 (Moon in Cancer to Leo 5:24 a.m.) You are close to completion; already you gain recognition as a courageous person. As a Scorpio, you make a deep impression. You dig deep for information and what you find will surprise you. Aries and Libra will play fascinating roles.

Saturday, August 18 (Moon in Leo) Saturday night excitement! Almost anything you touch feels good. You help people make a fresh start in a new direction, and you could be fatally attracted to a dynamic Leo. An Aquarius also plays a major role today; both Leo and Aquarius have these initials in names—A, S, J. Your lucky number is 1.

Sunday, August 19 (Moon in Leo to Virgo 4:52 a.m.) The new moon is in Leo on this Sunday, which relates to property, where you live, and your marital status. The tenth-house Leo moon compels you to review business, career, and promotions. Use your sense of showmanship and color coordination, and put your skills in advertising and publicity to work.

Monday, August 20 (Moon in Virgo) A pleasant Monday is due—the moon in Virgo represents your eleventh house, which sharpens your skill at collecting funding and making wishes come true. You might receive an award for something you have written and could receive an assignment to write about a fascinating subject.

Tuesday, August 21 (Moon in Virgo to Libra 4:18 a.m.) Details could mean the difference between success and failure, so proofread, checking subtle nuances in your search for the truth. What appeared impossible 36 hours ago can now be handled with aplomb. You will be regarded as exemplifying a success story.

Wednesday, August 22 (Moon in Libra)   Your recent good fortune in finance and romance buoys your confidence. You feel good. What was difficult will come easy today. Mercury-ruled people play roles, and Gemini and Virgo, who figure prominently, have these letters in their names—E, N, W. Stick with the number 5.

Thursday, August 23 (Moon in Libra to Scorpio 5:49 a.m.)   Be patient and diplomatic. The moon in your twelfth house represents institutions, hospitals, and the need to visit a loved one temporarily confined to home. Try singing in the shower; someone could notice or hear and you could be on your way! Libra is involved.

Friday, August 24 (Moon in Scorpio)   Go slow. Play the waiting game. People seek to intrigue you, but their motives are questionable. Make it crystal clear that you want nothing to do with a get-rich-quick scheme. You wonder, "What is it about me that attracts these people?" Pisces and Virgo figure in this scenario.

Saturday, August 25 (Moon in Scorpio to Sagittarius 10:59 a.m.)   A powerful Saturday night! The moon is in Scorpio, your sign, which represents your high cycle. Even as you read these lines, circumstances turn in your favor. The spotlight is on your personality and appearance, and something tonight about you that adds up to sex appeal. Your lucky number is 8.

Sunday, August 26 (Moon in Sagittarius)   Spiritual values surface. Events take place in a way that adds to income. People who formerly were wary of you will now trust you completely. Look beyond the immediate; make travel plans. Aries and Libra will play top roles.

Monday, August 27 (Moon in Sagittarius to Capricorn 8:01 p.m.)   Illuminate areas previously dark. Leo and Aquarius, who will play dramatic roles, have these letters in their names—A, S, J. Focus on independence and originality, and display your pioneering spirit. By tonight, you locate a valuable article that you lost 24 hours ago.

Tuesday, August 28 (Moon in Capricorn)   The spotlight is on your partnership and marriage, and on home buying or selling. Capricorn and Cancer, who figure prominently, will have these letters in their names—B, K, T. A Cancer, much attracted to you, states: "If only I could keep up with you, we might make a life together!"

Wednesday, August 29 (Moon in Capricorn)   For racing luck try these selections at all tracks: Post position special—number 7 p.p. in the third race. Pick six: 1, 2, 7, 5, 6, 2. Watch for these letters in the names of potential winning horses or jockeys: C, L, U. Hot daily doubles: 1 and 2, 2 and 7, 3 and 5. Long shots win; Sagittarian jockeys shine.

Thursday, August 30 (Moon in Capricorn to Aquarius 7:47 a.m.)   Taurus, Capricorn, and another Scorpio, who figure prominently, have these initials in their names—D, M, V. The puzzle pieces fall into place. Follow a pattern in order to gain enlightenment. You overcome obstacles relating to distance and language. Questions concern cosmetics.

Friday, August 31 (Moon in Aquarius)   On this last day of August, your views are verified via a long-distance call. Results are puzzling, but add up to good news. Focus on discovery, and on creative projects that include written material. The letters E, N, and W will appear in the names of persons playing special roles today.

Saturday, September 1 (Moon in Aquarius to Pisces 8:31 p.m.) Celebrate the first day of the month and the fact that the moon is in Aquarius, your fourth house. The number 3, with the Jupiter keynote means that your demeanor will be pleasant. People might even comment, "You look like you're feeling good today!" Enjoy yourself!

Sunday, September 2 (Moon in Pisces) The full moon is in Pisces, your fifth house, that section of your horoscope that relates to sexiness. It's a number 4, Pluto day, when you do things that narrowly escape the eyes of the law. Be near water, if possible. People are drawn to you; you might ask, "Do you sense something different about me?"

Monday, September 3 (Moon in Pisces) Be prepared for a quick change of plans involving trips, visits, and a variety of experiences. You will be musing, "This is not like any other Monday that I have experienced!" It's an excellent day for writing, reading, and teaching, and for expressing your true feelings. Your lucky number is 5.

Tuesday, September 4 (Moon in Pisces to Aries 8:57 a.m.) Young people you meet today will be independent and living out on their own. Taurus, Leo, and another Scorpio, who will figure prominently, could have these letters in their names—F, O, X. The accent is on art objects, luxury items, and music like you never heard before—it could even spark a new interest or hobby.

Wednesday, September 5 (Moon in Aries) Your vitality and vigor make a dramatic comeback. Get to know yourself! A period of introspection will be positive. Pisces and Virgo, who will play major roles today, could have these letters in their names—G, P, Y. Lucky lottery: 7, 13, 14, 12, 22, 18.

Thursday, September 6 (Moon in Aries to Taurus 8:16 p.m.)   A powerful Thursday! You feel good because you are doing something creative that suits your temperament and fulfills a major part of your ambitions. Capricorn and Cancer, who play important roles, could have these initials in their names—H, Q, Z. Invest in a business of your own.

Friday, September 7 (Moon in Taurus)   Time might appear to crawl, so get a handle on your personal rhythm. A project can be completed if you so desire, leading to more recognition and opening the doors of fame and fortune. Brush up on a foreign language; be with people who appreciate and perhaps love you.

Saturday, September 8 (Moon in Taurus)   Make a fresh start; the love spark will be rekindled. The spotlight is on legal affairs, public relations, partnership, and marriage. What seemed far away will now appear to be close—perhaps too close for comfort. Leo and Aquarius will play interesting roles. You will have luck with the number 1.

Sunday, September 9 (Moon in Taurus to Gemini 5:40 a.m.)   Make a decision in connection with your home or a creative project. A Cancer declares, "I could help you along the road of life, if you would so permit!" Remember karma and, at the very least, offer tea and sympathy. A Sunday-night dinner would fit the bill.

Monday, September 10 (Moon in Gemini)   Your forces are scattered; you will be versatile but likely to overlook important details. Gemini and Sagittarius, who play memorable roles, have these letters in their names—C, L, U. Give full play to your intellectual curiosity—you will locate lost objects.

Tuesday, September 11 (Moon in Gemini to Cancer 12:07 p.m.)   Take notice of this phenomenon when it occurs—Scorpio and another Sagittarius, who play major roles, could have these letters in their names—D, M, V. A missing locket will be located, causing you to wonder, "Why didn't I remember that I put it there?" Revise, review, and rewrite.

Wednesday, September 12 (Moon in Cancer)   If you did what you were supposed to do yesterday, you will feel very good today. Tear down in order to rebuild, and exude an aura of personal magnetism, sensuality and sex appeal. What at first seems out of place will eventually look just right. Lucky lottery: 5, 15, 21, 34, 6, 12.

Thursday, September 13 (Moon in Cancer to Leo 3:14 p.m.)   There's music in your life. You will be courted by a Libran who declares, "I would rather be with you than anyone else in the world!" The music plays, so dance to your own tune. It's an excellent day for viewing furniture and deciding how you want your home to look. Your lucky number is 6.

Friday, September 14 (Moon in Leo)   The moon in Leo equates to that section of your horoscope associated with promotion, production, career, and leadership. Define your plans, looking behind the scenes for answers. Refuse to be discouraged by someone who is a human wet blanket. Maintain an aura of mystery.

Saturday, September 15 (Moon in Leo to Virgo 3:38 p.m.)   Accent showmanship, color coordination, and an advertising or publicity campaign. People who at first said you could not do it will now be red faced. It turns out that you can do just about anything you say you can. Cancer and Capricorn will play intricate roles.

Sunday, September 16 (Moon in Virgo)   Participate in charitable or political activities. More than one person asks, "Why don't you run for office—you could do better than the other candidate?" Stress universal appeal, studying another language and the customs of people who live in foreign lands.

272

Monday, September 17 (Moon in Virgo to Libra 2:59 p.m.) Make a fresh start in a different direction, which will be necessary if you want to make progress. A new, different kind of love is on the horizon. Take a chance on romance! Leo and Aquarius, who play major roles in your life today, have these letters in their names—A, S, J.

Tuesday, September 18 (Moon in Libra) You did not keep your promise about diet and drinking—you will learn tonight that it does not pay to try to fool Mother Nature. Questions about marriage continue to loom large. Rehearse an answer or, better yet, write one and make duplicates, so you can hand them out when questions arise.

Wednesday, September 19 (Moon in Libra to Scorpio 3:27 p.m.) For racing luck, try these selections at all tracks: Post position special—number 5 p.p. in the seventh race. Pick six: 5, 7, 3, 9, 8, 4. Watch for these letters in the names of potential winning horses or jockeys: C, L, U. Hot daily doubles: 5 and 7, 6 and 3, 7 and 1. Longshot prices are featured; Sagittarian jockeys win photo finishes.

Thursday, September 20 (Moon in Scorpio) Refuse to be intimidated by a know-it-all. Your personal cycle is high, so designate where the action will be. Wear varying colors of green, from lime to emerald. Taurus, Leo, and another Scorpio, who play prominent roles, could have these letters in their names—D, M, V.

Friday, September 21 (Moon in Scorpio to Sagittarius 7:02 p.m.) The outcome of questions concerning your life and loves will be positive. A short trip is involved, which could be the result of a serious flirtation. You might hear these words: "I would do anything for you except love you again!" You will long remember this Friday in a happy way!

Saturday, September 22 (Moon in Sagittarius) The moon is in your money house, helping you locate a valuable object that appeared to be lost. An excellent day for increasing your income potential! What seemed like a lost cause will again be alive and kicking, giving you a second chance. Do it right this time! Your lucky number is 6.

Sunday, September 23 (Moon in Sagittarius) Spiritual values surface. The lunar position promises excellent results where money, investments are concerned. If you maintain your ethical standards, you cannot lose. Pisces and Virgo, who will play special roles, could have these letters in their names—G, P, Y.

Monday, September 24 (Moon in Sagittarius to Capricorn 2:48 a.m.) A promise made to you three months ago in an off-handed way could be fulfilled tonight. Remember what Jung said: Dreams can be our guideposts to the future. Take notes of your dreams upon awakening. Your past comes rushing up, containing lessons that help your future.

Tuesday, September 25 (Moon in Capricorn) A project is completed! The moon in Capricorn, in your third house, relates to ideas that click. Finish what you start, and try to become active in political or charitable campaigns. Aries and Libra, who play outstanding roles, have these letters in their names—I and R.

Wednesday, September 26 (Moon in Capricorn to Aquarius 2:04 p.m.) Lucky lottery: 26, 42, 12, 18, 7, 3. Make a fresh start, communicating with a relative who honestly feels that you are the only person who can help resolve a dilemma. A new love is on the horizon. If you are married, you rediscover your spouse in an emotional, mental, and physical way.

Thursday, September 27 (Moon in Aquarius) Don't attempt to please everyone—it won't work! The emphasis is on cooperative efforts, love, and marriage. The spotlight is on the value of property, remodeling, refurbishing, and getting ready to present a powerful sales pitch. Focus on food and conviviality, exercising self-restraint in connection with alcoholic beverages.

Friday, September 28 (Moon in Aquarius) The moon is in Aquarius, your fourth house, which equates to property, building, and a tedious job that must be done. Proofread and discover a mistake that could prove embarrassing and costly. Gemini and Sagittarius, who play significant roles today, have these initials in their names—C, L, U.

Saturday, September 29 (Moon in Aquarius to Pisces 2:49 a.m.) The lunar aspect coincides with subtle hints of sexuality. Someone attracted to you might do nothing for you. Taurus, Leo, and another Scorpio figure prominently. You could feel closed in—but this feeling will be only temporary. You'll have luck with the number 4.

Sunday, September 30 (Moon in Pisces) It's the last day of the month, with a number 5 keynote and the moon in Pisces, your fifth house. Today's scenario will be occupied by children and games of chance that rely on your intuitive intellect. Spiritual values are featured. Figure out why you are here and what you are doing about it.

OCTOBER 2001

Monday, October 1 (Moon in Pisces to Aries 3:06 p.m.) If you attempt to analyze this day, you will be puzzled. With a Pisces moon being in your fifth house, you exude personal magnetism, sensuality, and sex appeal. Imprint your style, refusing to follow others but letting them follow you, if they so desire. Wake Pisces!

Tuesday, October 2 (Moon in Aries)   The full moon in Aries equates to general health, working conditions, and your ability to resolve a dilemma that has haunted you for months. Gemini, Virgo, and Sagittarius, who play outstanding roles, are likely to have these letters in their names—E, N, W. Your lucky number is 5.

Wednesday, October 3 (Moon in Aries)   For racing luck, try these selections at all tracks: Post position special—number 2 p.p. in the fourth race. Pick six: 4, 1, 2, 2, 3, 8. Watch for these letters in the names of potential wining horses or jockeys: F, O, X. Hot daily doubles: 4 and 1, 4 and 2, 3 and 2. Home-grown jockeys will be in the money.

Thursday, October 4 (Moon in Aries to Taurus 1:59 a.m.)   People jump out of their categories. More persons will be on the move than in previous weeks, so deal with the unorthodox in as natural way as possible. Pisces and Virgo, who play outstanding roles, could have these letters in their names—G, P, Y.

Friday, October 5 (Moon in Taurus)   A money day for you! Legal affairs, public relations, and your marital status will all figure prominently. Deal gingerly with Cancer or Capricorn. Legal questions arise. An older person takes you into confidence and declares, "I believe you have the makings of success, and I'm with you all the way!"

Saturday, October 6 (Moon in Taurus to Gemini 11:10 a.m.)   Finish what you start, opening the lines of communication to overcome distance and language difficulties. Aries and Libra, who will play outstanding roles today, could have these letters in their names—I and R. Aries asserts, "I wish I could be with you longer."

Sunday, October 7 (Moon in Gemini)   Make yourself available! People want to see you and they have good news to relate. Imprint your style and stress your individuality. Whatever you do, do it with enthusiasm. Expect to be lectured to by Leo and Aquarius. Avoid heavy lifting, if possible.

Monday, October 8 (Moon in Gemini to Cancer 6:18 p.m.)   Expect a gourmet dinner tonight. A Cancer will do the cooking. Avoid a jealous rift. You'll be asked for a favor. What appeared to be long ago and far away will actually be at your doorstep. Know it, and be ready to take advantage of this knowledge. Your lucky number is 2.

Tuesday, October 9 (Moon in Cancer)   Take advantage of your intellectual curiosity—if you ask the right questions, you will get the answers you seek. Gemini and Sagittarius, who figure prominently, will have these letters in their names—C, L, U. You will receive calls relating to travel.

Wednesday, October 10 (Moon in Cancer to Leo 10:52 p.m.)   For you, this could be a day to embark on a journey. People express a desire to be with you, to travel with you, to dine with you, and make love with you. A relationship that was moribund will come back to life in a lively, stunning way. Another Scorpio is involved.

Thursday, October 11 (Moon in Leo)   Be ready for challenge, change, and a variety of sensations and experiences. Read and write, and learn through the process of teaching. Gemini, Virgo, and Sagittarius, who play leading roles, have these letters in their names—E, N, W. You'll have luck with the number 5.

Friday, October 12 (Moon in Leo)   There's music in your life, along with furniture arrangement, decorating, and remodeling. A domestic adjustment could include where you live or your marital status. A dispute is quickly settled, once you realize it is all about money. You receive a gift of an art object, which helps beautify your surroundings.

Saturday, October 13 (Moon in Leo to Virgo 12:56 a.m.)
Striving to understand the needs of a loved one could be
a gigantic task. Be receptive, go with the flow, and see
people and places and relationships in correct focus. You
will not be easy to fool, but you could be the victim of
self-deception. Lucky lottery: 7, 25, 16, 1, 12, 18.

Sunday, October 14 (Moon in Virgo)   Many of your
hopes and desires could come to fruition. The Virgo
moon in your eleventh house means that what you want
you can get—so be ready for it. This moon represents
reading material as well as good fortune in matters of
speculation. Your lucky numbers: 5, 6, 13, 22.

Monday, October 15 (Moon in Virgo to Libra 1:25 a.m.)
Stress universal appeal as you overcome distance and
language obstacles. People confide their most intimate
problems and expect you to come up with solutions. First
of all, don't blush so easily. Strive to understand the
subtleties of people from other lands.

Tuesday, October 16 (Moon in Libra)   Continue
knocking on the doors of fame and fortune. This time,
you could get an answer! Light will be shed on areas
previously dark. Let in fresh air and knowledge. Those
who said it was all in your imagination will be apologiz-
ing and will dine on crow. Stick with the number 1.

*Wednesday, October 17 (Moon in Libra to Scorpio 2:02
a.m.)*   Lucky lottery: 2, 17, 18, 22, 13, 14. A Libra
confides a marital problem. If you don't know what to
say, say nothing. If you want to complicate your life, then
begin to advise and consent. Cancer and Capricorn will
play outstanding roles.

Thursday, October 18 (Moon in Scorpio)   Your social
life picks up. The moon in your sign means your cycle
is high. You can designate where the action will be. You
emanate personal magnetism, as well as an aura of fun
and frolic. You'll be designated as the life of the party.

Gemini and Sagittarius will figure in today's dynamic scenario.

Friday, October 19 (Moon in Scorpio to Sagittarius 4:46 a.m.) Obstacles are removed as your cycle continues high, so stress originality, personality, and sex appeal. This will be one day you will long remember! Someone who once let you down will now seek your favor. Remain calm, cool, and collected. Taurus is in the picture.

Saturday, October 20 (Moon in Sagittarius) The emphasis is on advertising, publishing, getting across the fact that you will offer an unusual program. The accent is on the written word, communications from afar. Those who insist they do not believe will be taught cruel lessons. Lucky lottery: 5, 14, 23, 34, 16, 18.

Sunday, October 21 (Moon in Sagittarius to Capricorn 11:12 a.m.) Stick close to home, if possible. The moon in Sagittarius indicates that you will locate lost articles and get a raise in pay. Be careful, lest you fall into a trap—don't be in too much of a hurry to pick up money you see on the floor. It could be part of an intricate trap. Your honesty is being tested.

Monday, October 22 (Moon in Capricorn) You will be accused of dreaming. Take this criticism with a proverbial grain of salt, transforming the ordinary into the extraordinary. See people and relationships as they are, not merely as you wish they could be. Pisces and Virgo play meaningful roles.

Tuesday, October 23 (Moon in Capricorn to Aquarius 9:26 p.m.) Wake up! This could be your power-play day. Focus on promotion, production, leadership, and an increase in your income potential. In any matter of speculation, choose the number 8. If you are to follow any example, make it that of Capricorn! This applies especially if you have major planets in Capricorn.

Wednesday, October 24 (Moon in Aquarius) What was dear to you might go out of your life, to be replaced by new interests that will include a new love. Let go of a burden you should not have assumed in the first place. What started as a shot in the dark will prove accurate enough to hit the bull's-eye. Your lucky number is 9.

Thursday, October 25 (Moon in Aquarius) The Aquarian moon relates to that section of your horoscope associated with property value, real estate, and a sense of security. Leo and Aquarius, who play memorable roles, have these letters in their names—A, S, J.

Friday, October 26 (Moon in Aquarius to Pisces 9:54 a.m.) You did very well yesterday by sticking to your principles. Tonight you will receive praise from someone you admire. Before an hour has passed, you will be making deals with Cancer or Capricorn. Your reward: Gourmet dining and being told by a lovely member of the opposite sex, "I love you!"

Saturday, October 27 (Moon in Pisces) The Pisces moon relates to your fifth house, that section of your chart associated with change, children, and variety. You will be emitting an aura of personal magnetism, sensuality, and sex appeal. Your creative juices stir as you find an outlet for your hidden talent. Your lucky number is 3.

Sunday, October 28—Standard Time Begins (Moon in Pisces to Aries 9:13 p.m.) Some of your childhood dreams surface—signaling be the return of youth. Taurus, Leo, and another Scorpio, who pay fabulous roles, could have these letters in their names—D, M, V. Those who once crossed the street so as not to meet you will now seek to be on your good side.

Monday, October 29 (Moon in Aries) The good moon aspect coincides with public popularity and your ability to win the confidence of important people. A situation or relationship becomes mercurial—here today, gone tomorrow. In matters of speculation, stick with the number 5. Virgo will be in this picture.

Tuesday, October 30 (Moon in Aries)   Your general health report is favorable. Don't neglect back or head injuries. A pleasant surprise tonight! Music plays, and you will dance to your own tune. Taurus, Libra, and another Scorpio figure in this dynamic scenario. What appeared to be out of place will fit in perfectly, so relax and enjoy!

Wednesday, October 31 (Moon in Aries to Taurus 7:46 a.m.)   On this last day of October, use your imagination but do not let it run wild. Many people will celebrate Halloween, but magicians, both professional and amateur, will be celebrating this day in honor of Harry Houdini. A Pisces declares, "You are converting me to astrology!"

NOVEMBER 2001

Thursday, November 1 (Moon in Taurus)   November begins with a stimulating challenge. The full moon in Taurus is in your opposite sign, relating to legal affairs, public relations and your marital status. You'll be musing, "This is the kind of Thursday I really do enjoy!" Gemini, Virgo, and Sagittarius play roles.

Friday, November 2 (Moon in Taurus to Gemini 4:11 p.m.)   On this Friday, you will be saying to yourself, "At last I know I am not alone!" The Taurus moon stirs your creative talents, and coincides with a serious talk about marriage. You will be told by people you trust, "You are vibrant and you make others feel you really care about their welfare!"

Saturday, November 3 (Moon in Gemini)   The lunar position points to money, payments and collections, and your earning capacity. Special: Count your change! Neptune is involved; so is deception. Let go of dreams that you realize instinctively cannot be fulfilled.

Sunday, November 4 (Moon in Gemini to Cancer 10:42 p.m.)   On this Sunday, your mind covers various aspects of life, including how to survive on the money you earn. Dig deep for information. What you find will come as a stunning surprise. Capricorn and Cancer, who will play roles, have these letters in their names—H, Q, Z.

Monday, November 5 (Moon in Cancer)   The moon is in your ninth house, Cancer. Finish with packing and make your plans as if you already have been notified of a journey overseas. With the moon in its own sign, Cancer, you will receive a call saying, "Come on over; we look forward to your visit!"

Tuesday, November 6 (Moon in Cancer)   On this Tuesday, be ready for surprises. Family members decide to give you a going-away party. There also will be sentimental messages declaring, "We will miss you terribly!" Apparently, you are going to Paris, because someone asks, "Have you boned up on your French?"

Wednesday, November 7 (Moon in Cancer to Leo 3:32 a.m.)   Lucky lottery: 2, 12, 22, 13, 18, 5. The spotlight falls on travel, publishing, and advertising, and on letting the world know, "I am special; I want to be loved by all of you, even if that sounds impossible!" Cancer and Capricorn will play sensational roles.

Thursday, November 8 (Moon in Leo)   The moon in Leo, your tenth house, relates to business, career, prestige, and leadership. A major opportunity exists to take charge of your own destiny. The focus will be on entertainment and clothing, and on your appearance, exercise, diet, and nutrition. Sagittarius is involved.

Friday, November 9 (Moon in Leo to Virgo 6:48 a.m.)   You may be saying good-bye to someone who made love

282

to you. The strength of ties at home outweigh the love-making attraction. People say, "We will miss you, but hope you soon will be back!" You'll be musing, "What a day! I feel as if I am coming and going!" Another Scorpio is involved.

Saturday, November 10 (Moon in Virgo)   You will have more freedom of thought and action. A puzzle will be solved as you'll receive the answers to perplexing problems. All you need do is summon up the courage to ask! Read and write, teach and learn, and realize that Gemini and Virgo need attention. Your lucky number is 5.

Sunday, November 11 (Moon in Virgo to Libra 8:52 a.m.)   Many of life's puzzles will be handed to you to solve. Make a try, but know when to say, "Enough is enough!" Many of your fondest hopes and wishes can be fulfilled with the moon in Virgo, your eleventh house. Reading material is involved, and you could find a publisher for your work.

Monday, November 12 (Moon in Libra)   Look behind the scenes, for a pleasant surprise awaits you. What is creeping up on you is something you enjoyed, but previously neglected. Opportunity knocks twice for you! You are a special person, for very few people take the chance to correct past mistakes. Pisces is involved.

Tuesday, November 13 (Moon in Libra to Scorpio 10:44 a.m.)   A musical tune could be haunting. Seek the lyrics to go with the rhythm. Someone is trying to tell you something, if only you will listen. Capricorn and Cancer, who play significant roles, will have these letters in their names—H, Q, Z. Your fortunate number is 8.

Wednesday, November 14 (Moon in Scorpio)   You receive many offers—the key is to be selective. Your cycle is high, so choose the best. Circumstances turn in your favor even as you read these words. Wear shades of blue and green, making personal appearances and present your program or format. You'll receive a favorable reception.

Thursday, November 15 (Moon in Scorpio to Sagittarius 1:51 p.m.)   The new moon in your sign coincides with adventure and originality. Strive to be the best there is! Someone who once loved you will announce, "I cannot love you again!" Instead of making you sad, this actually lifts the emotional burden from your shoulders. Leo plays the top role.

Friday, November 16 (Moon in Sagittarius)   On this Friday, catch the stock market before it closes. The moon is in your lucky money house, which portends profit in matters of speculation. Capricorn and Cancer, who play important roles today, have these letters in their names— B, K, T.

Saturday, November 17 (Moon in Sagittarius to Capricorn 7:39 p.m.)   Saturday night will be live for you! Elements of timing and luck ride with you and you meet Gemini and Sagittarius who will liven up your life. There is much talk of travel, philosophy, theology, and publishing. Lucky lottery: 9, 19, 3, 30, 4, 18.

Sunday, November 18 (Moon in Capricorn)   Don't wander too far from home base, for indications are that you will be called back due to mechanical difficulties. A Capricorn is waiting for you with a frantic message. Aquarius and another Scorpio will also play roles. Calculate with care!

Monday, November 19 (Moon in Capricorn)   You discover that you are trying to do too much at one time! Gemini, Virgo, and Sagittarius, who will play meaningful roles and have these letters in their names—E, N, W. It's an excellent day for creative endeavors, including writing. The number 5 proves lucky.

Tuesday, November 20 (Moon in Capricorn to Aquarius 4:54 a.m.)   A dispute with a relative is settled and domestic harmony is restored. Be diplomatic, making intelligent concessions even though you know you are right. Remember recent resolutions about exercise, diet, and nutrition. Taurus, Libra, and another Scorpio will play important roles.

Wednesday, November 21 (Moon in Aquarius)   Lucky lottery: 7, 12, 11, 14, 18, 22. Your general health report is good. A valuable lesson will be learned—see people, relationships as they are, not merely as you wish they might be. Do not fall victim to self-deception. Pisces and Virgo figure in this scenario.

Thursday, November 22 (Moon in Aquarius to Pisces 4:51 p.m.)   Happy Thanksgiving! The moon in Aquarius, your fourth house, indicates that a celebration of this holiday at home would prove beneficial. Capricorn and Cancer, who will play significant roles, could have these letters in their names—H, Q, Z.

Friday, November 23 (Moon in Pisces)   You will win the confidence of a very important person. Stress universality, looking beyond the immediate and studying the language and habits of people in foreign lands. Others express a desire to be with you today, sharing questions and problems. Stick with the number 9.

Saturday, November 24 (Moon in Pisces)   The answer to your question: make fresh a start; highlight originality; walk where angels fear to tread. Display your pioneering spirit! You will prove an inspiration to those who have been too shy to try. Leo and Aquarius, who play dominant roles, have these letters in their names—A, S, J. Your lucky number is 1.

Sunday, November 25 (Moon in Pisces to Aries 5:20 a.m.)   A reunion tonight! It will be pleasant and much talk will be about old times. Cancer and Capricorn, who

are involved, could have these initials in their names—
B, K, T. Spiritual values surface; you will rediscover the
spark of love for your family. Enjoy dinner tonight!

Monday, November 26 (Moon in Aries)   Someone
who shares your basic interests will pay a meaningful
compliment. Much attention revolves around what to eat
and where to eat, and perhaps exotic recipes will be
traded. Social activities accelerate. Your popularity is on
the rise. A Sagittarian plays a top role.

*Tuesday, November 27 (Moon in Aries to Taurus 4:04
p.m.)*   On this Tuesday, you reflect, "I know what to
do and even know how to do it, but it is a question of
getting started!" Taurus, Leo and another Scorpio play
important roles, have these letters in their names—D,
M, V. Taurus talks about public relations, legal rights,
partnership, and marriage.

Wednesday, November 28 (Moon in Taurus)   Sev-
enth-house activities are spotlighted, including partnership, marital status, public relations, and publicity.
Participate in a clash of ideas. Someone, not exactly a
swindler, attempts to talk you into flirting with the law.
Don't do it! Your lucky number is 5.

Thursday, November 29 (Moon in Taurus)   For racing luck, try these selections at all tracks: Post position
special—number 2 p.p. in the fourth race. Pick six: 3,
6, 1, 2, 4, 7. Watch for these letters in the names of
potential winning horses or jockeys—F, O, X. Hot
daily doubles: 3 and 6, 2 and 4, 5 and 3. Hometown
jockeys win photo finishes; favorites will be in the winner's circle.

*Friday, November 30 (Moon in Taurus to Gemini 12:02
a.m.)*   Someone you desire for romance, partnership,
or marriage will be leaving town within 24 hours.
Sharpen your act; rehearse your lines. Do not wait until

286

it is too late! Attention revolves around your home, domestic harmony, art objects, and luxury items. Pisces is represented.

DECEMBER 2001

Saturday, December 1 (Moon in Gemini)   What begins as fun and games could turn serious. If using a device aimed at foretelling the future, the joke may not be too funny. Make a list for Christmas shopping. Those who pretend not to care about presents actually do care, and if you forget them, they will remember it as a slight.

Sunday, December 2 (Moon in Gemini to Cancer 5:29 a.m.)   Spiritual values surface and make their presence known. This will be one Sunday you won't soon forget! Take seriously your psychic impressions. Pisces and Virgo, who will play astounding roles, could have these letters in their names—G, P, Y. Be near water, if possible.

Monday, December 3 (Moon in Cancer)   On this Monday, you will feel as though you are awakening from a long slumber. What you have been waiting for will arrive. You'll also receive a compliment from someone who has sincere affection for you. Capricorn and Cancer figure in this scenario.

Tuesday, December 4 (Moon in Cancer to Leo 9:14 a.m.) Accent universal appeal, tossing aside narrow-minded concepts. Become more aware of how people live in other lands, giving special study to language and overcoming distance barriers. Participate in a political or charitable campaign. Aries plays a dramatic role.

Wednesday, December 5 (Moon in Leo)   The Leo moon in your tenth house relates to leadership and fulfillment of your ambitions. Make a fresh start, stressing independence and originality. New love is on the horizon, which could be different from anything you have ever experienced! Leo and Aquarius will play sensational roles.

Thursday, December 6 (Moon in Leo to Virgo 12:10 p.m.) On this Thursday, your cycle is high. Trust your judgment and intuition. Make a new start in a direction you have always wanted to take. Plan ahead for New Year's Eve, as well as for Christmas. Leo wants to become your ally and will, if you merely indicate the same goes for you.

Friday, December 7 (Moon in Virgo) Memories of historic events crowd your mind. Say to yourself, "The past is one thing, but we must live in the future!" Highlight diversity, versatility, and gaining information from published material. Gemini and Sagittarius elevate your ego with compliments.

Saturday, December 8 (Moon in Virgo to Libra 2:56 p.m.) What a powerful Saturday! You win friends and influence people. You sign a document that insures additional income. Capricorn and Cancer, who figure prominently, will have these letters in their names—H, Q, Z. Lucky lottery: 51, 4, 13, 12, 18, 19.

Sunday, December 9 (Moon in Libra) The emphasis on travel, movement, and finding an outlet for your creative urges, especially writing. Someone you once thought was indifferent will now show interest and might even state, "At times, I can hardly keep my hands off you!" Virgo is featured.

Monday, December 10 (Moon in Libra to Scorpio 6:08 p.m.) On this Monday, attention will revolve around your home, security, and the protection of your family. Long-ago and far-away places and people will return to your life. You will muse, "It certainly is an unusual, perhaps mystical Monday!" Taurus, Libra, and another Scorpio figure in today's dramatic scenario.

Tuesday, December 11 (Moon in Scorpio) Another mystical day! Toss aside preconceived notions, keeping an open mind without being gullible. Astrology will begin to play an even more important role in your life. Your cycle is high, so circumstances are turning in your favor, even as you read these words.

Wednesday, December 12 (Moon in Scorpio to Sagittarius 10:29 p.m.) For racing luck, try these selections at all tracks: Post position special—number 2 p.p. in the eighth race. Pick six: 1, 5, 3, 4, 2, 8. Watch for these letters in the names of potential winning horses or jockeys: G, P, Y. Hot daily doubles: 1 and 5, 3 and 2, 4 and 4. Capricorn and Cancer jockeys will be winners; favorites do not disappoint followers.

Thursday, December 13 (Moon in Sagittarius) Grab hold of an opportunity to elevate your prestige and to increase your income. You are going places, and people will admire and be envious. Aries and Libra, who figure prominently, have these letters in their names— I and R. A well-known athletic figure could meet with disaster.

Friday, December 14—Solar Eclipse (Moon in Sagittarius) A new moon, solar eclipse, falls in Sagittarius, your second house. Money and investments are involved. A valuable article will be lost for a short time and then found again. Make a fresh start in a different direction and hold tight to your valuables. Your lucky number is 1.

Saturday, December 15 (Moon in Sagittarius to Capricorn 4:47 a.m.) Sexual fireworks! The numerical symbol today relates to the moon, and the moon itself is in your power sector. Control your emotions and maintain your equilibrium. Decide about your future and the answers to questions about marriage. A Cancer plays the leading role.

Sunday, December 16 (Moon in Capricorn)   This will be a more social Sunday than in the recent past. Short trips and relatives are involved. Experiment, explore and give full rein to your intellectual curiosity. The spotlight is on advertising, publishing, and writing articles and stories. Gemini and Sagittarius figure prominently.

Monday, December 17 (Moon in Capricorn to Aquarius 1:43 p.m.)   This will not be a Blue Monday, but will require serious consideration about your future and your marital status. Before Monday is finished, you will say to yourself: "At last I have seen the light!" Taurus is in the picture.

Tuesday, December 18 (Moon in Aquarius)   A reunion with an Aquarian could prove eventful. A blend of your Pluto and the Aquarian Uranus might set the world on fire! Let people know, "I do not intend to stand still—I am moving on into the future!" Gemini, Virgo, and Sagittarius insert themselves into this scenario.

Wednesday, December 19 (Moon in Aquarius)   Attention revolves around your home, domestic issues, and the settling of a financial dispute. The facts are on your side, but avoid any tendency to rub it in. Taurus, Libra, and another Scorpio figure in this scenario. A discussion involves whether or not to move, to sell, or to purchase more furniture.

Thursday, December 20 (Moon in Aquarius to Pisces 1:09 a.m.)   Within 24 hours, the lunar position will encourage change, travel, and variety. Until then, play the waiting game, for time is on your side. Define your terms and make your position crystal clear. Follow through on psychic impressions. Pisces and Virgo will play major roles.

Friday, December 21 (Moon in Pisces) This could be your power-play day! The emphasis is on creativity, style, and physical attraction. Focus on design and appearance, consider where you want to go and what to do about it. Capricorn and Cancer, who will play stunning roles, could have these letters in their names—H, Q, Z.

Saturday, December 22 (Moon in Pisces to Aries 1:44 a.m.) Finish what you start. Let go of outmoded methods and appearances. Stress universal appeal, letting others know that you are here to stay! You could be knocking on the doors of fame and fortune. Discover your own style and stick to it, despite what others say.

Sunday, December 23 (Moon in Aries) Make a fresh start in a new direction. Seek what is new; let go of what you held a little too long. Leo and Aquarius, who figure in this scenario, could have these letters in their names— A, S, J. Make personal appearances, taking the initiative as you wear blends of yellow and gold.

Monday, December 24 (Moon in Aries) Christmas Eve! Focus on your family, your general well-being, and your ability to please your loved ones. Strive to maintain an even keel, avoiding the sensational. Cancer and Capricorn could dominate today's scenario. Both need reassurance that you do care about their welfare.

Tuesday, December 25 (Moon in Aries to Taurus 1:10 a.m.) A burden is lifted. Christmas Day is here, and you handle it with aplomb. Gemini and Sagittarius play leading roles and could have these letters in their names—C, L, U. Stress humor, versatility, and intellectual curiosity. You will be grateful for friends who are with you on this holiday.

Wednesday, December 26 (Moon in Taurus) You sigh with relief. The Taurus moon relates to a clash of ideas, cooperative efforts. You add up the money you spent and conclude that it was well worth it. Check details, proofread, and realize at last that you did get your money's worth. Another Scorpio is involved.

Thursday, December 27 (Moon in Taurus to Gemini 9:37 a.m.) As the year winds to an end, you conclude it was not so bad after all. Be analytical. Don't be satisfied to learn merely that something happened—find out why it happened. A long-lost article will be recovered. You'll muse, "I felt that if it had to be found, it would be, and now that I've found it, I will not be so careless in the future!"

Friday, December 28 (Moon in Gemini) Settle in your mind recent mysterious happenings. Find out, "What's going on here!" Be with convivial people. Plan ahead for a fun-filled and safe New Year's Eve. A relative announces, "Next year I will travel, and I hope some of you will come with me!" Taurus, Libra, and another Scorpio figure prominently.

Saturday, December 29 (Moon in Gemini to Cancer 1:38 p.m.) Get an accounting from someone who did your shopping. Look beyond the immediate; finding out who you are and what you are going to do about it. Rather than being moody, decide to meditate. See people and places as they are—not merely as you wish they could be. Your lucky number is 7.

Sunday, December 30—Lunar Eclipse (Moon in Cancer) The full moon, lunar eclipse, falls in Cancer, your ninth house, which is associated with travel, philosophy, and taking a stand on questions that border on the metaphysical. Spiritual values surface. You can transform what appears to be pure imagination into a solid product. Capricorn works into today's scenario.

Monday, December 31 (Moon in Cancer to Leo 5:08 p.m.) New Year's Eve! You have been waiting for it, and now it is here. Do the things you have been wanting

292

to do and say the things you have been wanting to say. Even if you do not entertain at home, don't go too far away. Aries and Libra, who play outstanding roles, are in the New Year's Eve scenario. Go easy on alcoholic beverages.

Happy New Year!

ABOUT THE AUTHOR

Born on August 5, 1926, in Philadelphia, Omarr was the only person ever given full-time duty in the U.S. Army as an astrologer. He also is regarded as the most erudite astrologer of our time and the best known, through his syndicated column (300 newspapers) and his radio and television programs (he is Merv Griffin's "resident astrologer"). Omarr has been called the most "knowledgeable astrologer since Evangeline Adams." His forecasts of Nixon's downfall, the end of World War II in mid-August of 1945, the assassination of John F. Kennedy, Roosevelt's election to the fourth term and his death in office . . . these and many others are on the record and quoted enough to be considered "legendary."

ABOUT THIS SERIES

This is one of a series of twelve
Day-by-Day Astrological Guides
for the signs of 2001
by Sydney Omarr